T0275893

Topological UML Modeling

Topological UML Modeling

An Improved Approach for Domain Modeling and Software Development

Janis Osis

Uldis Donins

ELSEVIER

Elsevier
Radarweg 29, PO Box 211, 1000 AE Amsterdam, Netherlands
The Boulevard, Langford Lane, Kidlington, Oxford OX5 1GB, United Kingdom
50 Hampshire Street, 5th Floor, Cambridge, MA 02139, United States

Designations used by companies to distinguish their products are often claimed as trademarks or registered
trademarks. In all instances in which Elsevier/Morgan Kaufmann Publishers is aware of a claim, the product
names appear in initial capital or all capital letters. Readers, however, should contact the appropriate
companies for more complete information regarding trademarks and registration.

The following are trademarks of the Object Management Group, Inc., in the United States and/or other
countries: CWM, MDA, MOF, OCL, OMG, UML, XMI.

Notices
Knowledge and best practice in this field are constantly changing. As new research and experience broaden
our understanding, changes in research methods, professional practices, or medical treatment may become necessary.

Practitioners and researchers must always rely on their own experience and knowledge in evaluating and using
any information, methods, compounds, or experiments described herein. In using such information or methods
they should be mindful of their own safety and the safety of others, including parties for whom they have a
professional responsibility.

To the fullest extent of the law, neither the Publisher nor the authors, contributors, or editors, assume any
liability for any injury and/or damage to persons or property as a matter of products liability, negligence or
otherwise, or from any use or operation of any methods, products, instructions, or ideas contained in the
material herein.

British Library Cataloguing-in-Publication Data
A catalogue record for this book is available from the British Library

Library of Congress Cataloging-in-Publication Data
A catalog record for this book is available from the Library of Congress

ISBN: 978-0-12-805476-5

For Information on all Elsevier publications
visit our website at https://www.elsevier.com/books-and-journals

Working together
to grow libraries in
developing countries

www.elsevier.com • www.bookaid.org

Publisher: Jonathan Simpson
Acquisition Editor: Jonathan Simpson
Editorial Project Manager: Lindsay Lawrence
Production Project Manager: Punithavathy Govindaradjane
Designer: Matthew Limbert

Typeset by MPS Limited, Chennai, India

DEDICATION

To the centenary of Latvian Republic.

CONTENTS

FOREWORD

In the early 1990s, the Object Management Group (OMG) undertook a worldwide survey. Given the craze at the time for object-oriented programming, object-oriented databases, object-oriented protocols—object-oriented anything, in fact—it seemed obvious that the myriad languages and methodologies for object-oriented analysis and design ought to be tracked down, compared, and cataloged. OMG started the process in 1993, and by 1994 had collected and published a useful guide, *Object Oriented Analysis & Design: Description of Methods.* Under the capable leadership of ICL's Andrew T.F. Hutt, OMG had moved past its early focus on distributed computing and middleware standards such as CORBA, focusing on software design methodologies and notations.

Unfortunately, the hue and cry that resulted from this simple and abundantly useful catalog was a huge surprise to Dr. Hutt, myself, and all of the OMG members and staff who participated in the production of the catalog. We were told that standardization would result in the freezing of forward momentum in software development methodology. Research remained fluid, we heard, and the researchers didn't want to see development stop in the face of new discoveries.

An important new idea came from the catalog, however: though development methodologies might have been in constant flux, all of the methodologies then in use could realize value from a shared *language* for expressing their processes. Language design, after all, was already well understood by 1994, and the race was then on to provide a standard language. Major consolidation in the software development methodology marketplace was just starting as well, which brought together erstwhile competitors to merge their thoughts and designs. The result was a new OMG standard, quite outside the middleware realm, for expressing software design—a key ingredient for any engineering practice after all is a way to express design, like blueprints for buildings and bridges. Abstract design languages allow analysis of the *design* from engineering viewpoints, much as a bridge design is checked for structural integrity from its blueprint, not after construction.

As I write this, the Unified Modeling Language (UML) is coming to the end of its first two decades as a world standard for software modeling. Twenty years have come and gone since, in September 1997, dozens of organizations came together to complete the first version of the language. Over the intervening years, newer versions have updated that first approach, increasing the expressibility of the language and at the same time simplifying its underpinnings. Though dozens of organizations and likely hundreds of individuals have had their fingers inside the UML standard, it remains robust and powerful and quite widely adopted in the software industry.

And, in fact, not just in the software industry—UML has been used in many other ways, as a way to express business processes, systems architectures, even electronic circuits. The success of a product (or in this case a standard) perhaps can be best measured as how broadly it is used both inside and outside of its intended purpose. UML has also spawned numerous related languages: the Meta-Object Facility (MOF) that underlies the UML is now the underpinnings also of other languages (like the Business Processing Model & Notation (BPMN) and others); the executable Functional UML (fUML), sufficiently precise to be directly executed like a programming language itself; UML has also been extended to explicitly support other modeling regimes like Systems Engineering (with the Systems Modeling Language, SysML) and work as of this writing is focusing on product architectures, business architectures, and others. UML (and MOF) in 2000 also became the major underpinning of the Model Driven Architecture (MDA), a model-based way to develop software, just as modeling and simulation underlie other engineering disciplines. Itself already approaching 20 years of age, the MDA is becoming a way to express *semantics*, and the UML is the key technology that makes that possible.

One weak spot for UML and MDA has always been the *computation-independent model* (CIM) layer that captures the design of a software engineering artifact without regard to how it is implemented. The CIM is then translated into a *platform-independent model* and thus to a *platform-specific model* which generally means some coding language, although it might be more complicated than that. Many methodologies have been developed over the past 20 years for CIM's that are sufficiently abstract to express design without regard to platform, but sufficiently precise to specify exactly one process. Solving that problem would allow another layer of automation—and thus success—for users of the Model Driven Architecture.

Topological modeling is one approach to capturing design in the abstract. It is a testament to the flexibility of the UML standard that topological modeling can actually be integrated directly into the language, using the native profiling mechanisms of the UML and its underlying MOF. This allows complete expression of system design, from a high-level abstraction, all the way down to low-level implementation, with a single language. That idea and a complete expression of the idea are the focus of this book, and an enduring testament to an OMG standard whose success continues to astound.

Richard Mark Soley, PhD
Chairman and Chief Executive Officer,
Object Management Group, Inc.,
Lexington, MA, United States
May 6, 2017

The analysis of problem domain and design of desired solution within software development process has a major impact of the achieved result—developed software. While the software developer community uses a set of tools and different techniques to create detailed specification of the solution, the proper analysis of problem domain functioning is ignored or covered insufficiently. One of such techniques is object-oriented software analysis and development which states that there are two fundamental aspects of systems modeling: analysis and design. The analysis defines what the solution needs to do within the problem domain to fit the customer's requirements, and the design states how the solution will be implemented. The design of object-oriented software is leaded by the Unified Modeling Language (UML). UML is an approved standard modeling notation for visualizing, specifying, constructing, and documenting the artifacts of a software–intensive system. While the UML has elements for designing and specifying artifacts of a software system, it lacks the ability to document the functioning of a problem domain by using computation independent constructs. To solve the previously mentioned UML issue, a new—extended—version of UML is developed—Topological Unified Modeling Language (Topological UML). Topological UML is a combination of UML and formalism of Topological Functioning Model (TFM). It captures system functioning specification in the form of topological space consisting of functional features and cause-and-effect relationships among them and is represented in a form of directed graph.

The main aim of improving UML is by transferring topology and mathematical formalism of TFM to UML thus strengthening the very beginning of the software development lifecycle. Sometimes it is very hard to pay appropriate resources and time at the very beginning of the software development lifecycle to detect and analyze aspects of desired software system as much as possible. If we pay appropriate attention at the beginning of the software development project, we tend to avoid wasting valuable resources, including time; otherwise it could lead to unnecessary reworking or even recoding parts of the system or the system as whole. Just like Benjamin Franklin has said:

"If you fail to plan, you are planning to fail!"

While the UML is a notation and as such its specification does not contain any guidelines of its application during software development process, the UML modeling driven methods fulfill this gap. Unfortunately, not every UML modeling driven method covers all the software development lifecycle. In addition—usually only a small part of UML diagrams is used to specify both problem and solution domains. Due to the partial UML and software development lifecycle coverage and the fragmentary application of UML diagrams the software developers are forced to combine UML with several modeling methods and techniques (instead of taking UML as a notation and one UML modeling driven method) thus the application of UML gets more complicated and incomprehensible. To address this issue the developed UML extension is provided together with a proper modeling method—Topological UML modeling.

Topological UML modeling for problem domain modeling and software systems designing is a model-driven modeling method. In the context of Model Driven Architecture (MDA), the Topological Functioning Model (TFM) considers problem domain information separate from the solution domain information and holistically represents a complete functionality of the system from the computation independent viewpoint while Topological UML has elements for representing system design at the platform independent viewpoint and platform specific viewpoint. The Topological UML modeling method covers modeling and specification of systems in computation independent and platform independent viewpoints. Problem domain analysis and software system design with Topological UML modeling method consists of six activities—the first one is problem domain functioning analysis followed by behavior analysis and design, structure analysis and design, state change and transition analysis, structuring logical layout of design, and concluding with components and deployment design.

STRUCTURE OF THE BOOK

Part I. Introduction

Takes a broad look at the UML—what it is (see Chapter 1: Unified Modeling Language—A Standard for Designing a Software), how to use it (see Chapter 2: Software Designing With Unified Modeling Language Driven Approaches), and how to adjust it to improve software modeling and design possibilities (see Chapter 3: Adjusting Unified Modeling Language). If you are familiar with UML and its application in software design, you can skip this part and go to Part II, Improving Domain Modeling, or Part III, Topological UML Modeling Explained.

Chapter 1. *Unified Modeling Language—A Standard for Designing a Software*

Chapter reviews UML evolution by paying most attention on the diagrams included in versions 1.x and 2.x as well as on the formalism development used to specify the language. Review shows the benefits and limitations of applying UML within software development lifecycle, and identifies UML extension mechanisms and scenarios.

Chapter 2. *Software Designing With Unified Modeling Language Driven Approaches*

UML is a notation and as such its specification does not contain any guidelines of software development process. This chapter discusses the current state of the art of UML-based software development approaches. Most attention is paid on the artifacts created by using the UML.

Chapter 3. *Adjusting Unified Modeling Language*

This chapter discusses UML improvement by using the metamodeling approach and its extensibility mechanism—profile. Since the UML specification is a specification of a notation and it does not include any guidelines for profile definition and specification, a set of profiles are reviewed to define a profile specification template.

Part II. Improving Domain Modeling

Takes a broad look at the Topological UML—what it is (see Chapter 4: Topological Unified Modeling Language) and how to use it (see Chapter 5: Topological UML Modeling).

Chapter 4. *Topological Unified Modeling Language*

Chapter defines Topological Unified Modeling Language (Topological UML) as a profile of UML thus answering *"What it is?"* The created profile provides a UML specific version of the metamodel that can be incorporated into standard UML modeling tools. Topological UML development is based on two steps: at first extend UML by using profile mechanism, thus creating Topological UML profile (this chapter), and then define guidelines for using Topological UML in practice, thus formalizing the way the Topological UML is used (next chapter).

Chapter 5. *Topological UML Modeling*

Defines method on how to apply Topological UML profile in practice thus answering *"How to use it?"* Problem domain analysis and software system design with Topological UML modeling method consists of six activities: (1) problem domain functioning analysis, (2) behavior analysis and design, (3) structure analysis and design, (4) state change and transition analysis, (5) structuring logical layout of design, and (6) components and deployment design.

Part III. *Topological UML Modeling Explained*

Describes in detail each of the Topological UML modeling activities. Within the Part III, Topological UML Modeling Explained, we use a case study of enterprise data synchronization system development. This part is supplemented with functioning description of enterprise data synchronization, functional requirements, and nonfunctional requirements.

Chapter 6. *Problem Domain Functioning Analysis*

Problem domain functioning analysis is the first activity within Topological UML modeling and it states that the analysis of the problem domain should be performed during which TFM gets developed. To do so, functioning description and functional requirements are used as prerequisites. This activity ensures that proper attention is paid at the very beginning of the software development lifecycle by capturing various aspects of the desired system. This part is supplemented with functioning description of enterprise data synchronization, functional requirements and nonfunctional requirements used throughout Part III, Topological UML Modeling Explained.

Chapter 7. *Behavior Analysis and Design*

Behavior Analysis and Design is the next activity within Topological UML modeling process. This activity is based on the results obtained within previous Topological UML modeling activity—problem domain functioning analysis. By basing behavior analysis on TFM, we are identifying and designing subsystems, use cases, actors, and relationships between them (topological use case diagram), messages and their sequence (sequence diagram), and workflows (activity and interaction overview diagram).

Chapter 8. *Structure Analysis and Design*

The main goal of structure analysis and design is to develop a topological class diagram which contains classes together with their attributes and responsibilities. To identify classes and assign the right responsibility to each one of them a TFM is used—initially TFM is transformed into communication diagram showing objects and messages they send each other, afterwards the communication diagram is further transformed into topological class diagram.

Chapter 9. *Object State Change and Transition Analysis*

This chapter describes object state change and transition analysis based on the state diagram development. The state changes and transitions within a system are formally analyzed by using TFM. The functional features together with topological relationships contain the necessary information to create state diagram which reflects the state changes within system.

Chapter 10. *Structuring Logical Layout of Software Design*

Logical layout of software design is structured in accordance with the defined subsystems in the behavior analysis and design activity and classes with their relationships as developed within structure analysis and design activity. The logical layout is depicted by using package diagram.

Chapter 11. *Components and Deployment Design*

Chapter describes components and deployment design activity which concludes the Topological UML modeling process. Components are designed in accordance with packages and nonfunctional requirements and is depicted by using component diagram. Deployment is planned for the designed components in accordance with nonfunctional requirements and is reflected by using deployment diagram.

Janis Osis and Uldis Donins

ACKNOWLEDGMENTS

We thank Richard M. Soley, Janis V. Barzdins, Janis Grundspenkis, Marite Kirikova, Dace Donina, Vicente Garcia Diaz, Peter J. Clarke, Artis Teilans, and Erika Nazaruka for comments and suggestions, and Lindsay Lawrence, Todd Green, and Punithavathy Govindaradjane for redactional assistance.

Introduction

CHAPTER 1

Unified Modeling Language: A Standard for Designing a Software

INFORMATION IN THIS CHAPTER:

- UML diagrams
- Formalism of UML
- Benefits and disadvantages of applying UML
- UML improvement options

1.1 INTRODUCTION

Unified Modeling Language—abbreviated as UML—is a graphical language officially defined by Object Management Group (OMG) for visualizing, specifying, constructing, and documenting the artifacts of a software system [106]. An artifact in software development is an item created or collected during the development process (example of artifacts includes use cases, requirements, design, code, executable files, etc.). UML offers a standard way to write system's blueprints, including conceptual things such as business processes and system functions as well as concrete things such as programming language statements, database schemas, and reusable software components [37]. Despite that UML is designed for specifying, visualizing, constructing, and documenting software systems, it is not restricted only for software modeling. UML has been used for modeling hardware, and is used for business process modeling, systems engineering modeling and representing organizational structure, among many other domains [125].

The first UML specification (version 1.1) was published by OMG at 1997. Since then there has been continuously ongoing work to improve both the language and its corresponding specification. Additionally, we should admit that UML versions 1.4.2 and 2.4.1 have been published under International Organization for Standardization (ISO) [44] and International Electronical Commission (IEC) [43] as a

Topological UML Modeling. DOI: http://dx.doi.org/10.1016/B978-0-12-805476-5.00001-0

standard. In year 2005, the version 1.4.2 was published as ISO/IEC 19501:2005 [46]. Following in year 2012, the version 2.4.1 was published as ISO/IEC 19505-1 [47] and ISO/IEC 19505-2 [48]. You should ask—why there are two separate ISO/IEC standards for single UML version? The answer hides in fact that beginning with UML version 2.0 its specification was divided in two parts (i.e., two separate documents)—so-called *Infrastructure* and *Superstructure*. Accordingly, the ISO/IEC standard is based on this separation. But what a surprise—UML version 2.5 specification [79] again is a single document.

During the two major and a number of revision versions of UML, the definition of UML is evolving. UML version 2.4.1 specification [77,78] defines the language as follows: *"UML is a visual language for specifying, constructing, and documenting the artifacts of systems. It is a general-purpose modeling language that can be used with all major object and component methods, and that can be applied to all application domains (e.g., health, finance, telecom, aerospace) and implementation platforms (e.g., J2EE, .NET)."*

The UML originally was developed in middle of 1990s as a combination of previously competing object-oriented analysis and design approaches:

- *Booch method* by Booch [13],
- *Object-Modeling Technique (OMT)* by Rumbaugh, Blaha, Premerlani, Eddy, and Lorensen [105],
- *Object-Oriented Software Engineering (OOSE)* by Jacobson, Christerson, Jonsson, and Overgaard [49], and
- Other contributions to modeling complex systems, e.g., *statecharts* by Harel [41].

The first version of UML (version 1.1) was approved by OMG in year 1997 [71]; afterwards UML has been revised with several releases (UML 1.3, 1.5, 2.0, 2.1.1, 2.1.2, 2.2, 2.3, 2.4.1, and 2.5 [81]) by fixing some problems and adding new notational capabilities. The latest standard released by OMG is UML version 2.5 (UML version 2.0 is a major rewrite of UML 1.x ("x" denotes the main version and any subversion of specification) and was released in 2015).

The UML became widely accepted as the standard for object-oriented analysis and design soon after it was first introduced [54] and still remains so today [22,103]. Since the release of first UML version a large number of practitioner and research articles and dozens of text-books have been devoted to articulate various aspects of the UML, including guidelines for using it. In fact, since the UML specification is a specification and thus it is written in a manner to specify every aspect of the language's constructs, it does not contain guidelines on how to apply the language elements in real-life situation. So just reading the language's specification does not give an insight of its application. We advise to read UML specification together with guidelines describing approach or methodology of applying UML diagrams throughout software development lifecycle. Since the UML as a language includes 14 kinds of diagrams and many elements building them up, the scope of UML-related research areas is wide:

- Formalization of UML semantics (e.g., [31,42] (both after UML 1.1 was released), and [122] (after UML 2.0 was released)),
- Extending the UML (e.g., [64,99], and review of a number of UML profiles developed by different researchers and groups [103]),
- Formalizing the way, the UML diagrams are developed (e.g., [88,96]),
- Ontological analysis of UML modeling constructs (e.g., [125]),
- Empirical assessments (e.g., [22,32]),
- Analysis of the UML's complexity (e.g., [30,111,112]),
- Difficulties of learning UML (e.g., [113]) and how to avoid them (e.g., [11]),
- Transformations between UML diagrams (e.g., [61,57,66]),
- Software code generation and related issues with generated code quality (e.g., [59,108,118]), and
- Experiments that evaluate aspects of UML models effectiveness (e.g., [17]).

The large number of researches regarding UML evolving and strengthening is caused by the basis on which UML was developed. According to Dobing and Parsons [22] the *"UML was not developed based on any theoretical principles regarding the constructs required for an effective and usable modeling language for analysis and design; instead, it arose from (sometimes conflicting) 'best practices' (e.g., Booch, OMT, OOSE) in parts of the software engineering community."*

The next section of this chapter introduces in brief with the diagrams found in UML specification. The review of elements that build up UML within this chapter is based on UML version 2.4.1

specification which is divided into two volumes (both volumes cross-reference each other and the specifications are fully integrated):

- *Infrastructure* [77]—defines a metalanguage core that can be reused to define a variety of metamodels, including UML, Meta-Object Facility (MOF) [74], and Common Warehouse Metamodel (CWM) [70]; and the core metamodel on which the *Superstructure* is based. The *Infrastructure* of the UML is defined by the *InfrastructureLibrary* package which consists of two subpackages:
  1. *Core*—contains core concepts which are used when metamodeling and
  2. *Profiles*—defines the mechanisms that are used to customize metamodels.
- *Superstructure* [78]—defines the notation and semantics for diagrams and their elements. The *Superstructure* metamodel is specified by the UML package, which is divided into a number of subpackages that deal with structural and behavioral modeling.

Although the UML specification 2.5 has been extensively rewritten from its previous version 2.4.1 by combining together the *infrastructure* and *superstructure* parts, the metamodel itself remains unchanged from UML 2.4.1 superstructure [79]. Thus, the amount and types of UML diagrams have not changed from version 2.4.1 to version 2.5.

1.2 UNIFIED MODELING LANGUAGE DIAGRAMS

A system should be specified from different viewpoints to get a broader and more comprehensive insight and understanding of the intended software. The more efforts are added to consider the system from different viewpoints at the very beginning of the software development lifecycle, the more risk of producing irrelevant or unnecessary software system is reduced or even avoided [98]. Another benefit of such approach hides in fact of reducing the need of overworking or overdoing things that seem to be completed. The bunch of UML diagrams allows us to take a look at the system from various viewpoints. *"A diagram is the graphical presentation of a set of elements, most often rendered as a connected graph of vertices (things) and arcs (relationships). A diagram is a projection into a system"* [15]. Additionally, the UML diagrams can be developed in different abstraction levels showing the most important aspects in each one of the level. The abstraction levels allow to describe and to show the system with the appropriate information amount for the stakeholders and developers.

In context of software development, there are five complementary views that are important in visualizing, specifying, constructing, and documenting software architecture [106]:

1. The use-case view,
2. The design view,
3. The interaction view,
4. The implementation view, and
5. The deployment view.

Each of these views involves structural modeling (static aspect of a system) as well as behavioral modeling (dynamic aspect of a system). Let's take a look at the diagrams included in UML specification and evolution history of them. The very first UML specification (version 1.1) released by OMG in 1997 [71] contained only nine diagram types. By evolving the UML, the amount of diagram types has also grown. The newest UML specification (version 2.5) [79] released by OMG in year 2015 contains 14 diagram types (see Fig. 1.1) which are organized in two major diagram types and one subtype:

- *Structure diagrams*—aimed to visualize, specify, construct, and document the static aspect of a system,
- *Behavior diagrams*—are used to visualize, specify, construct, and document the dynamic aspect of a system (modeling dynamic aspect of a system can be considered as representing its changing parts),
  - *Interaction diagrams*—show interaction, consisting of a set of objects and their relationships, including the messages that may be dispatched among them. By using interaction diagrams, it is possible to reason about flow of control within an operation, a class, a component, a use case, or the system as whole.

All of UML diagrams are briefly described in following subsections: Section 1.2.1 describes structure diagrams and Section 1.2.2—behavior diagrams.

1.2.1 Structure Diagrams
The UML's structural diagrams are aimed to visualize, specify, construct, and document the static aspect of a system [15,78,79].

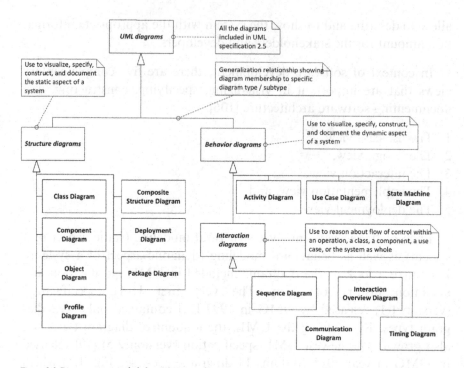

Figure 1.1 Diagram types included in UML specification version 2.5.

All structure diagrams are listed and described in the subsections of this section. Each subsection name denotes corresponding UML diagram and the contents include description, main elements, UML version in which the diagram is included, and an example of a diagram.

1.2.1.1 Class Diagram

Class diagram is the most common diagram found in object-oriented systems and it is used to illustrate the static viewpoint of a system. It shows a set of classes, interfaces, and their relationships. Class diagrams are also the foundation for a couple of related diagrams: component and deployment diagrams. The *class diagram* is included in UML specification since the first (1.1) version.

The class diagram includes following elements:

• *Class*—a template for creating objects, providing specification of attributes and operations that an instance of the class can complete. In the context of programming languages, the operation

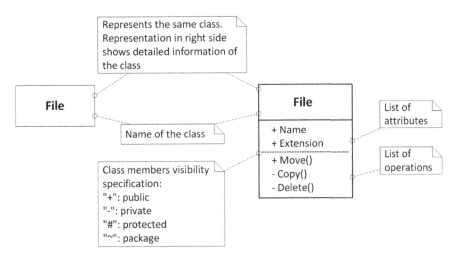

Figure 1.2 Example of a class representation.

is addressed as function or procedure. When an object is created by a constructor of the class, the resulting object is called an instance of the class. In certain circumstances it is needed to also model instances of classes at the specific moments in time—for those cases Object diagram should be used (see Section 1.2.1.2). See example of class representation using different notations in Fig. 1.2.

• *Interface*—specifies a contract consisting of a set of coherent public attributes and operations for a class. Any instance of a class that realizes the interface must fulfill that contract. Since interfaces are declarations, they are not instantiable. Instead, an interface specification is implemented by an instance of a class. Each class may implement more than one interface and each interface may be implemented by a number of different classes. Some object-oriented programming languages, such as .NET [68] and Java [19] uses interfaces to "implement" multiple inheritance. Multiple inheritance denotes that particular child can have more than one parent. Fig. 1.3 shows example of class diagram having multiple interfaces and classes realizing and requiring them.

• *Relationship*—a concept that specifies some kind of relationship between elements, i.e., it references one or more related elements. The relationship can model either physical or logical relations. The UML specification contains definition of multiple relationships that

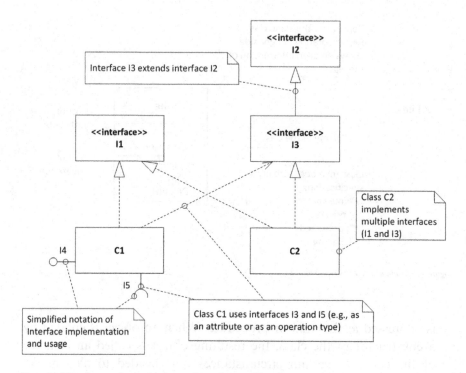

Figure 1.3 Class diagram showing implementation and usage of interfaces.

can exist between elements. The most important of relationships are the following three which are illustrated in Fig. 1.4:

1. *Generalization*—relates generalized classes to specialized classes, i.e., it shows the parent-child relations or the superclass-subclass relations.

2. *Association*—structural relationships among classes showing the physical structure of things. For example, transport vehicle has fuel tank. It shows also the multiplicity between things. For example, car has four tires.

3. *Dependency*—states that one entity uses the information and services of another entity. For example, car uses petrol station to fill fuel tank.

• *Enumerator*—used to specify definite set of available values. For example, Boolean can be specified as enumerator with two values *true* and *false* respectively (take a look at Fig. 1.5).

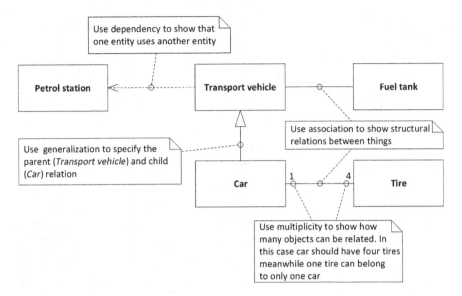

Figure 1.4 Example of relationships between classes.

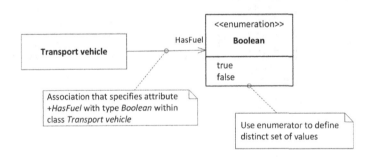

Figure 1.5 Enumerator definition for Boolean and its application.

Fig. 1.6 shows an example of class diagram which is developed as a part of data synchronization system development project which is later discussed in details in Part III, Topological UML Modeling Explained. It contains one abstract class (*DataSource*) with specialized classes of it (*SourceDataSource* and *TargetDataSource*), additional three classes and an enumerator which are tied together by associations and dependencies.

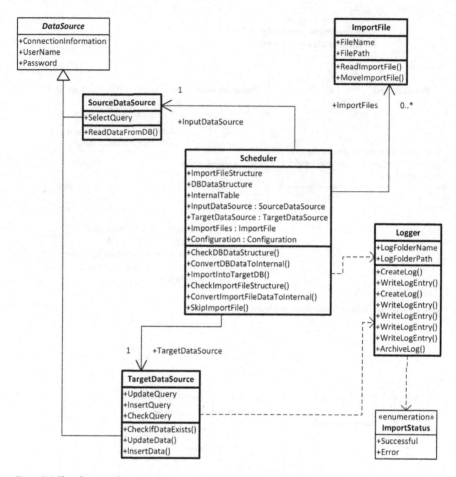

Figure 1.6 Class diagram of enterprise data synchronization system.

1.2.1.2 Object Diagram

While objects are instances of classes, an object diagram is a snapshot of the objects in a system at a specific point in time including the relations (links) between them. You should use object diagrams whenever it is needed to model or take a look on the values of attributes and state of the object at different stages during the execution of the software. They are very useful to model step-by-step execution of complex process or calculation operation. You can take a look at the initial stages of objects, during the process, and of course the final stages of objects to see the whole picture. Since it shows instances rather than classes, it is also called an instance diagram.

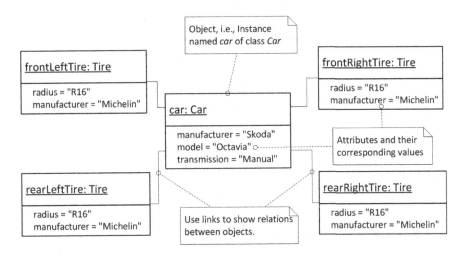

Figure 1.7 Object diagram showing car and all of its four tires.

The object diagram is included in UML specification since the first (1.1) version and it commonly contains following main elements: *object* and *link,* as you can see in Fig. 1.7. An association in class diagram becomes a link in object diagram. The example shows a car with four tires—the snapshot includes data about car itself (manufacturer and model) as well as tires (radius and manufacturer).

1.2.1.3 Package Diagram

The package is general-purpose mechanism for organizing modeling elements into groups, i.e., classes in groups or in namespaces and the relationships between them. Packages are used to arrange modeling elements (e.g., classes, interfaces, components, nodes, diagrams, collaborations, use cases, and other packages) into larger chunks that it is possible to manipulate them as a group. Packages can also be used to present different views of system's architecture and they can be incorporated into components to build up their internal structure. Well-designed packages group elements that are semantically close and tend to change together. Package diagram was first introduced in UML version 2.0. The elements that build up a Package diagram are as follows:

- *Name*—all packages should have a name that distinguishes them from other packages and allows to identify it. Since packages can be graphically displayed with slight differences—the name of package typically is placed in the middle of the package, or in the upper right side of the package (see examples in Fig. 1.8).

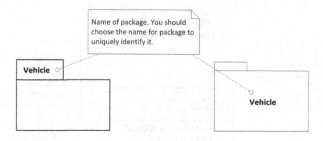

Figure 1.8 Name of package.

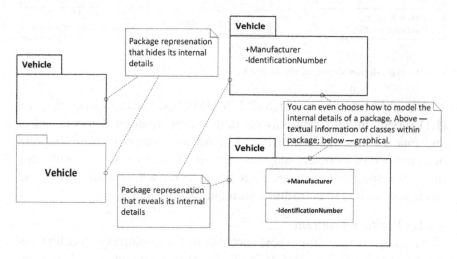

Figure 1.9 Packages.

- *Package*—a logical boundary of modeling elements to group together. You can either choose to show or hide the contents of a package. One way of how to organize packages—the commonly used namespaces of the classes. Graphically a package is drawn like a closed folder. Take a look at Fig. 1.9 to see the different ways of drawing package and revealing/hiding its details.
- *Element*—a package contains elements, i.e., classes, interfaces, components, nodes, use cases, diagrams, and other packages grouped into it. Every element that is included in the package is defined within it. If we destroy the package, all the elements within it are destroyed as well. Right side of Fig. 1.9 shows nested elements of package Vehicle while Fig. 1.10 gives an example of modeling package within package.

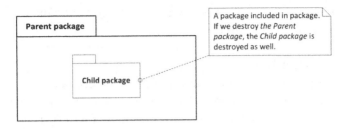

Figure 1.10 A package within a package.

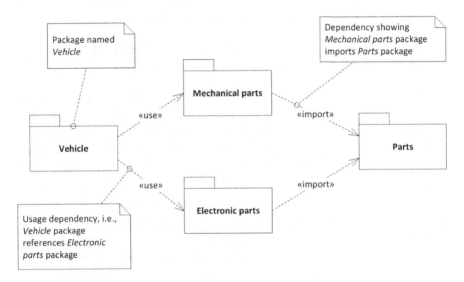

Figure 1.11 Package diagram showing packages and their relations.

- *Relationships*—several kinds of relationships are used when modeling packages: *import, export,* and *dependency use* relationship. If elements of one package uses elements of another package, then *import* or *use* relationship is used. If package contains public elements (e.g., public class *manufacturer* in Fig. 1.9) —it is called an *export.*

As you can see in Fig. 1.11, the package diagram is very useful to avoid unnecessary circular code references in the implementation. We should avoid circular references to enable normal code compilation— with such references both referenced classes must be recompiled every time either of them is changed. The role of package diagram is to identify as early as possible the situations where circular references could be used as a temporal solution (as we all know the temporal solutions are commonly with the most longest life) and to redesign the solution with the least efforts required.

1.2.1.4 Component Diagram

A component diagram shows the internal parts, connectors, and ports that implement a component. When the component is instantiated, copies of its internal parts are also instantiated. The UML component diagram shows how a software system will be composed of a set of deployable components—dynamic-link library (DLL) files, executable files, or web services—that interact through well-defined interfaces and which have their internal details hidden.

The *component diagram* is included in UML specification since the first (1.1) version and it contains the following elements:

- *Interface*—specifies a contract consisting of a set of coherent public attributes and operations for a class. Any instance of a class that realizes the interface must fulfill that contract. Since interfaces are declarations, they are not instantiable. Instead, an interface specification is implemented by an instance of a class. Each class may implement more than one interface and each interface may be implemented by a number of different classes. Fig. 1.12 shows example of component diagram having multiple interfaces and component providing and requiring them.
- *Component*—represents a modular part of a system that encapsulates its contents, it defines its behavior in terms of provided and required interfaces. As such, a component serves as a type whose conformance is defined by these provided and required interfaces (encompassing both their static as well as dynamic semantics). One component may therefore be substituted by another only if the two

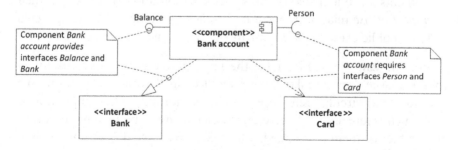

Figure 1.12 Component diagram showing component "Bank account" that provides and requires specific interfaces.

are type conformant. An example of component with provided and required interfaces is given in Fig. 1.13.

- *Port*—an explicit window into an encapsulated component. All of the interactions into and out of such component pass through ports. Each port provides or requires one or more specific interfaces. There can be multiple ports providing or requiring the same interface. It allows greater control over implementation and interaction with other components. Fig. 1.14 considers component with two named ports that each requires the same interface. The first port *Cash withdrawal* is used when bank's client takes out cash from automated teller machine (ATM) using his card. The other port named *Payment in shop* is used when making payments with card at shop.
- *Internal structure*—used to specify structure of a complex component, i.e., typically components are composed of smaller components thus building up the system. Fig. 1.15 gives example of an internal structure representation.
- *Part*—a component that builds up internal structure of a more complex component. You can consider part as a subcomponent. An example of showing parts within component is given in Fig. 1.15.

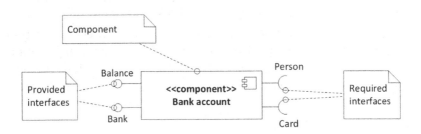

Figure 1.13 Example of component.

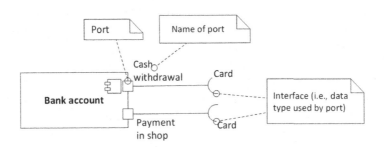

Figure 1.14 Component with two ports.

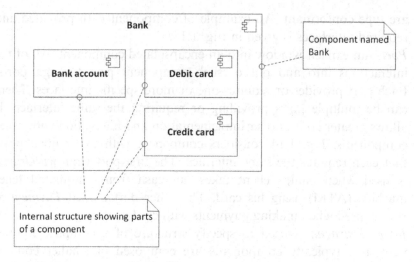

Figure 1.15 Internal structure of a component "Bank."

- *Connector*—a relation between ports of components. If one port provides interface required by the other port, they can be linked together. There are several types of connectors that we can draw between parts and components: A direct connector links together two ports of parts, connector by interfaces links together two ports by relating together required—provided interfaces using lollipop and socket notation, and delegation connector which links together port of a part and port of a component thus providing interface (i.e., provides services to other components) or requiring interface (i.e., consuming services of another component). Take a look at an example showing all three kinds of connectors in Fig. 1.16.

There is an additional diagram type within UML 2.x versions—*composite structure diagram.* It shows the internal structure of a class or collaboration and uses interface, component, port, and connector to show the internal structure. The difference between components and composite structure is tiny.

1.2.1.5 Deployment Diagram

A deployment diagram commonly is used to specify how the components of a system are distributed across the infrastructure and how they are related together. To model such a view deployment diagrams uses just two kinds of elements—nodes (i.e., components of a system

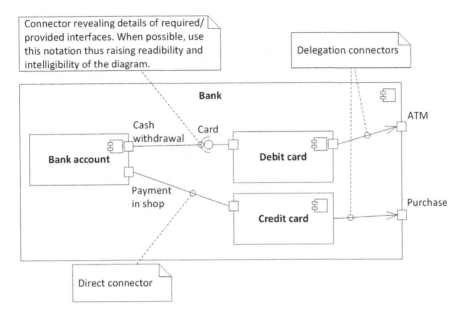

Figure 1.16 Example of connectors for parts and components.

or the infrastructure artifacts) and relationships that links nodes together. Deployment diagram shows the static deployment view of architecture. Deployment diagram typically is related to a component diagram in a way that nodes typically encloses one or more components. A deployment diagram is a diagram that shows the configuration of runtime processing nodes and the artifacts that live on them.

The *deployment diagram* is included in UML specification since the first (1.1) version and it includes following elements:

- *Node*—artifact of a software system (i.e., a component) or artifact of an infrastructure (e.g., server, network segment, sensors, etc.).
- *Relationship*—used to tie together nodes within deployment diagram thus building up a graph consisting of arcs (relationships) and vertices (nodes). Typically, association and dependency relationships are used.

An example of deployment diagram showing servers, their relationships and communication with client devices is shown in Fig. 1.17, which consists of three infrastructure layers—web-front-end servers, application server and data-storage server. The web-front-end servers contains all the components needed to render html pages on client

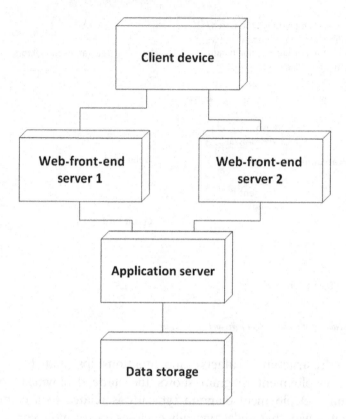

Figure 1.17 Deployment diagram showing servers as nodes and relations between them.

browsers, including communication with application layer to read and manipulate with data. The application layer (node of *Application server*) is hidden from the client thus improving security aspect of the deployment and contains all the artifacts that are required to work with data (i.e., implements read and write operations) while the *Data storage* node is responsible for storing and retrieving data bytes from the media. The *Client device* holds components such as internet browser for user to be able to interact with the system. The *Client device* node adds more understanding to the deployment diagram showing that the client can access data only using the web-front-end layer.

1.2.1.6 Profile Diagram
The profile diagram contains mechanisms that allow extending and adapting metaclasses from existing metamodels for different purposes; includes the ability to tailor the UML metamodel for different platforms or domains. The profile diagram is the most younger diagram

among the diagrams of UML—it is introduced only in version 2.2 thus finally allowing legally extending the UML metamodel—the profiles mechanism is consistent with the MOF. While there were no profile diagram the solution to "extend" UML was to rewrite the specification and add required elements. But this created additional headaches for bringing the new thing into practice—there were no standardized tool support for such new language specification. The UML profile diagram consists of following elements:

- *Metamodel*—a referenced model that is extended through the profile (e.g., UML).
- *Reference*—a dependency relationship with attached stereotype *"reference"* that is directed from profile to referenced metamodel.
- *Profile*—a special package that extends a referenced metamodel by adding stereotypes to it. Like packages in package diagram can be drawn at different abstraction levels revealing or hiding its content, the profile can be drawn in the same manner.
- *Metaclass*—a class that is extended by a stereotype. The metaclass is represented with the same node as regular class by attaching stereotype *"metaclass."*
- *Stereotype*—extends existing UML vocabulary by adding a new element to it and it describes how an existing metaclass can be extended enabling the integration of platform or domain-specific terminology or notation in the modeling language (a set of stereotypes build up the profile). A stereotype extension is used to indicate that the properties of a metaclass are extended through a stereotype. The stereotyped class is represented with the same node as regular class by attaching stereotype *"stereotype."*
- *Extension*—a special binary association, extension end is used to tie an extension to a stereotype when extending a metaclass. Extension relationship is directed from stereotyped class to the metaclass it extends.
- *Profile application*—a dependency relationship with attached stereotype *"apply"* between a package and a profile that allows to use the stereotypes from the profile in the model elements of the source package. Profile application relationship is directed from package that applies profile to the profile package.

Profiles in more details are explored in Chapter 3, Adjusting Unified Modeling Language, while an example showing generic profile with name *TestML* is given in Fig. 1.18. The example of profile extends

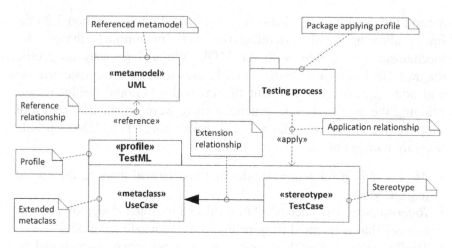

Figure 1.18 Profile diagram showing example of profile and profile application.

UML by adding stereotype *TestCase*. The stereotype *TestCase* extends metaclass *UseCase* by using extension relationship. The profile is applied by the package *Testing process*.

1.2.2 Behavior Diagrams

The UML behavior diagrams are used to visualize, specify, construct, and document the dynamic aspect of a system (modeling dynamic aspect of a system can be considered as representing its changing parts). Behavior diagrams include activity diagram, use case diagram, state diagram, and interaction diagrams. Interaction diagrams are a special subset of behavior diagrams and they are sequence, communication, interaction overview, and timing diagrams. An interaction diagram shows an interaction, consisting of a set of objects and their relationships, including the messages that may be dispatched among them. These diagrams share the same underlying model, although in practice they emphasize different things. By using interaction diagrams, it is possible to reason about flow of control within an operation, a class, a component, a use case, or the system as whole in two ways: (1) focusing on how messages are dispatched across time and (2) focusing on the structural relationships among the objects in an interaction and then consider how messages are passed within the context of that structure [15,37,78,79].

All behavior diagrams, including interaction diagrams, are listed and described in the subsections of this section. Each subsection name

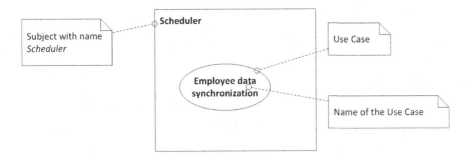

Figure 1.19 Example of use case *within* subject.

denotes corresponding UML diagram name and the contents includes description, main elements, UML version in which the diagram is included, and an example of a developed diagram.

1.2.2.1 Use Case Diagram

Use case diagram shows a set of use cases and actors and their relationships; it is used to organize and model the dynamic aspect—required usages—of a system. Each use case in use case diagram typically is supplemented by a full use case specification—a written statement detailing the preconditions (what must be true before the use case is performed), the sequence of events, including alternate sequence of events in case of exception or specific conditions, and the postconditions (what must be true after the use case has completed).

The use case diagram is included in UML specification since its first (1.1) version and it includes following elements:

- *Subject*—usually it is a system or subsystem, i.e., a set of use cases together describes the behavioral aspect of the subject under consideration. Fig. 1.19 contains example showing subject.
- *Use case*—it describes what a system or subsystem is doing, it does not include and does not specify how it is doing it. Commonly specification of use case is written in natural language, structuring the description as sequential steps performed by the actors and the subject involved in the use case scenario. Use case scenario includes both the main scenario and an alternative scenario which is used in the case of exception or specific conditions becoming true during the execution of it. The use case is drawn as an ellipsis showing the name of use case within it (see example in Fig. 1.19).

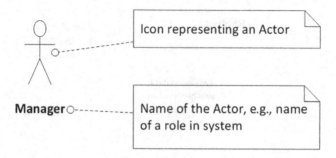

Figure 1.20 Actor.

- *Actor*—represents a coherent set of users, roles, external systems that interacts with the subject through specific use cases. Actors model entities that are outside the system. Taking a look from the subject's viewpoint—the external systems are also drawn as actors interacting with the use case. Fig. 1.20 shows a typical graphical representation of an actor although you can create a stereotype of the actor to visually represent in any form or image according to needs to better illustrate the actor.
- *Relationship*—there are three types of relationships used within use case diagram. The first one is between use cases showing dependency *extend* and *include* relations. The extend dependency is used to show an alternate flow of events in the case if specific conditions are met, e.g., an alternate scenario, while the include dependency is used to specify a common scenario included in multiple use cases (it avoids the duplications of the same scenarios/requirements). The second type of relationships is between use cases and actors, typically represented as associations showing the communication link between actor and use case. The last type is between actors—typically generalization is used to show the parent-child relationships between roles.

Fig. 1.21 shows an example of diagram which is developed as a part of data synchronization system development project described in detail in Part III, Topological UML Modeling Explained.

1.2.2.2 Activity Diagram

Activity diagram is used to model dynamic view of a system. It shows the control flow from step to step, i.e., from activity to activity. An activity shows set of actions, the sequential or branching control flow,

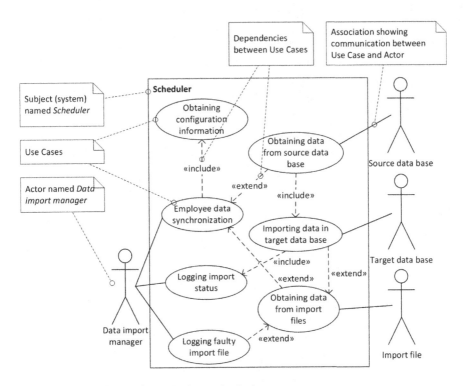

Figure 1.21 Use case diagram of enterprise data synchronization system.

and values that are produced or consumed by actions. The activity diagram is included in UML specification since the first (1.1) version, it includes following elements:

- *Activity*—specifies the flow of subordinate activities and actions, using a control and data flow model. The activity execution is started because of events happening outside that activity, e.g., other activities finish executing, objects and data becoming available. Each activity can include a set of preconditions, postconditions, and input and output parameters. Each precondition should be met for activity to start its execution (thus the availability of objects and data plays an important role). Activities may form invocation hierarchies invoking other activities, ultimately resolving to individual actions. In an object-oriented model, activities are usually invoked indirectly as methods bound to operations that are directly invoked. Activities may describe procedural computation. In this context, they are the methods corresponding to operations on classes.

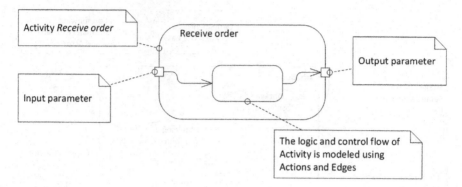

Figure 1.22 Activity.

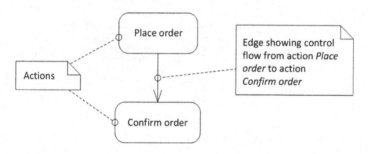

Figure 1.23 Actions and edges.

Activities may be applied to organizational modeling for business process engineering and workflow. In this context, events often originate from inside the system, such as the finishing of a task, but also from outside the system, such as a customer call. Activities can also be used for information system modeling to specify system level processes. An example of general activity is given in Fig. 1.22.

- *Action*—represents a single atomic step within an activity, i.e., it is the smallest step within activity and it is not further decomposed. The dynamics of activity is modeled by all the actions included within it. If there are common actions required in multiple activities, a call behavior action can be used to reference another activity. In this case, the execution of the call action involves the execution of the referenced activity and its actions. While an activity defines a behavior that can be reused in many places, whereas an action is only used once at a particular point in an activity. Example of actions is shown in Fig. 1.23.

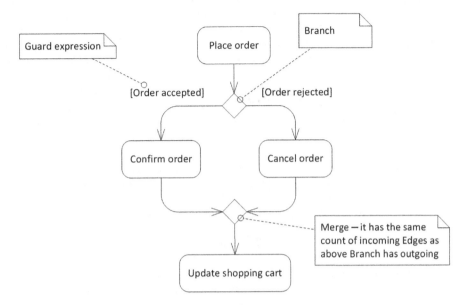

Figure 1.24 Branching and merging in activity diagrams.

- *Edge*—is used to model the control flow from activity to activity, i.e., it is a link between actions having arrowhead at the end of it pointing to the next action which is to be executed. In fact, an action may have sets of incoming and outgoing activity edges that specify control flow and data flow. An action will not begin execution until all of its input conditions are satisfied. A sample of edge connecting two actions is given in Fig. 1.23.
- *Branching and merging*—while actions and edges are used to model activity's behavior, the branching allows to introduce alternate execution paths based on conditions of each branch. A branch is represented in a form of a diamond, it has one incoming edge and two or more outgoing edges. Each outgoing edge has guard (a Boolean expression) to model which action will be executed next. Since activity diagrams beginning with UML version 2 is based on the formalism of Petri nets [21], all the branched flows should be merged together. Merge is represented with the same diamond as branch but it has two or more incoming edges and at least one outgoing edge. An example of branching and merging is illustrated in Fig. 1.24.
- *Forking and joining*—in the case of modeling concurrent control flows fork and join should be used. A fork has one incoming and

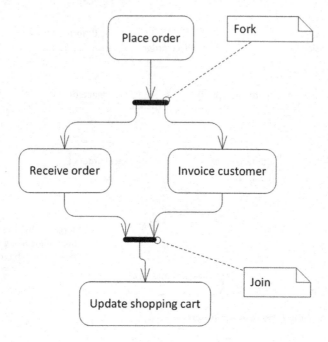

Figure 1.25 Forking and joining in activity diagrams.

two or more outgoing edges. Since activity diagrams is based on the formalism of Petri nets, all the forked flows should be joined together. The execution of an activity after join continues only when all the flows after fork have come to the join. A join has two or more incoming edges and one outgoing edge. Fork and join is represented using thick bar. An example illustrating use of fork and join is given in Fig. 1.25.

• *Initial and final nodes*—an initial node shows a starting point for executing an activity. One activity can have multiple initial nodes. In such case the invoking of the activity starts multiple flows—one at each initial node. Note that flows can also start at other nodes, e.g., the parameter node of activity (see example in Fig. 1.22). An initial node is represented in the form of circle. A final node is an abstract control node at which a flow in an activity stops—when a final node is reached the execution of activity is terminated. The execution termination occurs also in the case of forking—if one of the flow reaches final node, all the concurrent flows are terminated. The final node is represented with a filled circle within unfilled circle. If you need to terminate only one concurrent flow, a

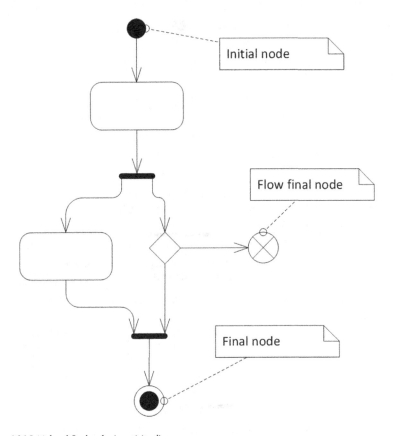

Figure 1.26 Initial and final nodes in activity diagram.

flow final node should be used. The flow final node is represented using X within a circle. See an example of initial and final nodes in Fig. 1.26.

Fig. 1.27 shows an example of activity diagram which is developed as a part of data synchronization system development project.

1.2.2.3 State Diagram

State diagram essentially is a state machine, consisting of states, transitions, events, and activities. While activity diagram shows a flow of control from activity to activity across number of objects involved in execution of those activities, state diagram shows flow of control from state to state within single object. State diagram specifies the sequences of states an object goes through during its lifetime in response to events, together with its responses to those events. The state diagram is

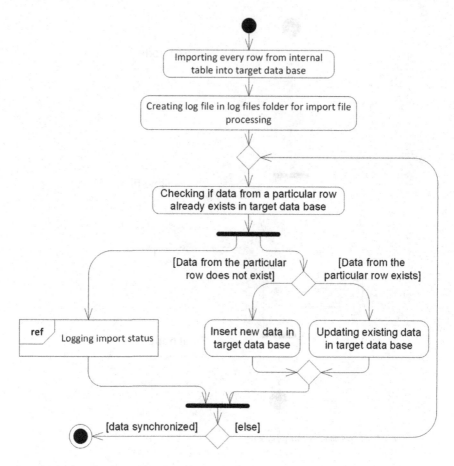

Figure 1.27 Activity diagram modeling data import in target data base.

included in UML specification since the first (1.1) version, it includes following elements:

- *State*—shows a state of an object. For an object to be in a particular state it should met some condition or situation in its lifetime, perform some activity, or wait for some event. If we take a look at file writing software, it could have a set of following states—*idle* (the software waits for a new file to be written in hard drive), *writing* (its writing bytes of file to hard drive), and *waiting* (the file is locked for writing by another process). Launching of such file writing software puts it in the situation where it is waiting for next operation thus setting the state to *Idle*. When user wants to write file, an event of this will be fired and the status is changed to *Writing*. If the software comes to condition where the file is exclusively locked for writing, it

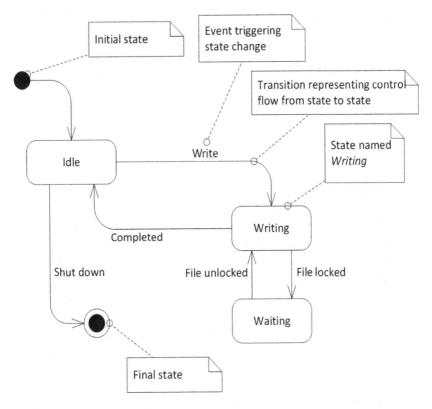

Figure 1.28 States of a file writing software.

is going to the state *Waiting*. After the file is unlocked the unlock event is fired and the software returns to *Writing*. See example in Fig. 1.28.

- *Event*—a specific occurrence or happening that plays a significant role in an object's lifetime and thus can trigger the state transition. See example in Fig. 1.28.
- *Transition*—a directed relationship between a source state and a target state showing that an object will transit from one specified state to another if specific conditions are met and specific events occur. See example in Fig. 1.28.
- *Initial and final states*—a special kind of states showing the initial state of an object and a final state. When the final state is reached, it means that the state machine is completed. These two states are similar to initial and final nodes in activity diagrams (see Section 1.2.2.2).

Fig. 1.28 shows an example of a state diagram showing states of file writing software.

1.2.2.4 Sequence Diagram

A sequence diagram is an interaction diagram that emphasizes the time ordering of messages sent between objects. It shows a set of objects or roles and messages sent and received by them. Sequence diagram has two features that distinguish them from communication diagrams—presence of lifeline and focus of control. The sequence diagram is included in UML specification since the first (1.1) version, it includes following elements:

- *Object or role*—shows object or role which is involved in the communication with other objects or roles.
- *Lifeline*—a vertical dashed bar showing the lifeline of object. The time dimension visually is going from top to down thus we can track the creation and destruction of an object along with the messages sent and received by it.
- *Message*—specifies a particular communication between objects or roles. It is represented as a directed relationship pointing from sender to receiver. Message can be an invocation of an operation, raising a signal, creating or destroying object. The message has a name and it can include also parameters. Using different notations of messages, we can model both synchronous and asynchronous interactions.
- *Control*—shows a period of time during which an object is performing an action requested by the message received, i.e., we can visually show the period of the execution of specific procedure; if we have nested procedure calls then we can visually as soon as possible show the possible bottlenecks raising performance issues in the future. Visually it is represented as a tiny vertical rectangle on the corresponding object's lifeline.
- *Structured control*—while control and messages allows us to model simple communication between objects, in many situations we need to model decision taking, parallel execution, and optional execution. To accomplish this modeling task, there are special graphical notation elements allowing us to model such cases.

Fig. 1.29 shows an example of diagram which is developed as a part of data synchronization system development project.

1.2.2.5 Communication Diagram

Communication diagram like sequence diagram pays attention on objects or roles involved in system and communication between them.

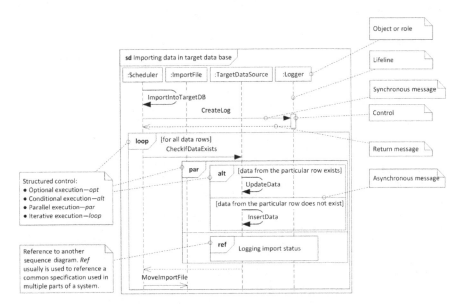

Figure 1.29 Importing data in target data base.

It accents structural organization of objects that send and receive messages; it shows a set of roles, connectors among roles, and messages sent and received by the instances playing these roles. Communication diagram have two features that distinguish them from sequence diagram—path and sequence number of messages (Sequence number indicates the time order of message). A communication diagram is a simplified version of the UML version 1.x collaboration diagram and it is included in UML beginning with version 2.0. It includes following elements:

- *Object or role*—shows object or role which is involved in the communication with other objects or roles.
- *Message*—specifies a particular communication between objects or roles. Since there are no timelines in communication diagram, the sequence of messages is numbered. Having a large communication diagram will lead to quite complex numbering of the messages.
- *Link*—shows a communication link between objects or roles. Communication direction between objects are represented with additional small arrow next to the link pointing from sender to receiver.

Fig. 1.30 shows an example of diagram which is developed as a part of data synchronization system development project.

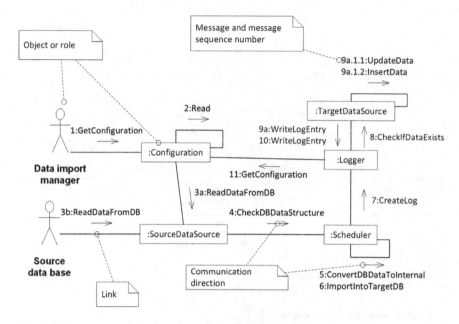

Figure 1.30 Communication diagram representing data synchronization with source data base.

1.2.2.6 Interaction Overview Diagram

Interaction overview diagram define interactions through a variant of activity diagram in a way that promotes overview of the control flow. The lifelines and the messages can be hidden at this overview level. Interaction overview diagrams are specialization of activity diagrams that represent interactions. Interaction overview diagram is introduced starting from UML version 2.0, it includes following elements:

- *Interaction*—emphasizes the time ordering of messages sent between objects. It shows a set of objects or roles and messages sent and received by them. Interaction is represented in a form of a rectangle with name tag, while the contents of this rectangle we can consider as a sequence diagram. Fig. 1.31 shows an example of interaction.
- *Interaction use*—a reference to an interaction. Interaction use hides the contents of the interaction. It is useful if we are using the same interaction across the system. Using interaction use we can define one interaction only once and reference it everywhere where it is needed. Representation of interaction use is given in Fig. 1.32.
- *Edge*—is used to model the control flow from activity to activity, i.e., it is a link between nodes having arrowhead at the end of it pointing to the next node which is to be executed. In fact, a node

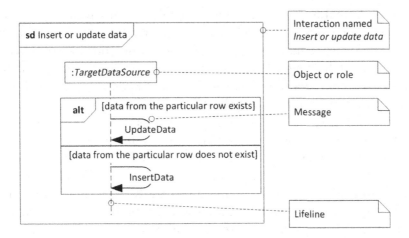

Figure 1.31 Interaction.

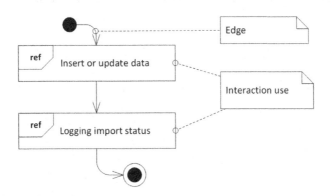

Figure 1.32 Interaction use.

may have sets of incoming and outgoing activity edges that specify control flow and data flow. A node will not begin execution until all of its input conditions are satisfied. An example of edges connecting interaction uses is given in Fig. 1.32.

- *Structured control*—while control and messages allows us to model simple communication between objects, in many situations we need to model decision taking, parallel execution, and optional execution. To accomplish this modeling task, there are special graphical notation elements allowing us to model such cases.
- *Initial and final nodes*—an initial node shows a starting point for executing interaction. An initial node is represented in the form of

circle. A final node is an abstract control node at which a flow in an interaction stops—when a final node is reached the execution of interaction is terminated. the execution termination occurs also in the case of forking—if one of the flow reaches final node, all the concurrent flows are terminated. The final node is represented with a filled circle within unfilled circle.

- *Branching and merging*—while interactions, interaction uses, and edges are used to model simple interactions, the branching allows to introduce alternate execution paths based on conditions of each branch. A branch is represented in a form of a diamond, it has one incoming edge and two or more outgoing edges. Each outgoing edge has guard (a Boolean expression) to model which action will be executed next. Merge is represented with the same diamond as branch but it has two or more incoming edges and at least one outgoing edge. Take a look at Fig. 1.33 which contains an example of branching and merging in interaction overview diagram.

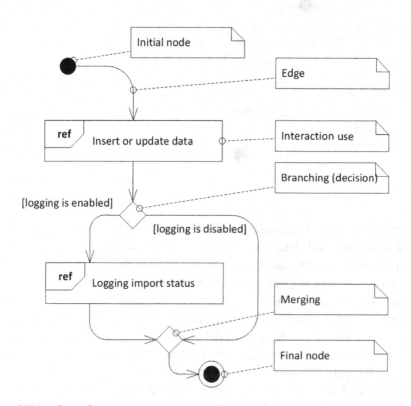

Figure 1.33 Branching and merging in interaction overview diagram.

- *Forking and joining*—in the case of modeling concurrent control flows fork and join should be used. A fork has one incoming and two or more outgoing edges. The execution after join continues only when all the flows after fork have come to the join. A join has two or more incoming edges and one outgoing edge. Fork and join is represented using thick bar. Fig. 1.34 includes an example of forking and joining.

Fig. 1.34 shows an example of interaction overview diagram.

1.2.2.7 Timing Diagram

Timing diagram is used to show interactions when a primary purpose of the diagram is to reason about time; it focuses on conditions changing within and among lifelines along a linear time axis. Timing diagram is a special form of a sequence diagram. The most notable graphical difference between timing diagram and sequence diagram is that time dimension in timing diagram is horizontal and the time is increasing from left to the right and the lifelines are shown in separate compartments arranged vertically. The timing diagram is available since UML version 2.0 and includes elements such as message, lifeline, timeline, and object or role.

1.3 BENEFITS OF APPLYING UNIFIED MODELING LANGUAGE

The use of UML for systems' modeling has following benefits [3,22,35,78,82]:

- The *UML is a modeling language and not a method, methodology, or technique,* thus making it independent of particular methods and programming languages. The UML specification defines a number of diagrams and the meaning of those diagrams. A method goes further and describes the steps required to develop the software, which diagrams are developed in what order, and who is responsible for completing certain tasks.
- The *UML is platform independent modeling language*—it can be used to design software for implementation in any programming language.
- It is a modeling language *created from* a set of *widely accepted object-oriented software design methods,* thus ending the endless choose between concurrent notations.
- The *UML is a set of standardized object-oriented models,* thus making communication between stakeholders more efficient and meaningful, i.e., if stakeholders are familiar with UML then the created

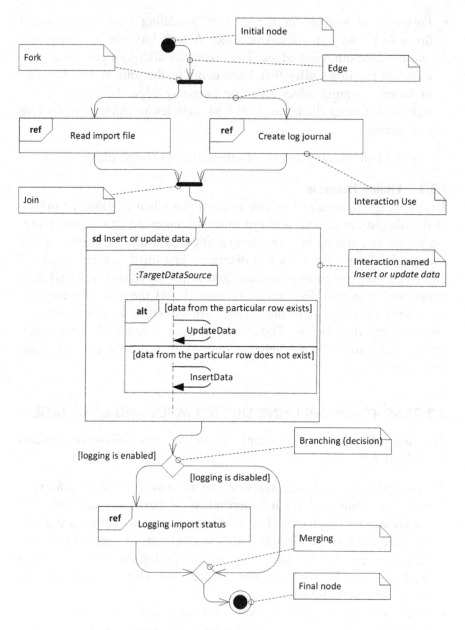

Figure 1.34 Interaction overview diagram.

models of system can be more easily communicated between different development teams, customers, and stakeholders.

- Starting with UML version 2.0 it contains *extension mechanisms*. If the set of models provided by UML are not enough for required solution, it is possible to extend UML in a number of allowed ways.

- The UML can be used for both large and complex systems modeling, as well as for small projects.
- As *UML is defined in accordance with XML Metadata Interchange (XMI)*, the models can be transferred between different tools from different tool vendors. Thus making users of UML less dependent on particular modeling tools.

Despite all above-mentioned benefits that the application of UML within software development has, it has also a number of disadvantages which are discussed in the next subsection.

1.4 DISADVANTAGES OF APPLYING UNIFIED MODELING LANGUAGE

The specification of UML and the UML itself is not developed basing on any theoretical principles regarding the constructs required for an effective and usable modeling language for analysis and design. UML arose from best practices in parts of the software engineering community; in fact, these best practices at some points are even conflicting [22]. Basically, this means that the UML goes without mathematics [83] (except activity diagrams, which are now (starting from UML version 2.0) based on the formalism and mathematics of Petri nets [78]). UML specification is described using the combination of languages—metamodeling, Object Constraint Language (OCL) [124], and the natural language. This has resulted in a language that contains many modeling constructs, which has thus been criticized on the grounds that it is excessively complex and large. At the same time, the UML has also been criticized for lacking the flexibility to handle certain modeling requirements in specific domains. As a result of this criticism, UML has evolved—starting from UML version 2.0 it allows the development of profiles [22].

Main disadvantages of UML are as follows [22,24,51,99]:

- *Size*—UML is a collection of notations that encompasses a wide range of notations. In addition, the provided extension mechanisms of UML allow modelers to add their own, often ad-hoc, extensions to the language. In short, *UML is large and growing.*
- *Incoherence*—UML has brought together a number of notations from different fields. For example, it is not clear how state diagram relates to class diagram and sequence diagram.

- *Different interpretations*—since the semantics of UML constructs are defined by using natural language, they are interpreted differently by different modelers.
- *Frequent subsetting*—organizations tend to define their own UML subset—guidelines on which parts to use; which not to use; own definitions of semantics where the standard is unclear, inconsistent or untenable for the organization concerned.
- *Lack of causality*—despite the fact that UML contains a set of 14 diagrams, none of the existing diagram allows to clearly trace cause-and-effect relationships between both problem and solution domains. This can be related to the fact, that only use case diagram deals with the requirements and computation independent viewpoint modeling.

In regards to the above listed disadvantages of UML, in [114] is presented a list of problems associated with using UML in software development; causes of these problems are various: ambiguous semantics, cognitive misdirection during the development process, inadequate capture of properties of system under consideration, lack of appropriate supporting tools and developer inexperience. By analyzing these problems in detail, part of the researchers claim that some of these problems can be addressed by formalizing UML semantics [122], and the most helpful sequencing of modeling techniques [26]. Others claim that a revision of the UML and its supporting tools is required [31]. Furthermore, it is assumed that largest part of these problems can be addressed to the ambiguous transition between analysis and design models [99].

1.5 FORMALISM OF UNIFIED MODELING LANGUAGE

The UML specification is defined by using a metamodeling approach which adapts formal specification techniques. A metamodel is used to specify the model that comprises the UML. In spite of using the metamodeling approach, the UML specification method lacks some properties of formal specification methods. The specification of UML cannot be considered as formal specification because of natural language (English) use in it. UML specification [77] underlines that the specification as a metamodel does not eliminate the option of specifying it later by using formal/mathematical language (e.g., notation Z [119], Prototype Verification System (PVS) [102], Rigorous Approach to Industrial Software Engineering (RAISE) [69]). Section 1.5.1 takes closer look at the formalism of UML version 1.x specification and

Section 1.5.2 takes closer look at the formalism of UML version 2.x (as the UML version 2.x is major revision of UML version 1.x).

1.5.1 Formalism of Unified Modeling Language Version 1.x

The specification of UML version 1.5 [72] contains language syntax and its static and dynamic semantics. The specification uses a combination of languages—a subset of UML, an OCL, and precise natural language to describe the abstract syntax and semantics of the full UML. Thus, the UML version 1.x specification uses a formal technique for preciseness improving but at the same time keeping readability of it. Despite that the language structure is described in precise specification that is necessary for tool interaction, it is needed to note that the existing description is not a completely formal specification (due to the use of natural language). As stated in [73], a common technique for specification of languages is to first define the syntax of the language and then to describe its static and dynamic semantics. The syntax defines what constructs exist in the language and how the constructs are built up in terms of other constructs. Static semantics of a language define how an instance of a construct should be connected to other instances to be meaningful while dynamic semantics define the meaning of a well-formed construct. These semantics are described using natural language (English).

Summarizing up the UML version 1.x specification, the metamodel of UML is described in a semi-formal way using three views [73]:

1. *Abstract syntax*—presented in a form of UML class diagram. The UML metamodel is defined with the set of interrelated packages. Abstract syntax shows the metaclasses defining the constructs and their relationships and also presents some of the well-formedness rules (mainly the multiplicity requirements of the relationships), and whether or not the instances of a particular subconstruct must be ordered. A short informal description in natural language describing each construct is supplied. The first paragraph of each of these descriptions is a general presentation of the construct that sets the context, while the following paragraphs give the informal definition of the metaclass specifying the construct in UML. Each metaclass has its attributes enumerated together with a short explanation. Besides that, the opposite role names of associations connected to the metaclass is also listed in the same way.

2. *Well-formedness rules*—the static semantics of UML metaclasses (except for multiplicity and ordering constraints) are defined as a set of invariants of an instance of the metaclass. These invariants have to be satisfied for the construct to be meaningful. The rules thus specify constraints over attributes and associations defined in the metamodel. Each invariant is defined by an expression written using OCL together with an informal explanation in English of the expression.
3. *Semantics*—defines meanings of the constructs using natural language (English). The constructs are grouped into logical chunks that are defined together. Since only concrete metaclasses have a true meaning in the language, only these are described in this section.

In summary, the UML metamodel is described in a combination of graphic notation, (precise) natural language, and formal language. The use of natural language for specifying language constructs makes its specification semiformal. This semiformal specification of UML can cause incorrectness and inaccuracy of system models defined with UML (due that statements in natural language can be interpreted with different meanings among different persons (in spite of trying to use it as precise as possible)).

1.5.2 Formalism of Unified Modeling Language Version 2.x
The main goal of major revision of UML within version 2.0 is to increase the precision and correctness of the specification. The set of UML modeling concepts is partitioned into horizontal layers of increasing capability called *compliance levels*. For ease of model interchange, there are only two compliance levels defined for infrastructure specification [77]:

- *Level 0 (L0)*—contains a single language unit that provides capabilities for modeling class-based structures encountered in object-oriented programming languages, and it provides an entry-level modeling capability, and
- *Metamodel Constructs (LM)*—adds an extra language unit for more advanced class-based structures used for building metamodels.

Superstructure specification adds three more compliance levels [78]:

- *Level 1 (L1)*—adds new language units and extends the capabilities provided by Level 0. Specifically, it adds language units for use cases, interactions, structures, actions, and activities.

- *Level 2 (L2)*—extends the language units already provided in Level 1 and adds language units for deployment, state machine modeling, and profiles.
- *Level 3 (L3)*—*represents the complete UML*. It extends the language units provided by Level 2 and adds new language units for modeling information flows, templates, and model packaging.

All compliance levels are defined as extensions to a single core *UML* package that defines the common namespace shared by all the compliance levels. Level 0 is defined by the top-level metamodel. The UML version 2.x specification is defined by using a metamodeling approach that adapts formal specification techniques. According to [77], the following are the goals of the specification techniques used to define UML 2.x:

- *Correctness*—improves the correctness of the metamodel by helping to validate it.
- *Precision*—increases the precision of both the syntax and semantics. The precision should be sufficient so that there is neither syntactic nor semantic ambiguity for either implementers or users.
- *Conciseness*—the specification techniques should be parsimonious, so that the precise syntax and semantics are defined without superfluous detail.
- *Consistency*—the metamodeling approach should be complemented by adding essential detail in a consistent way.
- *Understandability*—while increasing the precision and conciseness, the readability of the specification should also be improved. For this reason, a less than strict formalism is applied, since a strict formalism would require formal techniques.

The specification technique used in UML version 2.x describes the metamodel in the same way as the version 1.x does, i.e., it uses metamodeling approach and three views (abstract syntax, well-formedness rules, and semantics). Main language constructs are related to metaclasses in the metamodel. Other constructs, i.e., being variants of other ones, are defined as stereotypes of metaclasses in the metamodel. This mechanism allows the semantics of the variant constructs to be significantly different from the base metaclass. Another way of defining variants is the use of metaatributes.

The UML 2.x metamodel contains infrastructure library package which defines a reusable metalanguage kernel and a metamodel extension mechanism for UML. The metalanguage kernel can be used to specify a variety of metamodels, including UML itself, MOF, and CWM. In addition, the infrastructure library defines a profile extension mechanism that can be used to customize UML for different platforms and domains without supporting a complete metamodeling capability. The UML profile extension mechanism reduces notation size and efforts for specific task solution and allows creating additional constructs along with the benefit of profile reuse in ordinary UML modeling tools. The architectural alignment among UML, MOF, and XMI tries to solve the problem of UML model interchange between tools by using the rules of XMI specification.

In spite of trying to use natural language in more precise way, the specification of UML cannot be considered as formal specification because of natural language use—the problem considered in previous subsection still exists. The UML specification still underlines that the specification as a metamodel does not eliminate the option of specifying it later by using formal or mathematical language. However, the first steps of formalizing UML constructs are taken—starting from UML version 2.0 the activity diagram is formally based on Petri nets [79].

1.5.3 The Need of Additional Unified Modeling Language Formalization

Since the release of the first UML specification researchers are working and proposing approaches to improve formalization of UML. Researches on UML formalization are performed because the meaning of the language, which is mainly described in English, is too informal and unstructured to provide a foundation for developing formal analysis and development techniques, and because of the scope of the model, which is both complex and large [97]. Despite the fact that the latest UML specification is based on the metamodeling approach, the UML metamodel gives information about abstract syntax of UML but does not deal with semantics in formal way (as discussed previous, the semantics is expressed using natural language). Thus, it is hard to determine how a given change in a model influences its meaning and to verify whether a given model transformation preserves the semantics of the model or not. Since UML is method-independent, its specification tends to set a range of potential interpretations rather than providing an exact meaning [31,122].

According to [31], the formalization of UML specification has following benefits:

- *Clarity*—the formally stated semantics can act as a point of reference to resolve disagreements over intended interpretation and to clear up confusion over the precise meaning of a construct.
- *Equivalence and consistency*—a precise semantics provides an unambiguous basis from which to compare and contrast the UML with other techniques and notations, and for ensuring consistency between its different components.
- *Extendibility*—the soundness of extensions to the UML can be verified (as encouraged by the UML authors).
- *Refinement*—the correctness of design steps in the UML can be verified and precisely documented. In particular, a properly developed semantics supports the development of design transformations, in which a more abstract model is diagrammatically transformed into an implementation model.
- *Proof*—justified proofs and rigorous analysis of important properties of a system described in the UML require precise semantics. Proof and rigorous analysis are not currently supported by UML.
- *Tools*—the tools that make use of semantics, e.g., a code generator or consistency checker, require that semantics to be precise, whether it be expressed as part of the standard or invented in the code by the tool developer.

The current UML semantics are not sufficiently formal to realize all of the above listed benefits. Despite that researches on UML formalization have been made before the release of UML version 2.0, the UML version 2.x specification is not written as a formal specification of language. Therefore, there are a number of ongoing UML formalization researches trying to formalize it from different aspects.

1.5.4 Current Unified Modeling Language Formalization Attempts

After OMG accepted UML version 1.1 as a standard, a precise UML (pUML) group was found with main goal to bring together international researchers and practitioners who share the aim of developing the UML as a precise modeling language [31]. The aim of pUML group was to work firmly in the context of the existing UML semantics. As a formalization instrument they use several formal notations (e.g., OCL [124] or the formal language Z [119]). The pUML group is an example of researches focusing on formalization of UML semantics. Some of the formalization researches are restricted to the semantics of models, while the others are concerned with the issues of reasoning about models and model transformations. Currently there exist a number of approaches for specifying and formalizing semantics of UML:

- Specifying semantics by formal languages (e.g., using language Z [31] or Object-Z [52]),
- Using category theory—captures relationships between specification objects (e.g., [1,20]),
- Using stream theory—as streams is an adequate setting for the formalization of the semantics of concurrent systems (e.g., [16]),
- Using π-calculus or process algebra (e.g., [126]), and
- Using algebraic approaches (e.g., using mathematical notation [122])

As indicated by Evermann in [33], the researches on UML semantics formalization relate to the internal consistency of the UML, not to its relationship to problem domains. To address the relation of UML elements to problem domains, the researchers are ongoing on formalizing the way the software is developed by using UML diagrams (e.g., the problem domain formalization approach [89], or the software development with the emphasis on topology in constructed models [24]) and describing UML constructs by using ontology, thus relating them with problem domains (e.g., [33,125]).

By summarizing up the attempts to formalize UML, the following formalization directions emerge:

- Formalizing the semantics of UML,
- Formalizing the way, the UML is used, and
- Relating UML constructs to problem domains.

1.6 UNIFIED MODELING LANGUAGE IMPROVEMENT OPTIONS

According to the UML version 2.4.1 specification [77,78] and recent researches (e.g., [22,33,88,114,122,125]) in the field of strengthening UML, its use and analysis, the following UML improvement options arise:

- Extending UML by using UML's extensibility mechanisms,
- Formalizing the semantics of UML,

- Formalizing the way, the UML is used, and
- Relating UML constructs to problem domains.

The UML can be strengthened by using the mathematical topology. The use of topology reflects extending the UML to support topology in its diagrams, and formalizing the way the UML is applied during software development process. Since this work is dedicated to extend UML by its extensibility mechanisms and formalizing the software development process, the following two subsections discuss the UML extensibility mechanisms and its improvement by using mathematical topology.

1.6.1 Unified Modeling Language Extensibility Mechanisms

The UML version 2.4.1 extensibility mechanisms permit to extend the language in controlled ways; these mechanisms include stereotypes, tagged values, constraints, and profiles. If the enumerated four extension mechanisms does not solve the problem why the language should be extended, then UML metamodel can be extended using MOF. By extending UML using MOF there are no restrictions on what are allowed to do with a UML metamodel [15,77].

Stereotypes: A stereotype defines how an existing metaclass may be extended, and enables the use of platform or domain specific terminology or notation in place of, or in addition to, the ones used for the extended metaclass. In other words, a stereotype extends the vocabulary of the UML, allowing to create new kinds of building blocks that are derived from existing ones but that are specific to problem under consideration.

Stereotype can be considered as a type that defines other types, because each one creates equivalent of a new class in the UML metamodel. When an element is stereotyped (such as node or a class), the UML gets extended by creating a new building block just like the existing one but with its own special modeling properties (each stereotype may provide its own set of tagged values), semantics (each stereotype may provide its own constraints), and notation (each stereotype may provide its own icon). The stereotype *"stereotype"* specifies that the classifier is a stereotype that may be applied to other elements [15,77].

Tagged values: A tagged value extends the properties of a UML stereotype, thus allowing creation of new information in element's specification. By using stereotypes it is possible to add new things to the

UML; by using tagged values it is possible to add new properties to a stereotype. Tags that apply to individual stereotypes are defined so that everything with that stereotype has tagged value. A tagged value is not the same as class attribute. Rather, a tagged value can be considered as metadata because its value applies to the element specification, not to its instances [15].

Constraints: A constraint extends the semantics of a UML construct, thus allowing to add new rules or to modify existing ones. Each constraint consists of a textual description in natural language and may be followed by a formal constraint expressed in OCL. If it is not possible to express the constraint in OCL, then in such case the formal expression can be omitted [15,78].

Profiles: The profile mechanism has been specially defined for providing a lightweight extension mechanism to the UML specification. In UML version 1.1, stereotypes and tagged values were used as string-based extensions that could be attached to UML model elements in a flexible way. In subsequent revisions of UML, the notion of a profile was defined in order to provide more structure and precision to the definition of stereotypes and tagged values. Since the UML version 2.0 specification this has been carried further, by defining UML extension as a specific metamodeling technique. Stereotypes are specific metaclasses, tagged values are standard metaattributes, and profiles are specific kinds of packages. A profile defines a specialized version of UML for particular area or solution. Because it is built on standard UML elements, it does not present a new language, and it can be supported by ordinary UML tools [15,77,78].

According to UML version 2.4.1 specification [78], the profiles mechanism is not a first-class extension mechanism (i.e., it does not allow for modifying existing metamodels). Rather, the intention of profiles is to give a straightforward mechanism for adapting an existing metamodel with constructs that are specific to a particular domain, platform, or method. Each such adaptation is grouped in a profile. It is not possible to take away any of the constraints that apply to a metamodel such as UML using a profile, but it is possible to add new constraints that are specific to the profile.

The UML metamodel extension: First-class extensibility is handled by using MOF, where there are no restrictions on what are allowed to do with a UML metamodel (i.e., it is possible to add and remove metaclasses, constraints, and relationships as necessary) [77].

"There is no simple answer for when you should create a new metamodel and when you instead should create a new profile" [78].

1.6.2 Improving Unified Modeling Language by Using Topology

The UML improvement by using mathematical topology is based on topology and formalism of Topological Functioning Model (TFM) [86]. The TFM is a mathematical modeling language intended to design and analyze functionality of a system and it holistically represents a complete functionality of the system from a computation independent viewpoint. It considers problem domain information separate from the solution domain information. TFM has strong mathematical basis and is represented in a form of a topological space. Graphically, it is drawn as an oriented graph where nodes represent functional features of the system, while directed arcs represent their causal relationships. The TFM has topological characteristics: connectedness, closure, neighbor-hood, and continuous mapping. Despite that any graph is included into algebraic topology, not every graph is a TFM. A directed graph becomes the TFM only when theoretical substantiation of the systems is added to the above mathematical substantiation. The latter is represented by functional characteristics: cause-effect relations, cycle structure, and inputs and outputs [88,91].

It is acknowledged that every business and technical system is a subsystem of the environment. TFM enables careful analysis of system's operation and communication with the environment through analysis of functional cycles—a common thing for all system (technical, business, or biological) functioning should be the main feedback, visualization of which is an oriented cycle. Thus, it is stated that at least one directed closed loop (i.e., cycle) must be present in every topological model of system functioning. This cycle shows the main functionality that has a vital importance in the system's life. Usually it is even an expanded hierarchy of cycles. By interrupting this main cycle the system can no longer function or it functions faulty [86]. Therefore, a proper cycle analysis is necessary in the TFM construction, because it enables careful analysis of system's operation and communication with the environment. To better illustrate main cycle in graph representation of TFM, the arcs belonging to this cycle is drew with bolder lines [84].

The TFM and its construction steps are given in Chapter 4, Topological Unified Modeling Language, of this book.

The UML can be improved by supplementing it with the topological and functioning characteristics of TFM. To allow using topology in UML diagrams, it needs to be extended by using extensibility mechanisms. In such case a new kind of UML is created—*Topological Unified Modeling Language (Topological UML)*. The idea of Topological UML is adapted from [83]. The core framework proposal for Topological UML profile is presented in [99]. The first research results in [96] shows that *the transfer of topological and functioning characteristics from TFM to UML is sufficient for clearly tracing cause-and-effect relationships in both—problem and solution—domains.*

1.7 SUMMARY

The UML is a visual language for specifying, constructing, and documenting the artifacts of systems. It is a general-purpose modeling language that can be used with all major object and component methods, and that can be applied to all application domains and implementation platforms.

The UML version 1.x (the first version (1.1) is released in 1997) contains nine diagram types. UML version 2.0 (released in 2005) is a major rewrite of UML version 1.x with the main goal to increase the precision and correctness of the specification. The version 2.0 contains 13 diagram types, and the version 2.2 adds additional one diagram type—profile diagram (now in total UML has 14 diagram types). At the moment of writing this work, the newest version is 2.5 and it is released in 2015.

The specification of UML version 2.0 to 2.4.1 is divided into two volumes: infrastructure (core metamodel) and superstructure (notation and semantics for diagrams and their model elements). Actually, the superstructure specification is based on infrastructure specification. Specification version 2.5 is a rewritten version 2.4.1 combining together in a single document the infrastructure and the superstructure. The set of modeling concepts of UML is partitioned into horizontal layers of increasing capability called compliance levels. UML infra-structure specification defines only two compliance levels (for ease of model interchange): L0 and LM, while the superstructure specification adds three more compliance levels: L1, L2, and L3. In fact, the complete UML specification is given in compliance level L3.

While the application of UML within software development has a number of benefits, it also has some disadvantages. The main benefits are: UML is independent of software development methods, techniques, and platforms; it has an extension mechanism thus allowing to solve specific modeling tasks; and the models can be transferred between different tools from different tool vendors since UML is defined in accordance with XMI. The main disadvantages of UML application are its size, incoherence, different interpretations, frequent subsetting, and the lack of causality. From these disadvantages rises a set of problems like ambiguous semantics, cognitive misdirection during the development process, inadequate capture of properties of system under consideration, lack of appropriate supporting tools and developer inexperience, and inability to trace cause-and-effect relationships between the existing artifacts in problem domain and created artifacts in solution domain. By taking a closer look at benefits and disadvantages, it is visible that some benefits turn into disadvantages (e.g., independency of software development methods leads to cognitive misdirection during the development process). To address the listed disadvantages, a bunch of researches on UML strengthening and formalization are performed and are still ongoing, e.g., formalizing the semantics of UML, formalizing the way the UML is used, and relating UML constructs to problem domains.

The UML can be strengthened by using mathematical topology, thus addressing the disadvantage of lacking causality. Next chapter is dedicated to explore currently existing UML modeling driven software development approaches, thus addressing the disadvantages of UML's size, incoherence, different interpretations, and frequent subsetting.

CHAPTER 2

Software Designing With Unified Modeling Language Driven Approaches

INFORMATION IN THIS CHAPTER:

- UML modeling driven methods and approaches
- Comparison of UML application and usage
- Benefits and limitations of UML modeling driven methods and approaches

2.1 INTRODUCTION

The UML is a notation and as such its specification does not contain any guidelines for software development process (e.g., which diagrams to use and in what order to elaborate them). This is pointed out as a benefit of UML application in software development as well as a disadvantage in Chapter 1, Unified Modeling Language: A Standard for Designing a Software. Despite that UML is independent of particular methods and approaches, most of the UML modeling driven methods uses use case driven approach [22]. This might be caused by the originators (Booch, Rumbaugh, and Jacobson) of the UML since they recommend a use case driven process in their book *"The Unified Modeling Language User Guide"* [15]. A majority of UML modeling-driven approaches since then has endorsed this view, and most contain at least some further prescriptions for applying the UML in modeling (e.g., *"Applying UML and Patterns: An Introduction to Object-Oriented Analysis and Design and Iterative Development"* [58], *"UML for the IT Business Analyst"* [104], and *"Using UML: Software Engineering with Objects and Components"* [120]).

Since UML modeling-driven approaches are elaborated by different authors, their prescriptions sometimes differ. As indicated in UML usage research [22], *"while some accept the original view that only use cases are used to verify requirements with users, others explicitly or*

Topological UML Modeling. DOI: http://dx.doi.org/10.1016/B978-0-12-805476-5.00002-2

implicitly indicate that other UML diagrams can be used for this purpose, e.g., activity diagrams can be safely shared with customers, even those unfamiliar with software engineering." There is also difference in the use of use case narratives across various methods due to the lack of guidance on narrative format in the UML specification. The UML specification [79] only states that "*use cases are typically specified in various idiosyncratic formats such as natural language, tables, trees, etc. Therefore, it is not easy to capture its structure accurately or generally by a formal model.*"

A successful software development project can be measured against the deliverables that satisfy and possibly exceed expectations of customer, the delivery schedule that has occurred in a timely and economical fashion, and the created result is resilient to change and adaptation. For software development project to be successful by means of given measurements, it should satisfy the following two characteristics [14]:

- Solution should have a strong architectural vision and
- A well-managed development lifecycle should be used.

The International Organization for Standardization (ISO)/International Electronical Commission (IEC)/Institute of Electrical and Electronics Engineers (IEEE) architecture description standard [45] defines architecture as "*fundamental organization of a system embodied in its components, their relationships to each other, and to the environment, and the principles guiding its design and evolution.*" Besides this definition there exist a large number of architecture definitions. A system that has a good architecture has also a conceptual integrity. Good software architectures tend to have several attributes in common [14]:

- They are constructed in well-defined layers of abstraction,
- They have a clear separation of concerns between the interface and implementation of each layer, and
- The architecture itself is simple—common behavior is achieved through common abstractions and common mechanisms.

This chapter discusses the current state of the art of UML-based software development approaches by reviewing two aspects of each approach:

1. The process of software development and
2. The artifacts developed.

Most attention is paid on the artifacts created by using the UML.

2.2 CURRENT STATE OF THE ART

The review of software development methods discusses a number of existing UML modeling driven software development approaches paying the most emphasis and attention on the use and application of UML diagrams (i.e., which diagram types for what purpose are used and in which sequence they should be developed to create a blueprint of the information system under consideration). The analysis of UML diagram usage additionally shows if there are included transformation rules or guidelines between different diagram types. Each approach is reviewed by using following structure:

• At first a brief description of the approach is given,
• Overview and analysis is done of development steps involved in the approach, and
• Finally, analysis of used UML diagrams is given.

Currently exist dozens of UML modeling driven software development approaches, e.g.,

• Unified Process [107],
• Use case-driven methods [104],
• Model Driven Architecture (MDA) [53],
• Pattern-based development [58],
• Component-based development [120], and
• Conceptual modeling [82].

Overview of the current state of the art of UML-based software development approaches includes approaches that are well known in software development industry [22], formalizes the development process and problem domain [93], and are used in the conjunction of software development tools. The overview of UML modeling driven software development approaches includes a number of approaches thus covering different aspects of software development and its organization:

• Object-oriented analysis and design with Unified Process,
• Business Object-Oriented Modeling (B.O.O.M.),
• Object-oriented analysis and design with patterns,
• Conceptual modeling,
• Component-based development, and
• Topological Functional Model (TFM) for Model Driven Architecture (TFM4MDA).

2.2.1 Object-Oriented Analysis and Design With Unified Process

Object-oriented software development is a complete conceptual framework that covers the entire software development life cycle and it has the following characterization [104]:

- Affects the way in which the requirements are analyzed and modeled,
- Affects the way the software engineer designs the system specification, and
- Affects the way the code itself is structured—the software is implemented by using object-oriented programming languages (e.g., C++ [63], .NET language family (C#, Visual Basic .NET) [68], Java [19]).

One of the well-managed iterative and incremental development lifecycle is *Unified Software Development Process* (*Unified Process*), where each of the iteration includes its own requirements analysis, design, implementation, and testing activities.

2.2.1.1 Development Process

Unified Process is based on the enlargement and refinement of a system through multiple iterations, with cyclic feedback and adaptation. The system is developed incrementally over time, iteration by iteration, and thus this approach is also known as iterative and incremental software development. The iterations are spread over four phases where each phase consists of one or more iterations [4]:

- *Inception*—the first and the shortest phase in the project. It is used to prepare basis for the project, including preparation of business case, establishing project scope and setting boundaries, outlining key requirements, and possible architecture solution together with design tradeoffs, identifying risks, and development of initial project plan—schedule with main milestones and cost estimates. If the inception phase lasts for too long, it is like an indicator stating that the project vision and goals are not clear to the stakeholders. With no clear goals and vision the project most likely is doomed to fail. At this scenario it is better to take a pause at the very beginning of the project to refine the vision and goals. Otherwise it could lead to unnecessary make-overs and schedule delays in further phases.
- *Elaboration*—during this phase the project team is expected to capture a majority of system's requirements (e.g., in the form of use

cases), to perform identified risk analysis and make a plan of risk management to reduce or eliminate their impact on final schedule and product, to establish design and architecture (e.g., using basic class diagrams, package diagrams, and deployment diagrams), to create a plan (schedule, cost estimates, and achievable milestones) for the next (construction) phase.

- *Construction*—the longest and largest phase within Unified Process. During this phase, the design of the system is finalized and refined and the system is built using the basis created during elaboration phase. The construction phase is divided into multiple iterations, for each iteration to result in an executable release of the system. The final iteration of construction phase releases fully completed system which is to be deployed during transition phase, and
- *Transition*—the final project phase which delivers the new system to its end-users. Transition phase includes also data migration from legacy systems and user trainings.

Each phase and its iteration consists of a set of predefined activities. The Unified Process describes work activities as disciplines—a discipline is a set of activities and related artifacts in one subject area (e.g., the activities within requirements analysis). The disciplines described by Unified Process are as follows [107]:

- *Business modeling*—domain object modeling and dynamic modeling of the business processes,
- *Requirements*—requirements analysis of system under consideration. Includes activities like writing use cases and identifying nonfunctional requirements,
- *Analysis and design*—covers aspects of design, including the overall architecture,
- *Implementation*—programming and building the system (except the deployment),
- *Test*—involves testing activities such as test planning, development of test scenarios, alpha and beta testing, regression testing, acceptance testing, and
- *Deployment*—the deployment activities of developed system.

The disciplines and phases of Unified Process are given in Fig. 2.1 where the phases are columns and the disciplines are rows. It clearly shows that the relative effort across disciplines changes over time from

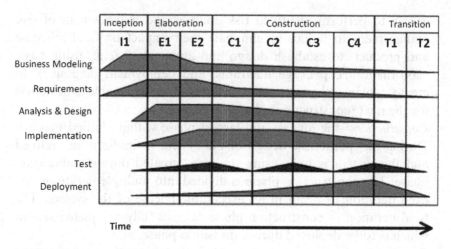

	Inception	Elaboration		Construction				Transition	
	I1	E1	E2	C1	C2	C3	C4	T1	T2
Business Modeling									
Requirements									
Analysis & Design									
Implementation									
Test									
Deployment									

Time ⟶

Figure 2.1 Disciplines and phases of Unified Process [123].

iteration to iteration, e.g., initial iterations apply greater relative effort on requirements and design while the latter—more on testing and deployment.

There exist a number of extensions and adaptions of Unified Process, e.g., Agile Unified Process (AUP) [2] and Rational Unified Process (RUP) [56].

2.2.1.2 Unified Modeling Language Diagrams Used

Since the Unified Process is a software development lifecycle by using it almost every UML diagram type is elaborated during software development process. Fig. 2.2 contains all the UML diagram types used within Unified Process, the oriented vertices between diagram types denotes their construction order and the source of the diagram. The root diagram is use case diagram which is constructed according to the functional requirements and business scenario narratives.

Detailed information of UML diagram types used within Unified Process and their intended use is given in Table 2.1.

2.2.2 Business Object-Oriented Modeling

Business Object-Oriented Modeling (B.O.O.M.) developed by Podeswa [104] is an UML modeling approach intended to relate business

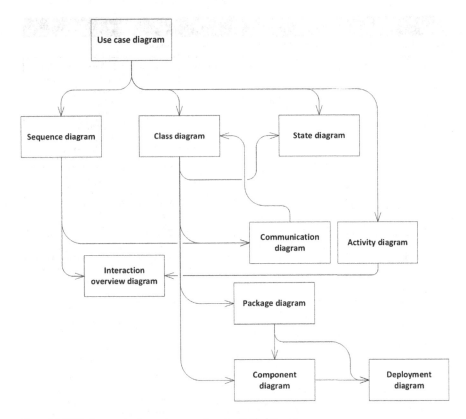

Figure 2.2 UML diagram development sequence by using Unified Process.

Table 2.1 UML Diagrams Used in Unified Process				
No.	Diagram Type	Sequence	Information for	Notes
1.	Use case diagram	1	Sequence diagram, class diagram, state diagram, activity diagram	Initial use cases are created during inception phase and later refined in elaboration and construction phases. Use cases help finding conceptual classes using noun phrase identification.
2.	Sequence diagram	2	Communication diagram, interaction overview diagram	Sequence diagrams are developed during elaboration and construction phases. They should be created for the main success scenario of the use case, and for frequent or complex alternative scenarios. Sequence diagram is generated from inspection of use case.

(Continued)

Table 2.1 (Continued)

No.	Diagram Type	Sequence	Information for	Notes
3.	Class diagram	3	Communication diagram, state diagram, package diagram, component diagram	Class diagram is developed during elaboration phase and refined later in construction phase. It is used to represent domain and a system design model. Domain model has conceptual classes with no operations; the key idea behind it is a visual dictionary of abstractions.
4.	State diagram	4	–	State diagrams are developed during elaboration and construction phases. The use of state diagrams is emphasized for showing system events in use cases, but they may additionally be applied to any class.
5.	Communication diagram	4	Class diagram	Communication diagrams are developed during elaboration and construction phases. They illustrate object interactions and help to analyze relations between classes.
6.	Activity diagram	4	Interaction overview diagram	Activity diagrams are developed during elaboration and construction phases. Used to visualize business workflows and processes, or use cases.
7.	Interaction overview diagram	5	–	Interaction overview diagrams are developed during elaboration and construction phases. Used to visualize business workflows and processes, or use cases.
8.	Package diagram	6	Component diagram, deployment diagram	Package diagram is developed during elaboration phase and refined later in construction phase. Each package groups a set of cohesive responsibilities.
9.	Component diagram	7	Deployment diagram	Component diagram is developed during elaboration phase and refined later in construction phase. It represents modular, deployable, and replaceable parts of a system.
10.	Deployment diagram	8	–	Deployment diagram is developed during elaboration phase and refined later in construction phase. It shows how instances of components are deployed on instances of processing nodes.

analysis documentation to the object-oriented software development. B.O.O.M. is use case driven analysis approach. A standard UML use case refers to an interaction with any type of system. While analyzing and specifying the system following question arises [104]: "*What type of system is being referring to?"* Therefore, use cases in B.O.O.M. are divided into two logical types: (1) business use cases and (2) system use cases (this distinction of use case types is not a part of the UML but is an UML extension). A business use case is an interaction with a business system while the latter one is an interaction with a software system. A system use case typically involves one active (primary) user and takes place over a single session on the computer. At the end of the system use case, the user should feel that he or she has achieved a useful goal. The main idea of the B.O.O.M. is to identify and describe business use cases that a planned system will affect, thus analyzing possible changes in business workflows and human roles. Each business use case is analyzed, looking for activities that the application will realize, and this information is specified as system use cases, which further will drive the whole development process.

2.2.2.1 Development Process
The software analysis and design with B.O.O.M. consists of two phases:

- *Initiation phase* involves creation and analysis of business use cases, initial identification of system use cases, and drawing a sketch of business objects involved into system in a form of class diagram. Processes defined by system use cases are identified by going back to the business use case workflow and selecting activities that can benefit from full or partial automation. Activity diagrams are used to model the workflow of each business use case in order to achieve consensus among developers and stakeholders of the business use cases. By the end of initiation phase developers should have overview of the project, initial list of system use cases together with knowledge on users involved within each system use case. System use cases are detailed only at the level to be able to estimate the project (e.g., whether the project development will take days, weeks, or months). The initiation phase includes following steps: (1) modeling business use cases, (2) modeling system use cases, (3) sketching static model (class diagram including key business classes), and (4) setting baseline for analysis.
- *Analysis phase* includes acquisition of detailed requirements from stakeholders, and analysis and documentation of elicited requirements for verification by stakeholders and for use by the developers. To achieve this goal a system use case specifications are created by

storyboarding the interaction between users and the proposed system. In parallel with system use case specification, a class diagrams describing key business concepts and business rules that apply to the business objects are developed. For better understanding of business objects life cycle, state diagrams are developed (state diagrams should be developed for at least every key business object). The analysis phase includes following steps: (1) dynamic and static analysis, (2) specifying test plan and implementation plan, and (3) setting baseline for development.

2.2.2.2 Unified Modeling Language Diagrams Used

The UML diagrams involved into B.O.O.M. application are listed in Fig. 2.3. Fig. 2.3 contains all the UML diagram types used within B.O.O.M., the oriented vertices between diagram types denotes their construction order and the source of the diagram. The root diagram is use case diagram. Since the B.O.O.M. covers the requirements and analysis phase of software development lifecycle, it uses diagrams only needed to analyze the business system and additionally a package diagram to organize developed artifacts.

Detailed information of UML diagram types used within B.O.O.M. and their intended use is given in Table 2.2.

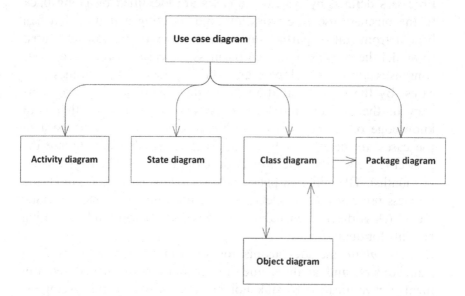

Figure 2.3 UML diagram development sequence by using B.O.O.M.

No.	Diagram Type	Sequence	Information for	Notes
			Table 2.2 UML Diagrams Applied Within B.O.O.M.	
1.	Use case diagram	1	Activity diagram, state diagram, class diagram, package diagram	Two types of use cases: business and system use cases. While the first one describes the functionality from a business perspective, the latter one describes functionality by the system perspective. Business use cases are developed before system use cases.
2.	Class diagram	1	Package diagram, object diagram	Describes key business concepts and rules that apply to business objects. A sketch of class diagram is made during initiation phase and later during analysis phase it is refined to include relationships.
3.	Package diagram	2	–	Package diagram is used as a container to group and organize other diagrams.
4.	Activity diagram	3	–	Activity diagram is used to help developers and stakeholders form a consensus regarding the workflow of each business use case.
5.	State diagram	4	–	The state change of objects in system is specified by using state diagram thus helping to avoid surmising objects behavior over time. State diagram should be created at least for every key business object.
6.	Object diagram	5	Class diagram	Object diagram is used instead of a class diagram in situations that involve more than one object of the same class acting in different roles. It is used while analyzing associations between classes.

2.2.3 Pattern-Based Software Design

A general approach in object design is to identify requirements, create domain model and add operations to software classes, and define the messaging between the objects to fulfill the requirements [36]. Deciding what operations belong to which class and how the objects should interact is important and not a trivial task—it takes careful analysis and explanation. According to [58] *"this is at the heart of what it means to develop an object-oriented system, not drawing domain model diagrams, package diagrams, and so on."* Operations of a class are addressed as responsibilities of this class. Responsibilities answer to two questions: *"What to do?"* and *"How to do?"*; and they are assigned to classes of objects during the object design. The translation of responsibilities into classes and operations is influenced by the granularity of the responsibility. A responsibility is not the same concept as an operation, but operations are implemented to fulfill assigned responsibilities. Responsibilities are implemented using operations that either act alone or collaborate with other operation and objects. In order to help assign responsibilities, patterns for object-oriented analysis and design has been created by a number of researchers and practitioners (e.g., [36,39,58,109]). In object-oriented analysis and design, a pattern is a named description of a problem and solution pair that is used to design object-oriented systems and can be applied to new contexts. Pattern can be considered as guidelines.

Set of nine GRASP (General Responsibility Assignment Software Pattern) patterns introduced in [58] are designed to address the assignment of responsibilities for objects and analysis of their interaction. The GRASP patterns are as follows:

- *Creator*—responsible for creating an object of a class,
- *Information expert*—leads placing responsibility on the class with the most information required to fulfill it,
- *Controller*—assigns responsibility for dealing with systems events (usually the controller is the first object beyond the user interface layer),
- *Low coupling*—assigns responsibilities in a way that coupling remains low (coupling is a measure of how strongly one element is connected to, has knowledge of, or relies on other elements),
- *High cohesion*—assigns responsibilities in a way that cohesion remains high (cohesion is a measure that shows how appropriate the assigned responsibilities of an element are),
- *Polymorphism*—defines variation of behaviors based on object's type (achieved by using polymorphic operations),
- *Pure fabrication*—creates a special class that has a highly cohesive set of responsibilities and that do not exist in the problem domain (i.e., an artificial class),
- *Indirection*—assign responsibility to an intermediate object to mediate between other components or services so that they are not directly coupled, and
- *Protected variations*—classes with predicted variation or instability are identified and responsibilities to these classes are assigned in a way to create a stable interface around them.

Since patterns can be used in the context of any software development lifecycle and the application of patterns and the order of pattern application are directly influenced by the used lifecycle, the subsection "Development Process" is not included for pattern-based design.

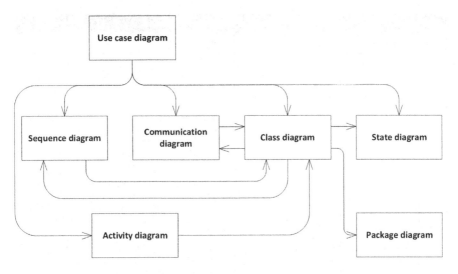

Figure 2.4 UML diagram development sequence by using pattern-based design.

2.2.3.1 Unified Modeling Language Diagrams Used

This section discusses UML diagrams addressed by GRASP design patterns. The UML diagrams used by GRASP design patterns are given in Fig. 2.4. Fig. 2.4 contains all the UML diagram types used within GRASP design patterns, the oriented vertices between diagram types denotes their construction order and the source of the diagram. The root diagram is use case diagram. The GRASP patterns in the context of Unified Process are focused on business modeling, requirements, and design disciplines, thus the GRASP design patterns uses only part of UML diagram types. This is due the fact that GRASP design patterns are intended for analysis and design of objects. The deployment diagrams are not addressed while they describe the logical structure of objects deployment and not the responsibilities assigned to objects. However, these diagrams are addressed by other patterns, e.g., pattern-oriented software architecture or architectural patterns. Example of architectural pattern is layer architecture [18] and model-view-controller pattern [36].

Detailed information of UML diagram types used within GRASP design patterns and their intended use is given in Table 2.3.

No.	Diagram Type	Information for	Notes
	Table 2.3 UML Diagrams Used by GRASP Design Patterns		
1.	Use case diagram	Sequence diagram, communication diagram, class diagram, state diagram, activity diagram	Use cases are used as an identification source of controller classes. Controller concept is described by controller pattern.
2.	State diagram	–	Describes allowed sequence of external system events that are recognized and handled by a system in the context of a use case. Additionally, state diagrams can be applied to any class.
3.	Sequence diagram	Class diagram	Sequence diagram is used to show the interaction between objects thus showing also the coupling between them. Sequence diagram is addressed by creator, controller, high cohesion, and indirection patterns.
4.	Communication diagram	Class diagram	Communication diagram is used to show the interaction and relations between objects. Communication diagram is addressed by creator, controller, high cohesion, and indirection patterns.
5.	Activity diagram	Class diagram	Used for visualizing business workflows and processes, or use cases.
6.	Class diagram	Sequence diagram, communication diagram, state diagram, package diagram	Since class diagram is the basis for domain model (in the context of Unified Process described in Section 2.2.1), it is addressed by all nine GRASP design patterns.
7.	Package diagram	–	Typical system is composed of a set of logical packages. Each package groups a set of cohesive responsibilities. This is the basic practice of modularization to support a separation of concerns.

2.2.4 Conceptual Modeling

Conceptual modeling can be viewed as an activity related to capturing the knowledge about the desired system functionality. According to [82], *"the conceptual schema of an information system is the specification of its functional requirements."* In the field of conceptual modeling exists a number of approaches (a set of conceptual modeling approaches are reviewed in *"On the Evolution of Quality Conceptualization Techniques"* [110]). Review of conceptual modeling in this section is based on *"Conceptual Modeling of Information Systems"* [82], where the development of conceptual schema is divided into two related parts:

• *Structural schema*—consists of a set of concepts used in a particular domain that constitutes a conceptualization (i.e., ontology) of a domain and

• *Behavioral schema*—specifies valid changes in the domain state together with the actions that the system can perform (changes in the domain state are domain events and a request to perform an action is an action request event).

The conceptual schema of software system should include the knowledge about the domain and the functions that the system has to perform in order to be able to perform the three main functions of software system:

- *Memory function*—ability to maintain a representation of the domain state,
- *Informative function*—ability to provide information about the domain state, and
- *Active function*—ability to perform actions that change the domain state.

The state of the domain consists of a set of relevant properties. The meaning of the relevant properties of the domain depends on the purpose for which the system is built. In the conceptual modeling of information systems, it is assumed that a domain consists of a number of objects and the relationships between them, which are classified into concepts. The state of a particular domain consists of a set of objects, a set of relationships, and a set of concepts into which these objects and relationships are classified.

2.2.4.1 Development Process
By looking at the conceptual modeling through the prism of UML and the diagram development sequence an interesting fact comes out—the first model to create is class diagram (i.e., the structural schema of software system). The software development process by using conceptual modeling is shown in Fig. 2.5 within the context of two kinds of conceptual schemas that are developed for each software system.

The development of class diagram is divided into several subactivities: (1) identification of entities, (2) their relationships (i.e., associations), (3) cardinalities on associations, (4) other relationship types, (5) derivation, (6) taxonomies (i.e., the class hierarchy), and (7) domain events. The domain events within classes are reflected as operations. Each entity identified in structural schema has its own state diagram (or multiple state diagrams) reflecting state changes of it. The set of use cases should be consistent with the set of requests defined in the behavioral schema. This consistency comprises two properties:

- Each request generated by use case should be defined in the behavioral schema.

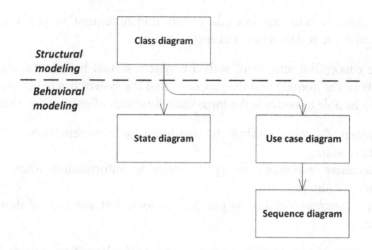

Figure 2.5 Modeling structural and behavioral schemas.

- Each request defined in the behavioral schema should be generated by one or more use cases.

   One way of documenting the mapping of use cases to requests is by including textual references to requests near the places in the use case specification where they are generated. Each use case (the request sequence) can be specified by using sequence diagram. A sequence diagram shows, for one particular scenario of a use case, the action requests that the actors generate and their temporal order. The state diagram, use case diagram, and sequence diagram together defines the behavioral schema of software system.

2.2.4.2 Unified Modeling Language Diagrams Used

Conceptual modeling of software systems uses only five UML diagram types: (1) class diagram, (2) state diagrams, (3) use case diagram, (4) sequence diagram, and (5) profile diagram. Fig. 2.6 contains all the UML diagram types used, the oriented vertices between diagram types denotes their construction order and the source of the diagram. In most cases the root diagram is the class diagram, but there can be scenarios where a domain specific language is created prior to constructing information system. In this scenario the root diagram is profile diagram which contains entity types (i.e., meta-entities) needed to build the system.

   Detailed information of UML diagram types used within conceptual modeling and their intended use is given in Table 2.4.

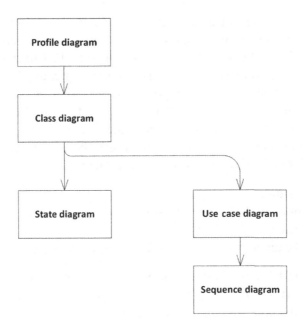

Figure 2.6 UML diagram development sequence by using conceptual modeling.

No.	Diagram Type	Sequence	Information for	Notes
	Table 2.4 UML Diagrams Used by Conceptual Modeling			
1.	Class diagram	1	State diagram, use case diagram (partly)	Reflects entities and their relationships. Each entity (class) has its own state diagram (or multiple state diagrams) reflecting state changes of it.
2.	State diagram	2	–	Each entity type may be associated with zero, one, or more state diagrams.
3.	Use case diagram	3	Sequence diagram	The set of use cases should be consistent with the set of requests defined in the behavioral schema.
4.	Sequence diagram	4	–	A sequence diagram shows, for one particular scenario of a use case, the action requests that the actors generate and their temporal order.
5.	Profile diagram	5	Class diagram	An entity type defined in the schema of system may also be an entity in the information base of the same system or of another system. A meta-entity type is an entity type whose instances are entity types.

2.2.5 Component-Based Development

The first promise of developed code reuse is object orientation—classes developed for one project should be usable in the next project. This supposed to deliver high-quality products on time and in budget.

Unfortunately, as revealed in recent research by Jones [50] this is not true—the software projects frequently overrun their budgets and software is developed behind the planned schedule. The next step in the direction of reusable software parts is components. According to Stevens and Pooley [120] a component is unit that can be reused or replaced. The ideal way to build a new system in the context of component-based development is to take existing components and plug them together. The *Catalysis Approach* [29] states that for a unit to be reusable it should have following characterization:

- High cohesion,
- Low coupling with the rest of the system,
- A well-defined interface, and
- It should be an abstraction of a well analyzed and understood concept.

Stevens and Pooley [120] describes component-based development in the context of *4 + 1 architecture view model* [55] which divides software architecture in five (4 + 1) views:

- *Logical view*—shows parts of the system and how they are related together with the functionality that is provided to system users, this view specifies the logical behavior of the system,
- *Process view*—reflects the dynamic aspects of the system, explains the system processes and how they communicate; it addresses several nonfunctional characteristics of system like concurrency, distribution, integrators, performance, and scalability,
- *Development view*—shows system from the perspective of developer and is concerned with software management,
- *Physical (deployment) view*—depicts the system from a system engineer viewpoint; concerned with the layout of software components on the physical layer, as well as the physical connections between these components, and
- *Scenario view (the +1 view)*—description of architecture is illustrated using a small set of scenarios which describe sequences of interactions between objects and processes; scenarios are used to identify architectural elements and to illustrate and validate the architecture design.

2.2.5.1 Development Process

Component-based development is oriented on creating reusable software components thus it can be used in the context of different software development lifecycles and architectural styles. By applying component-based development in the context of $4 + 1$ architectural style as suggested by Stevens and Pooley [120], the following UML diagrams are developed for each of the architecture view:

- *Scenario view*—use case diagram,
- *Logical view*—class diagram, interaction diagrams, and state diagram,
- *Process view*—interaction diagrams, state diagram, activity diagram, and deployment diagram (used to determine the threads of control of the system),
- *Development view*—component diagram and package diagram, and
- *Physical view*—deployment diagram.

The three case studies provided by Stevens and Pooley in [120] shows a part of a software development project. Within each case study the set of used diagrams differs and the order of diagram development also is different. Thus the guidelines of UML diagrams application and development sequence are left open and all the decisions about how to detail the system design should be taken by the project team. The three case studies together with developed diagrams are as follows:

1. *Study process administration*—use case diagram, class diagram, and activity diagram;
2. *Board games*—communication diagram, class diagram, and state diagram; and
3. *Discrete event simulation*—class diagram, use case diagram, state diagram, and communication diagram.

2.2.5.2 Unified Modeling Language Diagrams Used
The UML diagrams involved into component-based development are shown in Fig. 2.7. Since the use of UML diagrams vary from one case study to another (as discussed in previously), the development sequence of UML diagrams cannot be precisely specified.

Detailed information of UML diagram types used within component-based development and their intended use is given in Table 2.5.

2.2.6 Topological Functioning Modeling for Model Driven Architecture
Topological Functioning Modeling for Model Driven Architecture [92] is an approach intended for problem domain analysis and modeling in

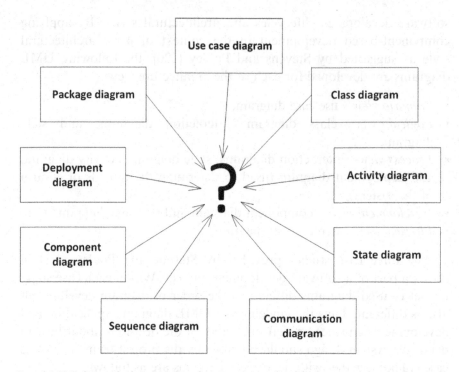

Figure 2.7 UML diagram development sequence by using component-based development.

No.	Diagram Type	Information for	Notes
Table 2.5 UML Diagrams Used in Component-Based Development			
1.	Use case diagram	?	Specifies a set of scenarios which describe sequences of interactions between objects and processes.
2.	Class diagram	?	Shows objects of the system and how they are related together with the functionality that is provided to system users.
3.	Activity diagram	?	Determines the threads of control in the system.
4.	State diagram	?	
5.	Communication diagram	?	Specifies the logical behavior of the system and determines the threads of control in the system.
6.	Sequence diagram	?	
7.	Component diagram	?	Shows the system from the viewpoint of developer.
8.	Deployment diagram	?	Shows the system from the viewpoint of system engineer by showing the topology of components on the physical layer.
9.	Package diagram	?	Shows the system from the viewpoint of developer by grouping together related elements.

the context of MDA [67], thus dealing with the weakest part of MDA—the computation independent model (CIM) and its formal transformation to platform independent model (PIM) [85,116]. In the context of MDA, TFM4MDA uses an extended version of MDA software lifecycle [84]. Extended MDA lifecycle is given in Fig. 2.8. In the standard MDA lifecycle [53] the feedback from deployment is going back directly to analysis (*"standard feedback"* in Fig. 2.8) and it is clearly visible that CIM is considered only as textual requirements without any formal relation to the functionality of the business system and that the requirements and desired behavior of system is not considered at all when changes are needed in the deployed software system.

To avoid ignorance of CIM and analysis of the business system in the context of MDA, TFM4MDA uses capabilities of the universal category logic and is based on the formalism of TFM [87] (TFM and

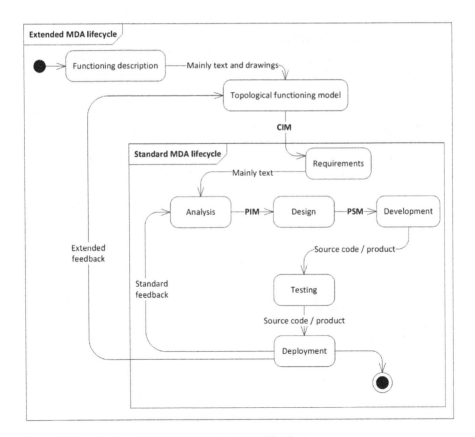

Figure 2.8 Extended and standard MDA software development lifecycle.

its construction steps are given in Chapter 4, Topological Unified Modeling Language, of this book). The main idea behind TFM4MDA is that the required functionality determines the structure of the planned system [88]. This corresponds to the opinion that there are two stages at the beginning of the problem analysis: the first one is *analysis of the problem domain* and the second one is *analysis of the application domain*. Having knowledge about a complex system that operates in the real world, a TFM of this system can be developed. This means that a TFM of the system is tested and can be partially changed and adjusted by functional requirements and vice versa. Usually changes in TFM are initiated if the software system introduces new functionality in the problem domain (e.g., in the context of library software development project discussed in [94]—sending of SMS notifications is a new functionality introduced to business process through the developed software system).

2.2.6.1 Development Process

The software development process within TFM4MDA approach begins with the analysis and formalization of problem domain as shown in Fig. 2.9, where the development is shown in the context of two kinds of information at the beginning of the problem analysis: the problem domain and the application domain.

Problem domain analysis and software modeling within the TFM4MDA approach consists following actions:

1. Development of TFM reflecting the problem domain functioning,
2. Functional requirement mapping onto TFM,

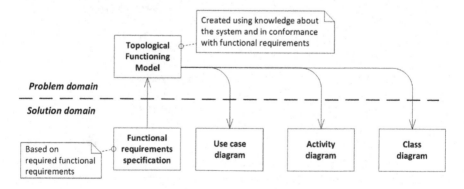

Figure 2.9 Software modeling within TFM4MDA approach.

3. Use case identification from a TFM,
4. Activity diagram development for each identified use case, and
5. Conceptual and controller class identification.

The formal development of TFM within TFM4MDA is given in Fig. 2.10.

After the development of TFM, the functional features are associated with business goals of the system. Associating functional features with business goals provides business use case and system use case identification according to the problem domain entities. Additionally, after those activities functional requirements can be traced back to the system use case diagram [7]. Problem domain concepts are selected and described in an UML Class diagram. The UML Class diagram is developed by performing two transformations: (1) TFM to problem domain objects graph and (2) problem domain objects graph to class

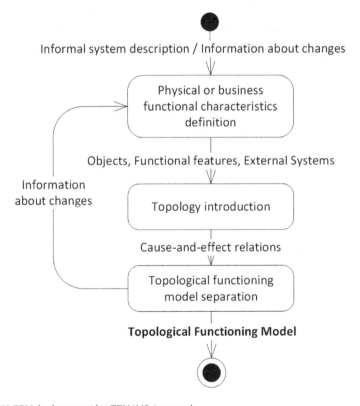

Figure 2.10 TFM development within TFM4MDA approach.

diagram. As a result of this transformation a class diagram reflecting conceptual classes (i.e., without attributes and operations) and nondirected associations between them is obtained.

2.2.6.2 Unified Modeling Language Diagrams Used

All the diagram types used within TFM4MDA are shown in Fig. 2.11, the oriented vertices between diagram types denotes their construction order and the source of the diagram. The root diagram is TFM which is constructed according to the problem domain functioning. TFM4MDA approach uses only three UML diagram types: use case diagram, activity diagram, and class diagram; and additional two diagrams: TFM and problem domain objects graph (the names of these two diagram types are given in italic in Fig. 2.11).

Despite the fact that TFM can be transformed to activity diagram, the author of TFM4MDA in [6] states that *"it is impossible to create fork and join nodes automatically because the TFM does not hold information of concurrency"* (thus TFM can be transformed into simple activity diagram). The transformation from TFM to class diagram is ambiguous while it is not clear how the control flow showing interaction between objects (i.e., cause-and-effect relationships) in TFM can be transformed into structural relationships (i.e., associations) between classes. The level

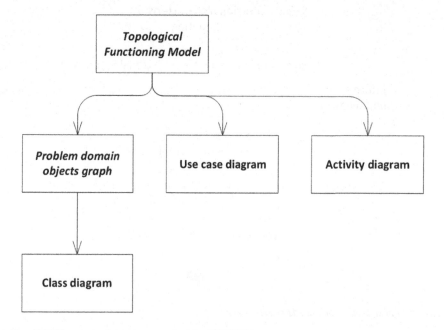

Figure 2.11 Diagram development sequence by using TFM4MDA.

Table 2.6 Diagrams Used in TFM4MDA Approach

No.	Diagram Type	Sequence	Information for	Notes
1.	Topological Functioning Model (TFM)	1	Problem domain objects graph, use case diagram, and activity diagram	TFM is used to formalize problem domain and thus it is the initial diagram developed when using TFM4MDA approach.
2.	Use case diagram	2	–	Since TFM4MDA approach is intended for problem domain analysis using TFM, it does not include guidelines for transformations between standard UML diagrams.
3.	Activity diagram	3	–	
4.	Class diagram	5	–	
5.	Problem domain objects graph	4	Class diagram	TFM is transformed 1:1 into problem domain object graph where each vertex shows only one type of objects.

of ambiguousness is even increased in the initial stage of TFM to class diagram transformation—the TFM to problem domain object graph transformation.

Detailed information of UML diagram types used within TFM4MDA and their intended use is given in Table 2.6.

2.3 BENEFITS AND LIMITATIONS OF UNIFIED MODELING LANGUAGE FOR MODELING DRIVEN APPROACHES

Since UML itself is a notation and as such it does not contain guidelines on how it can be applied in practice, the largest benefit of presence of UML modeling driven approaches is that the use of UML is made systematical. If UML is combined together with some approach, it can be used as a powerful tool to analyze and understand both business and software systems and to design planned software system. Despite the fact that UML modeling driven approaches provides a systematical use of UML diagrams, these approaches do cover different parts of a software development lifecycles. Whole software development lifecycle is covered only by the Unified Process, other methods focuses more on analysis (e.g., B.O.O.M., TFM4MDA, and conceptual modeling) while others—more on design and less on analysis (e.g., pattern-based design, component-based development). This impacts the number of UML diagram types that are used by each of the method. The summary of UML diagrams usage by each method is given in Fig. 2.12, where it can be seen that not every UML diagram type is used (UML in total has 14 diagram types). The greatest amount of applied diagram types is for the Unified process.

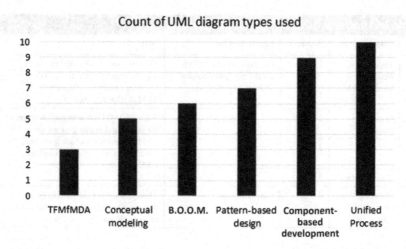

Figure 2.12 Number of UML diagrams used by UML modeling driven methods.

While the benefit of applying *Unified* process is the coverage of whole software development lifecycle, it has some limitations—the Unified Process promotes use case driven analysis of business system thus all the process is more or less use case driven (e.g., actors are identified by use cases, system class candidates are extracted from the use case narratives by using noun analysis). As such the Unified Process does not provide a formal way of analyzing and formalizing business system.

The only formal method for problem domain formalization among the reviewed methods is TFM4MDA. It uses TFM as a tool for both problem and solution domain analysis and formalization. When a TFM of system's functioning has been developed, it can be mapped onto functional requirements, goals and use cases. By mapping TFM onto functional requirements, the requirements get validated. As a result of this validation missing, overlapping, unrealizable, and conflicting require-ments are found. If there are requirements that do not map onto devel-oped TFM, then it is a signal that a new functionality is going to be introduced to the functioning of a business system through the new soft-ware. TFM can be transformed into activity diagram and class diagram (TFM4MDA addresses class diagram as conceptual class diagram). The conceptual class diagram contains conceptual classes (without attributes and operations) and associations between them.

While TFM4MDA has formalized the very beginning of software development lifecycle, its largest limitation is the conceptual class

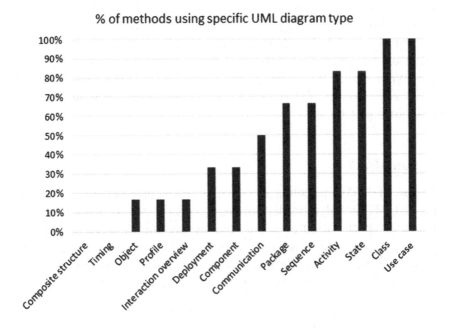

Figure 2.13 Percentage of UML diagram type application by UML modeling driven methods.

diagram and its development. TFM describes the functionality of the business and software system (including the responsibilities through the whole system). When TFM is transformed into conceptual class diagram this important information of responsibilities from TFM is not transferred to class diagram, thus raising a question: *"How the responsibilities carried by classes can be determined?"* The transformation from TFM to class diagram is ambiguous while it is not clear how the control flow showing interaction between objects (i.e., cause-and-effect relationships) in TFM can be transformed into structural relationships (i.e., associations) between classes. As underlined by Larman in [58]: *"deciding what operations belong where, and how the objects should interact, is terribly important and anything but trivial. This is a critical step - this is at the heart of what it means to develop an object-oriented system, not drawing domain model diagrams, package diagrams, and so forth."*

The analysis of UML application in software development industry [22] shows that the five most applied diagram type among UML diagrams are: (1) class diagram (84%), (2) use case diagram (71%), (3) sequence diagram (70%), (4) activity diagram (57%), and (5) state diagram (56%) (percentage in braces shows how many of the review's 135 respondents are using corresponding UML diagram type). This fact is tightly related with the UML modeling driven methods—the review of such methods shows that the five most applied UML diagram types within them are: (1) class diagram, (2) use case diagram, (3) activity diagram, (4) state diagram, and (5) sequence diagram as shown in Fig. 2.13.

2.4 SUMMARY

The use of UML modeling driven methods supplements the application of UML in software development. While UML is a notation and as such its specification does not contain any guidelines of its application during software development process, the UML modeling driven methods fulfill this gap. In fact, the application of modeling methods reduces and even solves disadvantages of UML identified in previous chapter:

• *Size*—systematic and consistent software development activities solves issue related with the large amount of UML diagrams and their elements (i.e., UML is applied gradually thus avoiding the need to read whole language specification at once),
• *Incoherence*—through the predefined actions the modeling method tries to develop diagram by diagram thus showing the seams and transitions between diagrams (e.g., developing state diagram for each class in class diagram),
• *Different interpretations*—UML semantics together with methodical application of UML diagrams creates shared understanding among stakeholders,
• *Frequent subsetting*—providing UML extension (e.g., profile) and a proper modeling method that uses this extension it is clearly visible how it is related to UML elements and diagrams and how software development can benefit from this extension, and
• *Lacking causality*—by tracing cause-and-effect relationships between both problem and solution domains the software system can be validated against the business needs and functional requirements. The only approach trying to deal with such cause-and-effect relationships is TFM4MDA. But the causality relationships are identified and analyzed only at the TFM and are not spread to UML diagrams during further analysis and design of the system.

Review of UML modeling methods shows that not every method covers all the software development lifecycle. Among the reviewed methods only Unified Process covers whole software development lifecycle while other methods cover just a specific part of it (e.g., analysis, design) thus impacting the number of UML diagram types that are applied by each of the method. While most of the reviewed UML modeling methods promotes use case driven software development process, the only formal method for business system (i.e., problem domain) formalization among the reviewed methods is TFM4MDA. It uses TFM as a tool for problem domain analysis and formalization. The TFM4MDA covers only TFM, use case, activity, and class diagram development. In fact, class diagram contains conceptual classes (without attributes and operations) and associations between them, thus the responsibilities of classes are not assigned.

The review of UML modeling driven methods leads to the following conclusions:

- None of reviewed method is sufficient for software development that allows to clearly trace cause-and-effect relationships in both problem and solution domains,
- Modeling methods determine the application of UML diagrams and not the UML itself (review of UML application in industry [22] and UML modeling methods review shows that the top five most applied UML diagrams are the same), and
- Due to the partial UML and software development lifecycle coverage and the fragmentary application of UML diagrams *the software developers are forced to combine UML with several modeling methods and techniques* (instead of taking UML as a notation and one UML modeling driven method) *thus the application of UML gets more complicated and incomprehensible.*

As stated in the Chapter 1, Unified Modeling Language: A Standard for Designing a Software, the UML can be improved by supplementing it with the topological and functioning characteristics of TFM. To allow using topology in UML diagrams, it needs to be extended by using extensibility mechanisms. In such case a new kind of UML is created—*Topological Unified Modeling Language* (*Topological UML*). If the UML disadvantage of *lacking causality* is solved by supplementing it with mathematical topology and thus creating Topological UML profile, then another UML disadvantage emerges—*frequent subsetting*. To address this issue, a new UML extension needs to be provided together with a proper modeling method—Topological UML modeling method. To address issues related with existing UML modeling methods, the Topological UML modeling method should include following aspects:

- It should ensure proper analysis of problem and solution domains thus enabling clearly tracing of cause-and-effect relationships in both domains (all software artifacts need to be an abstraction of a well analyzed and understood problem domain unit),
- It should cover most of the UML diagrams and software development lifecycle to eliminate the need to combine together several modeling methods,
- The developed artifacts should be with high cohesion (achieved through proper analysis of objects and their responsibilities throughout the system), and in addition
- Components of developed system need to have low coupling with the rest of the system and a well-defined interface.

CHAPTER 3

Adjusting Unified Modeling Language

INFORMATION IN THIS CHAPTER:

- UML metamodel
- Metamodeling principles and approaches
- Metamodel extension
- A new metamodel vs extension of existing one

3.1 INTRODUCTION

While the UML is intended to be a graphical language for visualizing, specifying, constructing, and documenting the artifacts of a system it has a number of advantages and a number of disadvantages as outlined in Chapter 1, Unified Modeling Language: A Standard for Designing a Software. The main disadvantages of UML which emerges the improvement of it have raised from the basis on which UML has been developed. The specification of UML and the UML itself is not developed basing on any theoretical principles regarding the constructs required for an effective and usable modeling language for analysis and design; instead UML arose from (sometimes conflicting) best practices in parts of the software engineering community [22]. In the field of improving UML and its application in software development the following improvement options are outlined:

- Extending UML by using UML's extensibility mechanisms,
- Formalizing the semantics of UML,
- Formalizing the way in which the UML is used, and
- Relating UML constructs to the problem domains.

According to the UML specification, the UML extension is divided into two ways: (1) *lightweight extension* and (2) *heavyweight extension* [77]. The lightweight extension is done by using profiles thus defining a new dialect of UML to customize the language for particular

Topological UML Modeling. DOI: http://dx.doi.org/10.1016/B978-0-12-805476-5.00003-4

platforms, domain and problem solutions. The heavyweight extension (or the first class extension) is done by using metamodeling based on Meta-Object Facility (MOF). In this case, all the benefits of creating profile are lost and it can be a difficult task to put it into the practice.

If there is need to extend the UML, at first it is needed to draw the scope of UML extension. If the new language will use most of the UML, then profiles are suitable choose for that solution. If the new language uses only small part of UML or there is need to use more complex features of UML such as redefinition, then creating a complete new language by using MOF metamodeling should be considered. The relationship between the UML and the new language under consideration is shown in Fig. 3.1. It clearly shows that if there is much overlap between the concepts in UML and those within the new language then UML should be extended and if there is little overlap, then MOF-based solution should be created. An example of using both approaches (UML profile-based extension and MOF-based solution) to develop a new language is demonstrated in the "*UML testing profile*" [75]. In other words, the UML testing profile specification defines the same language by using two different approaches.

The UML specification itself is defined by using metamodeling approach—a metamodel is used to specify the model that builds UML. One of the UML metamodel principles is its extensibility. In fact, the most common and suitable way for improving UML is to use its extensibility mechanisms—the profiles. By improving UML with the profile mechanism, it is possible to adapt and use ordinary UML compliant modeling tools [77]. Thus by creating a profile of UML the costs of adaption in industry for such new language is lowered and it can be

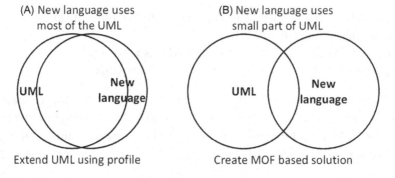

Figure 3.1 Overlap between UML, the new language under consideration, and the suggested language creation solution.

adapted faster (in comparison with creating a MOF-based solution which forces to implement new modeling tools along with the very new language).

Regardless of which UML extension way is used it is important to add mathematical foundations to the specification, thus making UML and its use more precise and formal. As outlined in Chapter 1, Unified Modeling Language: A Standard for Designing a Software, and as pointed out in *"Software Development with the Emphasis on Topology"* [24] and *"Formalization of the UML Class Diagrams"* [97], the UML can be strengthened by using the mathematical topology. The use of topology reflects extending the UML to support topology in its diagrams and formalizing the way the UML is used. Having more precise and formal language makes it less expensive to adapt in software development process and tools [38].

3.2 PROFILING UNIFIED MODELING LANGUAGE AND METAMODELING

The UML specification is defined using a metamodeling approach that adapts formal specification techniques (it is needed to notice that this approach lacks some of the rigor of a formal specification method, mainly due to the extensive use of natural language). The purpose of metamodeling is to use metamodel for specifying the model that comprises UML. UML specification (version 2.0 to 2.4.1) is organized in two parts: (1) *Infrastructure* [77] (represented by *InfrastructureLibrary*) and (2) *Superstructure* [78] (represented by *SuperstructureLibrary*). Although the UML specification 2.5 has been extensively rewritten from its previous version 2.4.1 by combining together the infrastructure and superstructure parts, the metamodel itself remains unchanged from UML 2.4.1 superstructure [79]. Thus the amount and types of UML diagrams have not changed from version 2.4.1 to version 2.5.

The infrastructure is represented by two packages: (1) *InfrastructureLibrary* (consists of two subpackages *Core* (contains core concepts used when metamodeling) and *Profiles* (defines the mechanisms that are used to customize metamodels)) and (2) *PrimitiveTypes* (consists of a few predefined primitive types that are commonly used when metamodeling) and it satisfies following design requirements [106]:

• Define a metalanguage core that can be reused to define a variety of metamodels,

- Architecturally align UML, MOF, and XML metadata interchange (XMI) so that model interchange is fully supported, and
- Allow customization of UML through profiles and creation of new languages (family of languages) based on the same metalanguage core as UML.

The *Core* package is a complete metamodel particularly designed for high reusability, where other metamodels at the same metalevel either import or specialize its specified metaclasses (see Fig. 3.2 where it is shown how UML, *Profiles*, and MOF each depends on a common core). Common core is defined as a *Core* package, thus enabling to share model elements between UML and MOF and ensuring that UML is defined as a model that is based on MOF as a metamodel.

The mechanisms and tools of improving and extending UML by using profiles are given in the *Profiles* package, which depends on the *Core* package. The *Profiles* package defines the mechanisms used to tailor existing metamodels toward specific platforms, domains, problem solutions or software process modeling. The primary target for profiles is UML, but it is possible to use profiles together with any metamodel that is based on (i.e., instantiated from) the common core. A profile must be based on a metamodel such as the UML that it extends. A profile of UML is a set of stereotypes, when defining a UML profile the stereotypes are defined to extend classes in the UML metamodel. A stereotype describes how an existing metaclass is extended thus enabling the integration of platform or domain specific terminology or notation in the modeling language.

The UML *Superstructure* metamodel is specified by the UML package *SuperstructureLibrary*, which is divided into a number of

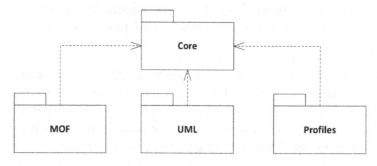

Figure 3.2 Dependencies between Core, MOF, UML, and Profiles packages.

packages that deal with structural and behavioral modeling. One of the primary uses of the UML *Infrastructure* specification is that it should be reused when creating other metamodels. The *SuperstructureLibrary* reuses the *InfrastructureLibrary* in two different ways: (1) all of the UML metamodel is instantiated from meta-metaclasses that are defined in the *InfrastructureLibrary* and (2) the UML metamodel imports and specializes all metaclasses in the *InfrastructureLibrary*.

Defining language by using metamodeling includes dealing with three meta-layers that always have to be taken into account:

1. Language specification: The metamodel,
2. User specification: The model, and
3. Objects of the model: The run-time instance of model.

This three-layer structure can be applied recursively, thus creating possibly infinite number of meta-layers. The metamodel in one case can be a model in another case (e.g., from the MOF viewpoint the UML is a model, from profile viewpoint the UML is a metamodel). The UML metamodel commonly is viewed as a four layer metamodel hierarchy [106]:

- *M3 meta-metamodeling layer*—defines a language for specifying a metamodel, e.g., MOF,
- *M2 metamodeling layer*—defines a language for specifying models (i.e., defines metamodel as an instance of a meta-metamodel, meaning that every element of the metamodel is an instance of an element in the meta-metamodel), e.g., UML, specific profile of UML,
- *M1 modeling layer*—defines languages that describe semantic domains, i.e., to allow users to model a wide variety of different problem domains, such as software, business processes, and requirements, e.g., user model which is an instance of UML metamodel, and
- *M0 run-time instances layer*—contains the run-time instances of model elements defined in a model.

Extending UML by developing a new profile has a number of positive and negative aspects. When a profiling has been chosen as an extension solution for the development of the new language the following aspects should be kept in mind:

- Positive aspects:
  - Profiles are well described in UML specification,

- Can add structure, additional constraints, and formal notation,
- Standard means for icons definition and well-defined display options,
- Application of profiles and how to use them is well defined, and
- Low development costs—profiles can be used within existing UML modeling tools.
- In some cases, it could be needed to remove some existing element or change its existing specification, then the negative aspects of profile application arise:
  - Cannot remove existing constraints,
  - Cannot redefine existing types, and
  - Cannot modify existing structures (i.e., existing relationships between language elements cannot be removed and changed).

3.3 OVERVIEW OF UNIFIED MODELING LANGUAGE PROFILES

The first UML profile was presented at UML'99 [38] under the title *"Towards a UML Extension for Hypermedia Design"* [12]. Since that a number of UML profiles are developed and published. They cover different problem domains, like business process, requirements, ontologies, device capabilities, parallel applications, and hypermedia. Most of the UML profiles have been presented at conferences which are specialized in conceptual modeling and software engineering. As Pardillo has underlined in his research *"A Systematic Review on the Definition of UML Profiles"* [103] the presentation of UML profiles *"shows a great disparity regarding both the profile definition process and the quality of the UML-profile presentation,"* thus leading to difficult comparison, discussion and usage of presented UML profiles.

To better understand the development and structure of UML profile specification this section holds an overview of four UML profiles which are created by different teams. The profiles for review are selected based on following criterions (at least one criterion for each profile is satisfied):

1. Widely accepted and used,
2. Developed at research or scientific institution, or
3. Published by Object Management Group (OMG) (i.e., publishers of UML specifications).

The review of UML profiles includes analysis of following UML profiles:

- *Executable UML (xUML)* [64] —satisfies the first criterion,
- *Topological Functioning Model for Model Driven Architecture (TFM4MDA)* [9] —satisfies the second criterion,
- *Object Management Group Systems Modeling Language (OMG SysML)* [80]—satisfies third criterion, and
- *Service Oriented Architecture Modeling Language (SoaML)* [76]— satisfies third criterion.

According to Pardillo, the systematic review of UML profiles should include two main aspects of UML profiling practices—(1) *profile definition process* and (2) *profile presentation quality*. Thus, the selected four profiles are measured against the following quantitative and qualitative criterions:

- Qualitative criterions:
  1. *Purpose of the profile*—briefly describes the purpose and goal of the profile,
  2. *Problem domain addressed*—identifies problem domain addressed and the specific task which needs to be solved by the profile,
  3. *Formalization of UML semantics*—identifies if semantics of existing UML elements are formalized,
  4. *Formalization of profile semantics*—identifies if semantics of the new elements (i.e., stereotypes) are expressed in formal statements,
  5. *Extension approach*—evaluates the applied UML extension approach, and
  6. *Specification structure*—evaluates the profile definition structure and whether it follows some specification guidelines or style.
- Quantitative criterions:
  7. *Metaclasses extended*—count of metaclasses that are extended,
  8. *Stereotypes defined*—count of stereotypes defined in profile,
  9. *Diagrams extended*—number of UML diagrams that are extended,
  10. *Diagrams introduced*—count of diagrams that are new to profile (i.e., defined in profile and does not exist in UML specification), and
  11. *Total count of diagrams*—total count of diagrams included into profile.

The result of the evaluation against qualitative criteria is given below in Table 3.1.

Table 3.1 Evaluation of Qualitative Criteria for Selected Profiles

No.	Criterion	Profile	Evaluation
1.	Purpose of the profile	xUML	Graphically specifies a system at high level of abstraction, abstracting away both specific programming languages and decisions about the organization of the software. The models are testable, and can be compiled into a less abstract programming language to target a specific implementation. It supports MDA through the specification of PIM, and the compilation of the PIM into PSM. Together with model compiler, xUML models are executable—model compiler turns xUML model into an implementation using a set of decisions about the target hardware and software environment.
		TFM4MDA	An attempt to raise the formalization level of problem domain modeling within MDA at the CIM level and CIM-to-PIM transformation. It includes a new type of diagram: Topological Functioning Model (TFM); thus allowing to analyze and model problem and solution domain functioning. According to [88] within software development process this diagram should be created before any other diagram gets constructed. This conforms to the extended MDA lifecycle [83].
		OMG SysML	A general-purpose modeling language for systems engineering applications. It supports the specification, analysis, design, verification, and validation of a range of systems (e.g., hardware, software, information, processes, personnel, and facilities) and it is particularly effective in specifying requirements, structure, behavior, allocations, and constraints on system properties to support engineering analysis. The authors of OMG SysML anticipate that it will be customized to model domain-specific applications (e.g., such as automotive, aerospace, communication, and information systems).
		SoaML	A language for designing services within a service-oriented architecture (SOA). It supports range of modeling requirements for SOAs, including the specification of services systems, individual service interfaces, and service implementations. This is done in a way to support automatic generation of derived artifacts following MDA-based approach.
2.	Problem domain addressed	xUML	Software modeling and development within MDA.
		TFM4MDA	Formal problem and solution domain modeling and analysis.
		OMG SysML	Systems engineering.
		SoaML	Modeling of SOA and services.
3.	Formalization of UML semantics	xUML	None.
		TFM4MDA	None.
		OMG SysML	None.
		SoaML	None.

(Continued)

No.	Criterion	Profile	Evaluation
4.	Formalization of profile semantics	xUML	Semantics and constraints expressed in natural language.
		TFM4MDA	Semantics and constraints expressed in natural language and OCL.
		OMG SysML	Semantics and constraints expressed in natural language.
		SoaML	Semantics and constraints expressed in natural language.
5.	Extension approach	xUML	Elements of UML are supplemented with action language and action concepts to make the UML diagrams executable.
		TFM4MDA	UML is extended only where it is necessary to introduce new elements for definition of TFM and elements related to it.
		OMG SysML	Since the OMG SysML profile does not use every modeling element and every diagram which is included in UML version 2.0, initially a narrowed version of UML (UML4SysML) is developed. The OMG SysML specification defines the language architecture in terms of the parts of UML 2 that are reused and the extensions to UML 2.
		SoaML	UML is extended only where it is necessary to accomplish the goals and requirements of SOA and service modeling.
6.	Specification structure	Executable UML	Since this profile is created basing on UML version 1.4, which contains no profile diagram and the profiling mechanism, the specification style is not convenient with UML specification style. All of the new concepts are defined only using natural language. For the diagrams and elements the authors of xUML try to keep the following specification points: 1. UML diagram (description of which can be supplemented by set of definitions), 2. Diagram element (description of which are supplemented by set of definitions), and 3. How to apply diagram in software development process.
		TFM4MDA	Specification of TFM4MDA includes profile diagram which shows metaclasses and stereotypes extending them. Each stereotype has brief description of its semantics in natural language and constraints in OCL. A standalone metamodel is defined for TFM.
		OMG SysML	Specification structure follows the style in which the UML specification itself is written. Specification is divided into parts that contain specific modeling aspects; each part contains definition of elements needed to construct specific diagram. Elements are described in the same way as in UML specification, thus containing determined specification parts.
		SoaML	The same as used for OMG SysML (see above).

Table 3.1 (Continued)

The result of the evaluation against quantitative criteria is given in Table 3.2.

Summary of positive and negative aspects for each evaluated profile is given in Table 3.3.

The review of profiles shows that there is no unified profile definition template or approach—each author defines profile on its own. After doing systematic review of UML profiles, Pardillo in his research [103] has outlined that *"the low presentation quality point out the need of more formal methods and templates to present UML profiles."* Only two of four reviewed profiles (OMG SysML and SoaML) have huge similarities in the profile specification (the specification structure

Table 3.2 Evaluation of Quantitative Criteria for Selected Profiles

Criterion \ Profile	xUML	TFM4MDA	OMG SysML	SoaML
Metaclasses extended	?	6	25	12
Stereotypes defined	?	8	40	20
Diagrams extended	?	0	3	0
Diagrams introduced	0	1	2	0
Total count of diagrams	8	14	9	13

Table 3.3 Positive and Negative Aspects of Selected UML Profiles

No.	Aspect	Profile	Evaluation
1.	Positive aspects	xUML	Models are testable and executable. Profile contains approach of applying it.
		TFM4MDA	Profile has an approach (called TFM4MDA) for its use in software development.
		OMG SysML	Profile definition structure.
		SoaML	Profile definition structure.
2.	Negative aspects	xUML	Profile definition style—no stereotypes and extended metaclasses modeled.
		TFM4MDA	TFM4MDA approach uses problem domain graph as intermediate model between TFM and class diagram but in the same time this graph is not included in TFM4MDA profile.
		OMG SysML	The introduced requirements diagram is just a repository of textual requirements.
		SoaML	Names of stereotypes are the same as for the metaclasses they extend. It could lead to confusion of used element and misunderstanding of developed diagrams.

is about 85% the same). The specification of these two profiles follows the overall specification structure of UML; thus if the reader is familiar with the UML specification understanding of these profiles is relieved. Summarizing issues related to UML profile specification techniques and templates, the next section provides guidelines for profile development.

3.4 DEVELOPING A PROFILE FOR UNIFIED MODELING LANGUAGE

Developing a profile for UML should be done in consistent way by using some unified profiling approach or template. Since UML specification contains only the definition of elements that are building up a profile and does not provide guidelines or process on how to apply these elements, before creating a profile for UML it is needed to define guidelines of profile development. While this section summarizes up the contents of profile in the terms of used elements from UML specification [78], the next section gives guidelines of contents for a profile specification.

The UML profile diagram consists of following elements:

- *Metamodel*—a referenced model that is extended through the profile. A graphical representation is shown in Fig. 3.3 where UML is used as a metamodel to extend.
- *Reference*—a dependency relationship with attached stereotype *«reference»* that is directed from profile to referenced metamodel. An example of reference relationship is given in Fig. 3.4 where a profile named *TestML* references metamodel of UML. This example shows that *TestML* profile is created by extending UML.
- *Profile*—a special package that extends a referenced metamodel by adding stereotypes to it. Like packages in package diagram can be

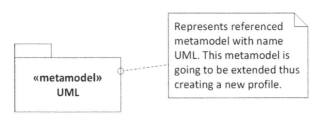

Figure 3.3 Metamodel representation.

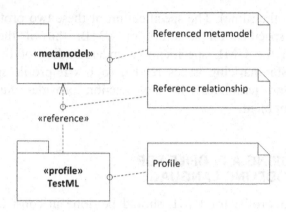

Figure 3.4 Metamodel reference relationship.

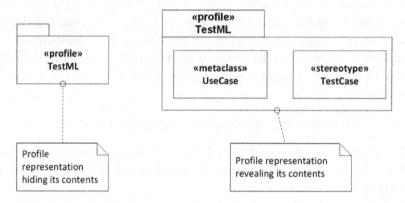

Figure 3.5 Profile illustration variations.

drawn at different abstraction levels revealing or hiding its content, the profile can be drawn in the same manner. Fig. 3.5 gives an example of profile *TestML* showing on the left side just the profile node and on the right side—profile together with its contents.

- *Metaclass*—a class that is extended by a stereotype. The metaclass is represented with the same node as regular class by attaching stereotype *«metaclass»*. An example of regular class and metaclass is illustrated in Fig. 3.6.
- *Stereotype*—extends existing UML vocabulary by adding a new element to it and it describes how an existing metaclass can be extended enabling the integration of platform or domain specific terminology or notation in the modeling language (a set of stereotypes build up the profile). A stereotype extension is used to indicate that

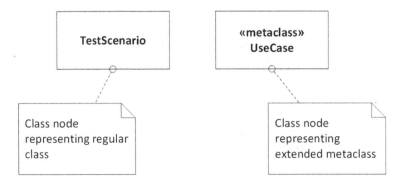

Figure 3.6 Class nodes showing regular class and metaclass.

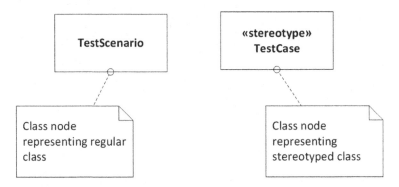

Figure 3.7 Class nodes showing regular class and stereotyped class.

the properties of a metaclass are extended through a stereotype. The stereotyped class is represented with the same node as regular class by attaching stereotype *«stereotype»*. An example of regular class and stereotyped class is given in Fig. 3.7.

- *Extension*—a special binary association, extension end is used to tie an extension to a stereotype when extending a metaclass. Extension relationship is directed from stereotyped class to the metaclass it extends. An example of extension relationship is given in Fig. 3.8 where a stereotyped class named *TestCase* extends metaclass *UseCase*.
- *Profile application*—a dependency relationship with attached stereotype *«apply»* between a package and a profile that allows to use the stereotypes from the profile in the model elements of the source package. Profile application relationship is directed from package that applies profile to the profile package. Take a look at profile application example in Fig. 3.9.

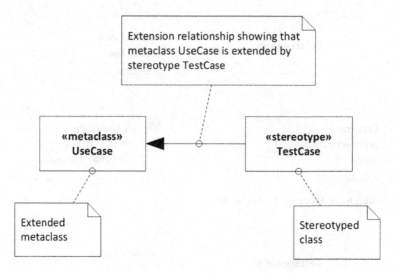

Figure 3.8 Extension relationship.

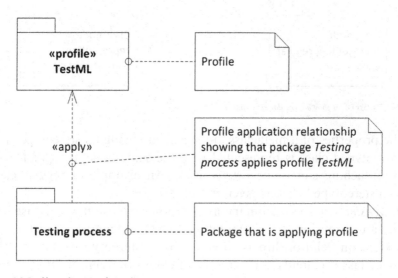

Figure 3.9 Profile application relationship.

An example showing generic profile with name *TestML* is given in Fig. 3.10. The example of profile extends UML by adding stereotype *TestCase*. The stereotype *TestCase* extends metaclass *UseCase* by using extension relationship. The profile is applied by the package *Testing process*.

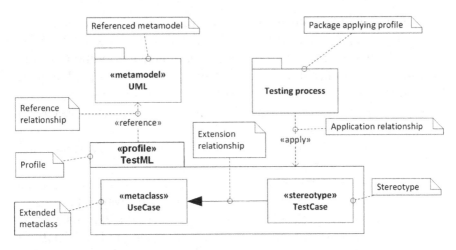

Figure 3.10 Example of profile and profile application.

3.5 PROFILE SPECIFICATION TEMPLATE

As shows the specification of OMG SysML [80] and SoaML [76] the best practice for UML profile specification is to use the same structure as used for UML specification, thus if the reader is familiar with UML specification it is easier to read and understand the specification of specific UML profile. UML specification is created by keeping in mind following aspects [77]: correctness, precision, conciseness, consistency, and understandability.

The profile specification should start with profile diagram showing the referenced metamodel and how the profile extends it. After profile diagram, one or more package diagrams should be provided showing the packages of which the profile consists. UML elements within its metamodel and specification also are grouped into packages. At this point it is advised to reuse the package specification style used in UML specification. Each package and each class in the UML specification (both infrastructure [77] and superstructure [78] specifications) has following structure:

- *Package*—this clause provides information for each package and each class in the UML metamodel or profile. Each package specification contains one or more of the following subclauses (*Classes, Diagrams*, and *Instance model*).
  - *Classes*—contains a list of the classes specifying all the constructs defined in package. This subclause begins with one diagram or

several diagrams depicting the abstract syntax of the constructs (i.e., the classes and their relationships) in the package, together with some of the well-formedness requirements (multiplicity and ordering). Then follows a specification of each class in alphabetic order. Each class specification has following subclauses:

- *Description*—an informal definition of the metaclass specifying the construct in UML.
- *Attributes*—list of all attributes for metaclass. Attributes are given together with a short explanation.
- *Associations*—list of all member ends of associations connected to this class (associations are listed in the same way as attributes).
- *Constraints*—well-formedness rules of the metaclass. These rules specify constraints over attributes and associations defined in the metamodel. Mostly they are defined by using OCL expressions together with an informal explanation of the expression.
- *Additional operations (optional)*—contains any additional operations on the class which are needed for the OCL expressions.
- *Semantics*—the meaning of a well-formed construct is defined using natural language (can include formal definition of construct's semantics).
- *Semantic variation points (optional)*—objective of a semantic variation point is to enable specialization of that part of UML for a particular situation or domain.
- *Notation*—presents the notation of the construct (i.e., class).
- *Presentation options (optional)*—if there are different ways to show the construct, these ways are described in this subclause.
- *Style guidelines (optional)*—describes non-normative conventions that are used in representing some part of a model.
- *Examples (optional)*—examples of how the construct is to be depicted.
- *Rationale (optional)*—if there is a reason why a construct is defined like it is, or why its notation is defined as it is, then it is given in this subclause.

- *Diagrams*—this subclause is included into specification to describe specific kind of diagram, if this diagram uses the constructs that are defined in this package.
- *Instance model*—shows an example of applying constructs defined in this package.

3.6 SUMMARY

When extending UML it is needed to draw the scope of required extension: if the new language will use most of the UML, then profiles are more suitable; and if the new language uses only small part of UML or there is need to use more complex features of UML such as redefinition, then creating a complete new language by using MOF metamodeling should be considered. In fact, UML specification itself is defined using metamodeling approach (a metamodel is used to specify the model that builds UML). One of the UML metamodel principles is its extensibility. The most common and suitable way for improving UML is to use its extensibility mechanisms—the profiles (in this scenario it is possible to adapt and use ordinary UML compliant modeling tools). Thus, by creating a profile of UML, the costs of adapting it in practice is lowered and it can be adapted faster (in comparison with creating a new modeling language which leads to implementing new modeling tools).

Since the UML specification is a specification of a notation, it does not include any guidelines for profile definition and specification, thus leading to current situation when UML profiles are developed in inconsistent ways. This makes it hard to read and understand profiles proposed and created by different authors. To overcome identified issue, a set of UML profiles are analyzed resulting in profile specification template—*the best practice for UML profile specification is to use the same structure as used for UML specification.* Thus, if the reader is familiar with UML specification it is easier to read and understand the specification of specific UML profile.

Improving Domain Modeling

CHAPTER 4

Topological Unified Modeling Language

INFORMATION IN THIS CHAPTER:

- Topology in UML diagrams
- Extending UML
- Defining Topological UML
- Metamodels of Topological UML diagrams

4.1 TOPOLOGICAL UNIFIED MODELING LANGUAGE: AN UNIFIED MODELING LANGUAGE IMPROVEMENT

Topological Unified Modeling Language (Topological UML) is a combination of Unified Modeling Language (UML) and formalism of Topological Functioning Model (TFM) and is based on the principles of metamodeling and Meta-Object Facility (MOF). Idea of Topological UML is adapted from [83] where it is shown that *"there is a lack of mathematical formalism by drawing UML diagrams."* The main aim of improving UML is by transferring topology and mathematical formalism of TFM to UML, thus strengthening the very beginning of the software development lifecycle. Sometimes it is very hard to pay appropriate resources and time at the very beginning of the software development lifecycle to detect and analyze aspects of desired software system as much as possible. Especially in the world in which the result is required as soon as possible. As the end-user demands his or her software, the analysis, design, etc. is just a side-product for which the customer needs to pay—and it creates undesirable costs. But keep in mind, every single design decision which should be taken will be taken! If it happens as early as possible, it avoids wasting valuable resources, including time; otherwise it could lead to unnecessary reworking or even recoding parts of the system or the system as whole.

TFM enables careful analysis of system's operation and communication with the environment through analysis of functional cycles and it

Topological UML Modeling. DOI: http://dx.doi.org/10.1016/B978-0-12-805476-5.00004-6

allows to pay the required attention at the very beginning of the software development lifecycle. While using the TFM as a tool to carefully analyze the problem domain and design the solution domain, it is very important to not lose the information gathered during construction of the TFM. The best way to do this is to transfer all the design decisions from TFM to other design diagrams and of course to the software code. In such case, we are going from more abstract models to more specialized models, thus adding more and more development specific artifacts to design to get us to the executable software. Our research *"An Innovative Model Driven Formalization of the Class Diagrams"* [96] shows that it is possible to transfer topology from TFM into UML class diagrams thus creating a new diagram type called *topological class diagram* and that this diagram can be refined to have all necessary information for software development as outlined in *"Towards the Refinement of Topological Class Diagram as a Platform Independent Model"* [28].

The Topological UML is developed as a profile of UML and its specification takes advantage of the package merge feature of UML to merge extensions into UML. The created profile provides a UML specific version of the metamodel that can be incorporated into standard UML modeling tools as stated in UML's specification [77]. Since there is no specific profile definition method or approach the Topological UML profile definition is done by using results of profile definition analysis as given in Chapter 3, Adjusting Unified Modeling Language. Topological UML development is based on following steps:

- Extend UML by using profile mechanism, thus creating Topological UML profile and
- Define guidelines for using Topological UML in practice (thus formalizing the way the Topological UML is used).

This chapter covers extending UML while next—defining guidelines.

Despite that together with Topological UML is defined method on how to apply it in practice, the Topological UML language is intended to support multiple approaches and methods (e.g., structured, object-oriented, and conceptual). It is assumed that each methodology may impose additional constraints on how a Topological UML construct or diagram may be used and applied.

The analysis of UML diagrams included in the version 2.4.1 shows which of the diagrams already have elements that can reflect cause-and-effect (topological) relationships and which diagrams should be extended. The extension of a number of UML diagrams is necessary to develop a framework for Topological UML and later define Topological UML profile diagram for it. The analysis of existing UML diagrams is given in Table 4.1.

UML diagrams which already have constructs that reflect cause-and-effect relationships are the following six: (1) activity,

No.	Diagram	Has Cause-and-Effect Relationship	Requires Extension	Description
Table 4.1 Cause-and-Effect Relationships in UML Diagrams
Structure Diagrams
1.	Class diagram	No	Yes	Relationships which are used in class diagrams do not reflect cause-and-effect relations between classes, e.g., dependency shows that one class uses another without any clues how this class and for what is used, association shows structural relationships between classes (i.e., the structure), generalization shows inheritance between classes. By adding topological relationship to class diagram, it is possible to model cause-and-effect relations between classes.
2.	Component diagram	No	No	Component diagram shows relationships between logical components (by using interfaces and ports), i.e., it shows how a software system will be composed of a set of deployable components. Therefore, component diagram do not need to include topological relationship.
3.	Composite structure diagram	No	No	A composite structure diagram shows the internal structure of a class or collaboration. Since the difference between components and composite structure is small, composite structure diagram do not need to include topological relationship.
4.	Deployment diagram	No	No	A deployment diagram shows a set of nodes and their relationships. They are used to illustrate the static deployment view of architecture. Therefore, they do not need to include topological relationship.
5.	Object diagram	No	No	Object diagram shows instance of classes in class diagram with objects and their corresponding relationships (i.e., a snapshot taken at specific time). Since triggering of topological relationship causes a change in system the snapshot taken is altered thus creating a new snapshot. Therefore, object diagram do not need to include topological relationship.

(Continued)

Table 4.1 (Continued)

No.	Diagram	Has Cause-and-Effect Relationship	Requires Extension	Description
6.	Package diagram	No	No	Package diagram models contents of packages and relationships between packages, i.e., the structure of packages. Relationships used in package diagrams are import and export. If an element of one package uses element from another package, then there is a relationship between the two packages. Relations between packages are used to enable reuse of package contents. Therefore, package diagram do not need to include topological relationship.
7.	Profile diagram	No	No	Since Profile diagram allows to define a new language belonging to UML language family, it allows to add new language elements or extend existing ones and it does not include information about functioning of systems. The profile diagram is not used to model and design systems. Therefore, profile diagram do not need to include topological relationship.
Behavior Diagrams				
8.	Activity diagram	Yes	No	Cause-and-effect relations in activity diagram is reflected by the control flow from one node to another. Therefore, activity diagram do not need to include additional topological relationship.
9.	Use case diagram	No	Yes	Associations between actors and use cases show that there can be interaction (message sending) between actor and use case. Actor can be a user or another system. Addition of topological relationship to use case diagram enables to design and show formally defined communication between the use case and actor thus showing who is triggering the communication.
10.	State diagram	Yes	No	Topological relationship within state diagram is reflected by transition relationship between two states indicating that an object in the first state will perform certain actions and enter the second state when a specified event occurs and specified conditions are satisfied. Therefore, state diagram do not need to include additional topological relationship.
Behavior Diagrams: Interaction Diagrams				
11.	Sequence diagram	Yes	No	Message sending from one lifeline to another (i.e., a series of messages) establishes a chain of causality in sequence diagram, thus it already has constructs to reflect cause-and-effect relationships. Therefore, sequence diagram do not need to include additional topological relationship.

(Continued)

No.	Diagram	Has Cause-and-Effect Relationship	Requires Extension	Description
				Table 4.1 (Continued)
12.	Communication diagram	Yes	No	Since both sequence diagram and communication diagram derive from the same information in UML metamodel, message sending from one lifeline to another (i.e., a series of messages) establishes a chain of causality in communication diagram, thus it already has constructs to reflect cause-and-effect relationships. Therefore, communication diagram do not need to include additional topological relationship.
13.	Interaction overview diagram	Yes	No	Interaction overview diagram combines aspects of activity diagrams and sequence diagrams, thus it already has constructs to reflect cause-and-effect relationships. Therefore, interaction overview diagram do not need to include additional topological relationship.
14.	Timing diagram	Yes	No	Timing diagrams describe behavior of both individual classifiers and interactions of classifiers, focusing attention on time of occurrence of events causing changes in the modeled conditions of the lifelines. Therefore, timing diagram already has constructs to reflect cause-and-effect relationships and do not need to include additional topological relationship.

(2) state (or state machine), (3) sequence, (4) communication, (5) interaction overview, and (6) timing diagram. According to the intended use of component diagram, composite structure diagram, deployment diagram, object diagram, package diagram, profile diagram, and state diagram they do not require to be extended in order to introduce cause-and-effect relationships. The analysis of UML diagrams provides results of diagrams which are missing topological relationships and which one of those should be extended. Extension should be provided for two UML diagrams: (1) class diagram and (2) use case diagram.

By extending the class diagram and use case diagram to include cause-and-effect relationships, it is possible to model topological relations between classes and enables to design and show formally defined communication between the use case and actor thus showing who is triggering the communication. This is a very important aspect while these both are the most widely used UML diagrams, as identified in Chapter 2, Software Designing With Unified Modeling Language Driven Approaches: (1) class diagram (84%) and (2) use case diagram (71%).

4.2 TOPOLOGICAL UML PROFILE

According to the Topological UML base idea to combine formalism of TFM with UML and to create Topological UML in accordance with UML extension mechanisms, the new language includes all diagram types from UML and a new diagram type—TFM (thus making a family of 15 diagrams). The analysis of topology in UML diagrams shows that there are two diagrams which should be extended in order to include topological relationship: (1) class diagram and (2) use case diagram. Extension of these two diagrams means that it is possible to reflect cause-and-effect relations by using these diagrams. The extended versions of these two diagrams are called *topological class diagram* and *topological use case diagram*.

The diagrams included into Topological UML language specification are as shown in Fig. 4.1: (1) topological class diagram, (2) component diagram, (3) object diagram, (4) composite structure diagram, (5) deployment diagram, (6) package diagram, (7) profile diagram, (8) TFM, (9) activity diagram, (10) topological use case diagram, (11) state diagram, (12) sequence diagram, (13) communication diagram, (14) interaction overview diagram, and (15) timing diagram. Bolder lines in Fig. 4.1 denotes the new diagram (TFM) and two extended diagrams (topological class diagram and topological use case diagram).

The profile diagram specifying Topological UML language consists of eight stereotypes and two enumerations which are divided into four packages. The top-level profile diagram of Topological UML is given in Fig. 4.2 which shows the related metamodel and relationships between packages in profile. The packages are used to group together elements based on their intent and semantics and to ease the evolution of Topological UML (i.e., creation of new Topological UML versions). The packages that build up Topological UML profile are as follows:

- *TopologicalRelationships*—contains constructs related to relationships,
- *TopologicalStructure*—contains constructs related to structure representation,

Figure 4.1 Topological UML diagrams.

- *TopologicalBehavior*—contains constructs related to behavior modeling, and
- *TopologicalModels*—contains diagram types added to UML by Topological UML profile.

The Topological UML profile packages are designed to provide the necessary constructs to create TFM, topological class diagram, and topological use case diagram. Stereotypes included into each package are used across multiple diagram types thus making Topological UML profile more compact and without needless constructs. Stereotypes are related to corresponding metaclasses by extension relationship. The following subsections describe each of the Topological UML package and gives specification of all the stereotypes and enumerations used to create Topological UML profile.

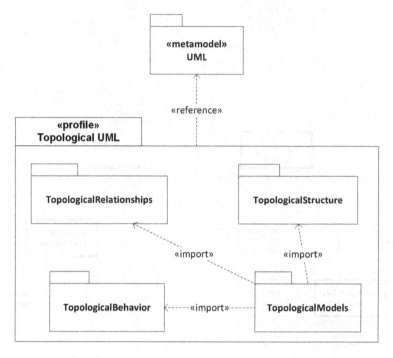

Figure 4.2 Topological UML profile top level package.

4.2.1 Topological Relationships Package

The topological relationships package contains all relationships that are created by Topological UML profile. These relationships provide the necessary constructs to create TFM, topological class diagram, and topological use case diagram. The relations introduced are used across multiple diagram types thus making Topological UML profile more compact and without needless constructs. The topological relationships package is given in Fig. 4.3 as package *TopologicalRelationships*.

The topological relationships package contains following stereotypes:

- *TopologicalRelationship*—topological relationship is a binary relationship that shows a cause-and-effect relation between two elements: (1) source element and (2) target element. A topological relationship is assertion that indicates that the effect element can be triggered only by the cause element thus showing that effect element is executed only after the cause element executes.
- *LogicalRelationship*—logical relationship represents logical relation between two or more topological relationships belonging to TFM (an instance of *TopologicalFunctioningModel*). It can show conjunction (*and*), disjunction (*or*), and exclusive disjunction (*xor*).

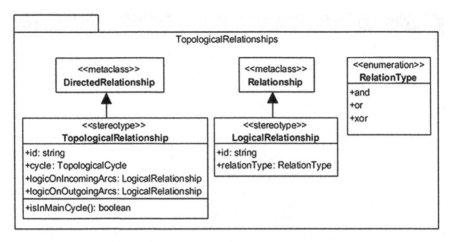

Figure 4.3 TopologicalRelationships *package.*

Topological relationship in Topological UML is reflected by stereotype *TopologicalRelationship*. Specification of *TopologicalRelationship* is given in Table 4.2.

Logical relationship in Topological UML is reflected by stereotype *LogicalRelationship*. Specification of *LogicalRelationship* is given in Table 4.3.

4.2.2 Topological Structure Package

The topological structure package contains all structure elements that are created by Topological UML profile. These elements provide the necessary constructs to create TFM, topological class diagram, and topological use case diagram. The elements introduced are used across multiple diagram types thus making Topological UML profile more compact and without needless constructs. The topological structure package is given in Fig. 4.4.

Topological structure package *TopologicalStructure* contains following stereotypes:

- *TopologicalCycle*—topological cycle represents directed functional cycle of system; it consists of elements and relationships between them. It can show the main functionality that has a vital importance in the functioning of system, i.e., by interrupting the main cycle the system can no longer function or its functioning is deformed.
- *TopologicalOperation*—topological operation is a behavioral feature of classifier that specifies the name, type, parameters, and

Table 4.2 Specification of Stereotype *TopologicalRelationship*

Clause	Specification
Description	Topological relationship represents a cause-and-effect relationship between two elements: (1) source and (2) target element. Extends «metaclass» *DirectedRelationship*.
Attributes	• + id: string [1] • Specifies the identifier of topological relationship.

Associations	• + cycle: TopologicalCycle [0..*]
	   • Specifies the cycle to which this topological relationship belongs. Topological relationship can belong to many cycles at a time.
	• + logicOnIncomingArcs: LogicalRelationship [0..*]
	   • Specifies logical relationship to which this logical relationship belongs. Topological relationship can belong to many logical relationships at a time.
	• + logicOnOutgoingArcs: LogicalRelationship [0..*]
	   • Specifies logical relationship to which this logical relationship belongs. Topological relationship can belong to many logical relationships at a time.

Constraints	1. Logical relationship *logicOnIncomingArcs* should belong to TFM (an instance of *TopologicalFunctioningModel*). 2. Logical relationship *logicOnOutgoingArcs* should belong to TFM (an instance of *TopologicalFunctioningModel*). 3. If *TopologicalRelation* relates instances of *UseCase* and *Actor*, then source cannot be the same type and/or instance as target. 4. If *TopologicalRelation* relates instances of *UseCase* and *Actor*, then target cannot be the same type and/or instance as source.
Additional operations	• + isInMainCycle(): Boolean • Check that topological relationship belongs to main functioning cycle.
Semantics	Topological relationship is a binary relationship that shows a cause-and-effect relation between two elements: (1) source element and (2) target element. A topological relationship is assertion that indicates that the effect element can be triggered only by the cause element thus showing that effect element is executed only after the cause element executes.
Notation	Topological relationship is shown as arrow with filled arrowhead pointing from cause element to effect element (the arrowhead is placed at the effect side); it is directed only in one way—from cause to effect. **Cause element** ⟶ **Effect element**

Presentation options	In the case of topological class diagrams where behavioral features (operations) are related with topological relationship, multiple topological relationships can be merged by listing cause and effect behavioral features together with their identifiers on the ends of relationship (identifier for related behavior features on both ends of relationship is the same). Identifiers are local to one topological relationship; it can be any user-specific symbol.
	
	Class A 1 OperationA1 1 OperationB1 Class B
	        2 OperationA2 2 OperationB2
	        3 OperationA3 3 OperationB3
	
	OperationA2 is related to OperationB2, both share the same identifier – 2

constraints for invoking an associated behavior, and related functional features and topological relationships for specifying cause-and-effect relations within system, thus allowing a cause-and-effect relations to be modeled within the system by means of behavioral features (e.g., in topological class diagram).

Table 4.3 Specification of Stereotype *LogicalRelationship*	
Clause	**Specification**
Description	Logical relationship represents a logical relation between two or more topological relationships. It extends «metaclass» *Relationship*.

Attributes	• + id: string [1]
	  ◦ Specifies the identifier of logical relationship.
	• + relationType: RelationType [1]
	  ◦ Specifies the type of logical relation; defined values: *and, or,* and *xor*.

Associations	No additional associations.
Constraints	1. Minimal count of related elements is two (i.e., relatedElement: Element [2..*]). 2. relatedElement can be only of type *TopologicalRelationship*. 3. Related topological relationships should belong to TFM (an instance of *TopologicalFunctioningModel*). 4. Either target element or source element of related topological relationships should be the same.
Semantics	Logical relationship represents logical relation between two or more topological relationship belonging to TFM (an instance of *TopologicalFunctioningModel*). It can show conjunction (and), disjunction (or), and exclusive or (xor).
Notation	Logical relationship is drawn as solid line connecting related topological relationships. If topological relationship is included in logical relationship, a point is set on the place where line representing logical relationship crosses arrow representing topological relationship. Next to the line of logical relationship is added label denoting the type of it. Topological relationship / Logical relationship / Type of logical relationship (diagram with A, B, C nodes and AND label)

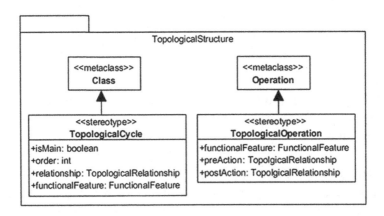

Figure 4.4 TopologicalStructure *package.*

Table 4.4 Specification of Stereotype *TopologicalCycle*

Clause	Specification
Description	Topological cycle represents directed functional cycle of system; it consists of elements and relationships between them. Extends «metaclass» *Class*.
Attributes	• + isMain: Boolean [1] · Indicates if cycle is main functioning cycle of system. • + order: Integer [1] · Shows the order of functioning cycle.
Associations	• + relationship: TopologicalRelationship [2..*] · Contains all topological relationships belonging to this functioning cycle. • + functionalFeature: FunctionalFeature [2..*] · Contains all functional feature belonging to this functioning cycle.
Constraints	1. Only one main functional cycle is allowed in system. 2. Can contain elements and relations between them which form the oriented cycle.
Semantics	It is acknowledged that every business and technical system is a subsystem of the environment. Besides that a common thing for all system functioning should be the main feedback, visualization of which is an oriented cycle. Therefore, it is stated that at least one directed closed loop (main functioning cycle) must be present in every topological model of system functioning. It shows the main functionality that has a vital importance in the functioning of system, i.e., by interrupting the main cycle the system can no longer function or its functioning is deformed.
Notation	There is no general notation for a *TopologicalCycle*. It is formed by elements and relationships between them.
Presentation options	The main topological cycle (isMain = true) can be highlighted by drawing bolder lines of relationships belonging to it.
Examples	Example shows diagram with two cycles—one main cycle and one ordinary cycle.

Topological cycle in Topological UML is reflected by stereotype *TopologicalCycle*. Specification of *TopologicalCycle* is given in Table 4.4.

Topological operation in Topological UML is reflected by stereotype *TopologicalOperation*. Specification of *TopologicalOperation* is given in Table 4.5.

4.2.3 Topological Behavior Package

The topological behaviors package contains all behavioral constructs that are created by Topological UML profile that are necessary to create TFM, topological class diagram, and topological use case diagram.

Clause	Specification
Table 4.5 Specification of Stereotype *TopologicalOperation*	
Description	Topological operation is extension of «metaclass» *Operation* which is a behavioral feature of a classifier that specifies the name, type, parameters, and constraints for invoking an associated behavior, and related functional features and topological relationships for specifying cause-and-effect relations within system.
Attributes	No additional attributes.

Associations	• + functionalFeature: FunctionalFeature [1]
	  ∘ Reference to functional feature which specifies this operation.
	• + preAction: TopologicalRelationship [0..1]
	  ∘ Specifies relationship to cause action for this action.
	• + postAction: TopologicalRelationship [0..1]
	  ∘ Specifies relationship to effect action of this action.

Constraints	1. If topological relationship specifying cause action belongs to main functioning cycle (preAction.isMain → true), then this operation cannot be suppressed. 2. If topological relationship specifying effect action belongs to main functioning cycle (postAction.isMain → true), then this operation cannot be suppressed.
Semantics	Topological operation is a behavioral feature of classifier that specifies the name, type, parameters, and constraints for invoking an associated behavior, and related functional features and topological relationships for specifying cause-and-effect relations within system, thus allowing a cause-and-effect relations to be modeled within the system by means of behavioral features (e.g., in topological class diagram).
Notation	No additional notation—uses the same as extended «metaclass» *Operation*.

The relations introduced are used across multiple diagram types thus making Topological UML profile more compact and without needless constructs. The topological behaviors package is given in Fig. 4.5 as package *TopologicalBehavior*.

Topological behaviors package *TopologicalBehavior* contains following stereotypes:

• *FunctionalFeature*—functional feature is a description of an atomic business action (i.e., it cannot be separated into a number of other business actions). Each functional feature is a unique tuple (stereotype *FunctionalFeature* is an abstraction of this tuple).
• *Condition*—condition shows precondition and postcondition within system. To enter the execution of behavior (e.g., functional feature) all preconditions of it should be true and to exit the execution of this behavior all postconditions should be evaluated to true. In the context of business system a condition also can be atomic business rule.
• *ActionResult*—action result specifies a result of object's action together with affected objects. For example, by registering customer in the registration journal a registration entry is created.

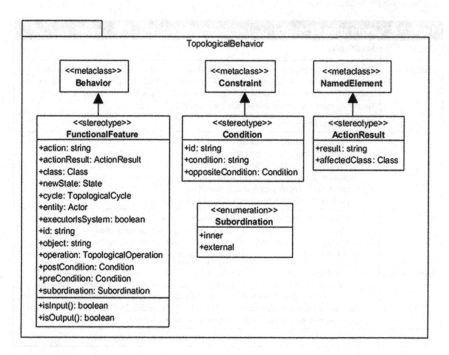

Figure 4.5 TopologicalBehavior *package.*

Functional feature in Topological UML is reflected by stereotype *FunctionalFeature*. Specification of *FunctionalFeature* is given in Table 4.6.

Precondition and postcondition in Topological UML are reflected by stereotype *Condition*. Specification of *Condition* is given in Table 4.7.

Result of action in Topological UML is reflected by stereotype *ActionResult*. Specification of *ActionResult* is given in Table 4.8.

4.2.4 Topological Models Package
The topological models package contains additional model that are introduced to UML by Topological UML profile—TFM. *TopologicalModels* package contains one stereotype:

- *TopologicalFunctioningModel*—It represents TFM by using UML metamodeling constructs. TFM is a mathematical model that shows functioning of a system in the form of directed graph consisting of functional features and topology between them. Functional features

Table 4.6 Specification of Stereotype *FunctionalFeature*

Clause	Specification
Description	Stereotype *FunctionalFeature* extends «metaclass» *Behavior* and is an abstraction of functional feature.

Attributes	• + action: string [1]
	  · Action performed by object (see attribute this.object).
	• + executorIsSystem: Boolean [1]
	  · Indicates if execution of action could be automated (i.e., performed without human interaction).
	• + id: string [1]
	  · Identifier of functional feature.
	• + object: string [1]
	  · Object that receives the result or that is used in action (e.g., a role, a time period, a catalogue, etc.).
	• + subordination: Subordination [1]
	  · Specifies subordination of functional feature, can be *inner* or *external*.

Associations	• + actionResult: ActionResult [0..1]
	  · Result of action (this.action) performed by object (this.object).
	• + class: Class [0..1]
	  · Represents object (this.object) in static viewpoint of system (can be specified when the class diagram is synthesized).
	• + newState: State [0..1]
	  · Represents the new state of object (this.object) after performing action (this.action).
	• + cycle: TopologicalCycle [0..*]
	  · Shows the functioning cycles to which this functional feature belongs.
	• + entity: Actor [1]
	  · Entity responsible for performing action specified by this functional feature.
	• + operation: TopologicalOperation [0..1]
	  · Specifies functionality defined by action (this.action). Operation can be specified when the class diagram is synthesized.
	• + preCondition: Condition [0..*]
	  · Set of preconditions, where precondition can be an atomic business rule.
	• + postCondition: Condition [0..*]
	  · Set of postconditions, where precondition can be an atomic business rule.

Constraints	1. Each functional feature is participating in at least one topological relationship either as a target or as a source. 2. In order for control flow to enter into functional feature, if any precondition is present it should be evaluated to true. 3. In order for control flow to leave functional feature, if any postcondition is present it should be evaluated to true.

Additional operations	• + isInput(): Boolean
	  · Check if functional feature is input functional feature.
	• + isOutput(): Boolean
	  · Check if functional feature is output functional feature.

Semantics	Functional feature is a description of an atomic business action (i.e., it cannot be separated into a number of other business actions). Each functional feature is a unique tuple (stereotype *FunctionalFeature* is an abstraction of this tuple).
Notation	Functional feature is represented in a form of circle with label inside showing identifier of it. ⑦
Presentation options	Functional feature can be represented as a class showing its stereotype name «FunctionalFeature» above the identifier or identifier with action of functional feature. The format of displaying functional feature name is as follows: $<id>[$': '$<action>]$ «FunctionalFeature» **7** «FunctionalFeature» **7: Checking due date**

Table 4.7 Specification of Stereotype *Condition*

Clause	Specification
Description	Condition is an abstraction of precondition and postcondition in system. It extends «metaclass» *Constraint*.

Attributes	• + id: string [1]
	  ◦ Identifier of condition.
	• + condition: string [1]
	  ◦ Boolean expression written in natural language or machine readable language.

Associations	• + oppositeCondition: Condition [0..1] ◦ Relation to opposite condition of this condition, i.e., this.condition = this. oppositeCondition.condition.
Constraints	No additional constraints.
Semantics	Condition shows precondition and postcondition within system. To enter the execution of behavior (e.g., functional feature) all preconditions of it should be true and to exit the execution of this behavior all postconditions should be evaluated to true. In the context of business system a condition also can be atomic business rule.
Notation	There is no notation for condition. It is shown only as attribute of functional feature.

Table 4.8 Specification of Stereotype *ActionResult*

Clause	Specification
Description	Action result is an abstraction of result which is achieved by object performing action as specified by functional feature. Extends «metaclass» *NamedElement*.
Attributes	• + result: string [1] ◦ Textual description of result of action performed by object specified in functional feature.
Associations	• + affectedClass: Class [0..1] ◦ Related class which is affected by the result of action performed by object specified in functional feature.
Constraints	1. Instance of *ActionResult* should belong to instance of *FunctionalFeature*.
Semantics	Action result specifies a result of object's action in functional feature specification. The action result shows also affected objects during its execution. For example, by registering customer in the registration journal a registration entry is created.
Notation	There is no notation for action result. It is shown only as attribute of functional feature.

embed information of systems functioning and its structural description while topology defines cause-and-effect relations between them thus embedding the behavior of the system.

The topological models package is shown in Fig. 4.6.

Specification of TFM's stereotype *TopologicalFunctioningModel* is given in Table 4.9.

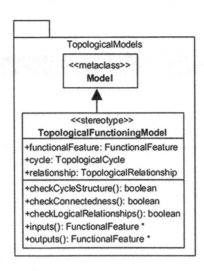

Figure 4.6 TopologicalModels *package.*

Table 4.9 Specification of Stereotype *TopologicalFunctioningModel*	
Clause	**Specification**
Description	*TopologicalFunctioningModel* is an abstraction of Topological Functioning Model (TFM) in the metamodeling terms; it extends «metaclass» *Model*.
Attributes	No additional attributes.

Associations	• + functionalFeature: functionalFeature [2..*]
	  ◦ Functional feature is an atomic business action (i.e., it cannot be separated into a number of other business actions).
	• + cycle: TopologicalCycle [1..*]
	  ◦ Topological cycle represents directed functional cycle of system; it consists of functional features and relationships between them.
	• + topologicalRelationship: TopologicalRelationship [2..*]
	  ◦ Topological relationships relating functional features.

Constraints	1. Instances of *TopologicalRelationship* can relate only instances of *FunctionalFeature* (i.e., source and target of *TopologicalRelationship* can only be of type *FunctionalFeature*). 2. *TopologicalFunctioningModel* should contain at least two elements of type *FunctionalFeature*. 3. *TopologicalFunctioningModel* should contain at least two elements of type *TopologicalRelationship*. 4. *TopologicalFunctioningModel* should contain at least one instance of type *TopologicalCycle*. 5. *TopologicalFunctioningModel* should contain one instance of type *TopologicalCycle* with its attribute isMain set to value true (isMain = true).

Additional operations	• + checkCycleStructure(): Boolean
	  ◦ Check that created model contains functioning cycles.
	• + checkConnectedness(): Boolean
	  ◦ Check that all functional features are connected with cause-and-effect relationships.
	• + checkLogicalRelationships(): Boolean
	  ◦ Identify and set logical relations within model. In addition identification of logical relations does an additional model checking by verifying correctness and allowance of specified preconditions and postconditions.
	• + inputs(): FunctionalFeature *
	  ◦ Array of functional features that are input functional features (this.functionalFeature [].isInput).

(Continued)

Table 4.9 (Continued)	
Clause	**Specification**
	• + outputs(): FunctionalFeature * ◦ Array of functional features that are output functional features (this.functionalFeature [].isOutput).
Semantics	*TopologicalFunctioningModel* represents TFM by using UML metamodeling constructs. TFM is a mathematical model that shows functioning of a system in the form of directed graph consisting of functional features and topology between them. Functional features embed information of systems functioning and its structural description while topology defines cause-and-effect relations between them thus embedding the behavior of the system.
Notation	TFM is displayed as a directed graph showing functional features as circles and topological relationships (i.e., cause-and-effect relations) between them. Topological relationship is denoted with solid line and filled arrowhead to the target (i.e., effect) functional feature. Additionally logical relations can be shown between topological relationships. Logical relationship is drawn as solid line connecting related topological relationships (connection with topological relationship is denoted by bold point). TFM in diagram header is denoted with keyword tfm.
Style guidelines	The main topological cycle (isMain = true) can be highlighted by drawing bolder lines of relationships belonging to it. Example shows diagram with two cycles—one main cycle and one ordinary cycle.
Examples	

4.3 METAMODELS OF TOPOLOGICAL UML DIAGRAMS

This section gives metamodels of Topological UML diagrams which are new to UML or which have been extended—TFM, topological class diagram, and topological use case diagram.

4.3.1 Metamodel of Topological Functioning Model

To better understand the metamodel of TFM at first let's take a look at the TFM itself, i.e., what it is and what can we do with it. TFM is a mathematical modeling language intended to design and analyze functionality of a system and it holistically represents a complete functionality of the system from a computation independent viewpoint. It considers problem domain information separate from the solution domain information. TFM has strong mathematical basis and is represented in a form of a topological space. Graphically it is drawn as an oriented graph where nodes represent functional features of the system, while directed arcs represent their causal relationships. The TFM has *topological characteristics*: (1) connectedness, (2) closure, (3) neighborhood, (4) and continuous mapping. Despite that any graph is included into algebraic topology, not every graph is a TFM. A directed graph becomes the TFM only when theoretical substantiation of the systems is added to the above mathematical substantiation. The latter is represented by *functional characteristics*: (1) cause-effect relations, (2) cycle structure, and (3) inputs and outputs [88, 90].

It is acknowledged that every business and technical system is a subsystem of the environment. TFM enables careful analysis of system's operation and communication with the environment through analysis of functional cycles—a common thing for all system (technical, business, or biological) functioning should be the main feedback, visualization of which is an oriented cycle. Thus, it is stated that at least one directed closed loop (cycle) must be present in every topological model of system functioning. This cycle shows the main functionality that has a vital importance in the system's life. Usually it is even an expanded hierarchy of cycles. By interrupting this main cycle the system can no longer function or it functions faulty [86]. Therefore, a proper cycle analysis is necessary in the TFM construction, because it enables careful analysis of system's operation and communication with the environment. To better illustrate main cycle in graph representation of TFM, the arcs belonging to this cycle is drew with bolder lines [84].

4.3.1.1 Formal Definition of Topological Functioning Model

TFM is represented in a form of a topological space (see Eq. 4.1 [86]), where X is a finite set X of functional features X_{id} (see Eq. 4.4) of the system under consideration, and Θ is the topology that satisfies axioms of topological structures and is represented in a form of a directed graph (i.e., Θ is a finite set of topological relationships T_{id} [10] (see Eq. 4.3) between functional features):

$$G = (X, \Theta). \tag{4.1}$$

Topological space Z represents functioning of the system under consideration and its surrounding environment (i.e., finite set of TFMs exists in topological space where each TFM shows functioning of a specific system). The topological space Z is a system represented by Eq. (4.2) [86], where N is a set of internal system functional features and M is a set of functional features of other systems that interact with the system or of the system itself, which affect the external ones:

$$Z = N \cup M. \tag{4.2}$$

The necessary condition for constructing the topological space Z is a meaningful and exhaustive verbal, graphical, or mathematical system description. The adequacy of a model describing the functioning of a specific system can be achieved by analyzing mathematical and functional properties of such abstract object [86]. To create a TFM that reflects the system under consideration, the necessary information can be taken from different sources such as verbal descriptions like documents [86], interviews, user stories, business use cases (discussed in [104]), diagrams, ontologies, schemas, business process descriptions, requirements specifications, as well as from mathematical expressions and expert knowledge about the system.

To analyze and show functioning of specific system, TFM of this system should be separated from topological space Z. Separation of the TFM from the topological space Z of a problem domain is performed by applying the closure operation over a set of system's inner functional features (the set N) as it is shown by Eq. (4.3) [86], where X_η is an adherence point of set N and capacity of X is the number n of adherence points of N:

$$X = [N] = \bigcup_{\eta=1}^{n} X_\eta \tag{4.3}$$

An adherence point of the set N is a point, whose each neighborhood includes at least one point from the set N. The neighborhood of a vertex Y in a directed graph is the set of all vertices adjacent to Y and the

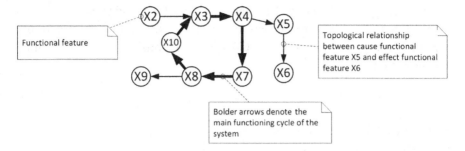

Figure 4.7 Example of TFM.

vertex Y itself. It is assumed here that all vertices adjacent to Y lie at the distance d = 1 from Y. An example of TFM is given in Fig. 4.7.

4.3.1.2 Formal Definition of Functional Features

Functional feature is a description of atomic business action (i.e., it cannot be separated into a number of other business actions). In [5] it is suggested that each functional feature is a unique tuple; in [97] this tuple is extended to include class and operation reference (elements *Cl* and *Op*). This research redefines tuple to include all necessary elements needed when constructing TFM (the new elements are *Id, St, Es,* and *S*). Unique tuple definition of functional feature X_{id} is a shown by Eq. (4.4):

$$X_{id} = <\text{Id, A, Op, R, O, Cl, St, PreCond, PostCond, E, Es, S}> \quad (4.4)$$

where,

- *Id*—identifier of functional feature,
- *A*—action of object O,
- *Op*—operation which will provide functionality defined by action A (can be acquired when the class diagram is synthesized),
- *R*—result of action A,
- *O*—object that receives the result or that is used in action A (e.g., a role, a time period, a catalogue),
- *Cl*—class which will represent object O in static viewpoint of system (can be acquired when the class diagram is synthesized),
- *St*—new state of object O after performing action A,
- *PreCond*—is a set of preconditions C_{id} (see Eq. 4.5),
- *PostCond*—is a set of postconditions C_{id} (see Eq. 4.5),
- *E*—entity responsible for performing action A,
- *Es*—indicates if execution of action A could be automated (i.e., performed without human interaction), and
- *S*—subordination of functional feature (can be internal or external).

4.3.1.3 Formal Definition of Preconditions and Postconditions

Each precondition or postcondition is a condition C_{id} described by unique tuple given in Eq. (4.5). Condition is considered as an atomic business rule.

$$C_{id} = \; < Id, \; Cond, \; oCond >, \text{ where} \qquad (4.5)$$

- *Id*—identifier of condition,
- *Cond*—condition or an atomic business rule, and
- *oCond*—identifier of opposite condition, i.e., $C_i = C_j$.

4.3.1.4 Formal Definition of Topological Relationships

Cause-and-effect relationship T_{id} is a binary relationship relating two functional features X_{id} and are represented as arcs of a directed graph that are oriented from a cause vertex to an effect vertex. The synonym for cause-and-effect relationship is topological relationship. Each cause-and-effect relationship is a unique tuple represented by Eq. (4.6):

$$T_{id} = \; < Id, \; X_c, \; X_e, \; L_{out}, \; L_{in} >, \text{ where} \qquad (4.6)$$

- *Id*—unique identifier of topological relationship,
- X_c—cause functional feature,
- X_e—effect functional feature,
- L_{out}—set of logical relationships between topological relationships on outgoing arcs of cause functional feature X_c (optional), and
- L_{in}—set of logical relationships between topological relationships on incoming arcs of effect functional feature X_e (optional).

4.3.1.5 Formal Definition of Logical Relations

Logical relation L_{id} shows the logical relationship conjunction (*and*), disjunction (*or*), or exclusive or (*xor*) between two or more topological relationships T_{id}. The type of logical relation denotes system execution behavior (e.g., decision making, parallel actions). Each logical relation is a unique tuple represented by Eq. (4.7):

$$L_{id} = \; < Id, \; T, \; Rt >, \text{ where} \qquad (4.7)$$

- *Id*—identifier of logical relationship,
- *T*—set of topological relationships belonging to this logical relationship, and
- *Rt*—logical relationship type (*and, or,* or *xor*).

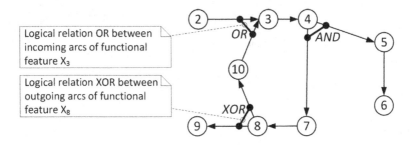

Figure 4.8 Example of logical relations between topological relationships.

Identification of logical relations L_{id} between cause-and-effect (i.e., topological) relationships T_{id} consists of two activities:

1. Identification of logical relations L_{out} between topological relationships T_{id} that are outgoing from functional feature X_{id} and
2. Identification of logical relations L_{in} between topological relationships T_{id} that are incoming to functional feature X_{id}.

Example of logical relations between topological relationships is given in Fig. 4.8.

4.3.1.6 Definition of Topological Functioning Model Metamodel
The metamodel of TFM represents it as an instance of the metaclass *TopologicalFunctioningModel*. In order to define metamodel of TFM the following UML version 2.4.1 metaclasses has been extended: *Model, Class, NamedElement, Behavior, Constraint, Relationship*, and *DirectedRelationship*.

Metamodel of TFM is given in Fig. 4.9 showing all stereotypes, metaclasses and enumerations involved into definition of TFM. Mappings between elements of unique tuple (see Eq. 4.4) and attributes of stereotype *FunctionalFeature* which is defining functional features is given in Table 4.10.

Mappings between elements of unique tuple (see Eq. 4.5) and attributes or properties of stereotype *Condition* which is defining precondition and postcondition of functional feature is given in Table 4.11.

Mappings between elements of unique tuple (see Eq. 4.6) and attributes or properties of stereotype *TopologicalRelationship* which is defining topological relationships between functional features is given in Table 4.12.

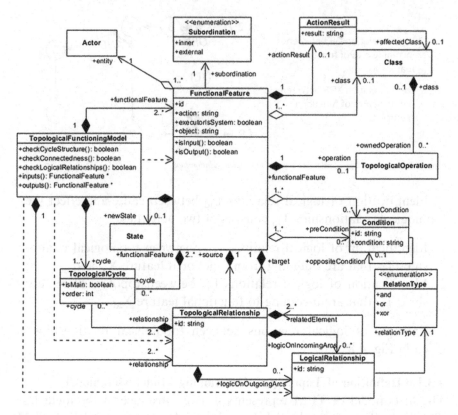

Figure 4.9 Metamodel of TFM.

No.	Tuple Element	Class Attribute or Property With Type	Multiplicity
Table 4.10 Mappings Between Tuple and Stereotype Elements for Functional Feature X_{id}			
1.	Id	id:string	1
2.	A	action:string	1
3.	Op	operation:Operation	0..1
4.	R	actionResult:ActionResult	0..1
5.	O	object:string	1
6.	Cl	class:Class	0..1
7.	St	newState:State	0..1
8.	PreCond	preCondition:Condition	0..*
9.	PostCond	postCondition:Condition	0..*
10.	E	entity:Actor	1
11.	Es	executorIsSystem:boolean	1
12.	S	subordination:Subordination	1

Table 4.11 Mappings Between Tuple and Stereotype Elements of Precondition and Postcondition C_{id}

No.	Tuple Element	Class Attribute or Property With Type	Multiplicity
1.	Id	id:string	1
2.	Cond	condition:string	1
3.	oCond	oppositeCondition:Condition	0..1

Table 4.12 Mappings Between Tuple and Stereotype Elements of Topological Relationships T_{id}

No.	Tuple Element	Class Attribute or Property With Type	Multiplicity
1.	Id	id:string	1
2.	Xc	source:FunctionalFeature	1
3.	Xe	target:FuntionalFeature	1
4.	Lout	logicOnOutgoingArcs:LogicalRelationship	0..*
5.	Lin	logicOnIncomingArcs:LogicalRelationship	0..*

Table 4.13 Mappings Between Tuple and Stereotype Elements of Logical Relationships L_{id}

No.	Tuple Element	Class Attribute or Property With Type	Multiplicity
1.	Id	id:string	1
2.	T	relatedElement:TopologicalRelationship	2..*
3.	Rt	relationType:RelationType	1

Mappings between elements of unique tuple (see Eq. 4.7) and attributes or properties of stereotype *LogicalRelationship* which is defining logical relations between topological relationships is given in Table 4.13.

According to metamodel of TFM in order to create TFM an instance of class *TopologicalFunctioningModel* should be instantiated. Each instance consists of at least two functional features (instances of class *FunctionalFeature*), two cause-and-effect relationships (instances of class *TopologicalRelationship*), and at least one functioning cycle (instance of class *TopologicalCycle*).

4.3.2 Metamodel of Topological Class Diagram

Metamodel of topological class diagram is given in Fig. 4.10, where classes with bolder lines show elements that are added to the metamodel of regular UML class diagram.

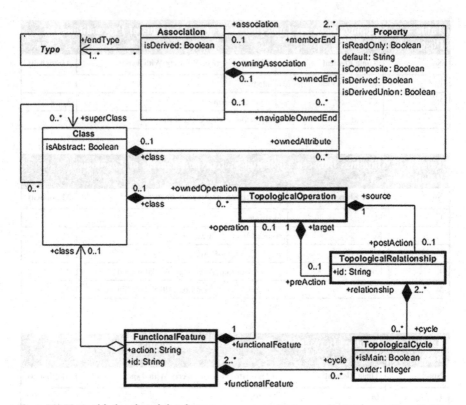

Figure 4.10 Metamodel of topological class diagram.

Topological class diagram is based on UML class diagram—it is extended to include topological relationships thus allowing to trace causality relations between problem and solution domains. Additionally, topological class diagram is able to show functioning cycles of a system (including the main functional cycle), input and output classes (classes which are communicating with the external environment). The presence of functional cycles allows classifying classes thus the classes participating in functional cycles can be marked and highlighted in the solution.

To achieve above described goal a class *TopologicalOperation* is used instead of class *Operation* thus allowing to relate two operations with topological relationship (similarly as association relationship relates at least two properties). Each operation specifies a cause and an effect of it (the cause is specified by using attribute *preAction* and the effect is specified by using attribute *postAction*). Attribute *preAction* leads to related topological relationship and the attribute target of this relationship leads to pre-operation (the cause), while attribute *postAction* leads to related topological relationship and the attribute source of this relationship leads to post-operation (the effect). The topological relationship defines the causality within topological class diagram while association defines the structure of objects (more precisely their specification—classes).

Each topological operation is related with functional feature that specifies it. This relation allows establishing direct traceability between TFM and topological class diagram. Besides that, relationships in topological class diagram are perceived formally from problem domain.

4.3.3 Metamodel of Topological Use Case Diagram
Topological use case diagram extends ordinary UML use case diagram by adding topological relationship between actor and use case (i.e., between classes *Actor* and *UseCase*) thus allowing to define actor for use case diagram directly from TFM by automatically relating functional features with corresponding use case. Since both classes *Actor* and *UseCase* are generalizations of class *BehavioredClassifier*, the source and target of topological relationships (i.e., both ends of a binary relationship) is connected to the *BehavioredClassifier*.

The metamodel of the topological use case diagram is represented in Fig. 4.11, where classes with bolder lines show elements that are added to the metamodel of regular UML use case diagram.

Topological use case diagram allows development of use cases based on the functional features and functionality they describe, functional features are mapped onto use cases. The input and output functional features define communication with the external environment. When functional features have been mapped onto use cases, the identification of actors is performed. The actors in topological use case diagram are entities from functional features.

Additionally *«include»* and *«extend»* relationships between use cases can be added automatically by analyzing topological and logical relationships between the mapped functional features. The scope of subsystems is defined formally by analyzing the functional cycles within TFM. If more than one functioning cycle is found, subsystems are designed in a way that each subsystem includes functionality of one

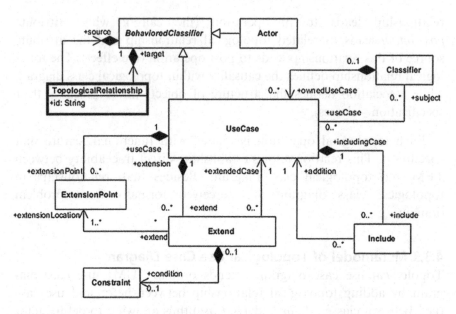

Figure 4.11 Metamodel of topological use case diagram.

functional cycle. Thus, the topological use case diagram is developed in strong accordance with the functioning of the problem and solution domains.

4.4 SUMMARY

The most common and suitable way for improving UML is to use its extensibility mechanisms—the profiles (in this scenario, it is possible to adapt and use standard UML compliant modeling tools). Thus, by creating a profile of UML, the costs of adapting it in practice is lowered and it can be adapted faster (in comparison with creating a new modeling language which leads to implementing new modeling tools). Since the UML specification is a specification of a notation, it does not include any guidelines for profile definition and specification, thus leading to current situation when UML profiles are developed in inconsistent ways. To overcome this, in Chapter 3, Adjusting Unified Modeling Language, you will find a solution.

Topological UML is a combination of UML and formalism of TFM. The main aim of improving UML is by transferring topology and mathematical formalism of TFM to UML thus strengthening the very beginning of the software development lifecycle. Sometimes it is very hard to pay appropriate resources and time at the very beginning of the software development lifecycle to detect and analyze aspects of desired software system as much as possible. If we pay appropriate attention at the beginning of the software development project, we tend to avoid wasting valuable resources, including time; otherwise it could lead to unnecessary reworking or even recoding parts of the system or the system as whole. Just like Benjamin Franklin has said back in 18th century:

"If you fail to plan, you are planning to fail!"

TFM enables careful analysis of system's operation and communication with the environment through analysis of functional cycles and it allows to pay the required attention at the very beginning of the software development lifecycle. While using the TFM as a tool to carefully analyze the problem domain and design the solution domain, it is very important not to lose the information gathered during construction of the TFM. The best way to do this is to transfer all the design decisions from TFM to other design diagrams and of course to the software code. In such case, we are going from more abstract models to more specialized models, thus adding more and more development specific artifacts to design to get us to the executable software. While this chapter specifies Topological UML profile, the next chapter defines a modeling method for applying Topological UML profile in practice.

CHAPTER 5

Topological UML Modeling

INFORMATION IN THIS CHAPTER:

- Topological UML modeling method
- Top-down design with Topological UML diagrams
- Seams between diagrams
- Topological UML modeling in comparison with other modeling methods

5.1 TOPOLOGICAL UML MODELING: A METHOD FOR DESIGNING SOFTWARE

Topological UML modeling for problem domain modeling and software systems designing is a model-driven modeling method which combines Topological Functioning Model (TFM) and its formalism with elements and diagrams of Topological UML. In the context of Model Driven Architecture (MDA), the TFM considers problem domain information separate from the solution domain information and holistically represents a complete functionality of the system from the computation independent viewpoint while Topological UML has elements for representing system design at the platform independent viewpoint and platform-specific viewpoint. The Topological UML modeling method covers modeling and specification of systems in computation independent and platform independent viewpoints.

The application of Topological UML modeling ensures proper analysis of system functioning by identifying and analyzing functioning cycles. The functioning cycle is a common thing of all system (technical, business, or biological) functioning. Therefore, it is stated that at least one directed closed loop must be present in every TFM of system functioning [86]. It shows the main functionality that has a vital importance in the system's life (i.e., by destroying the main functioning cycle the system can no longer function or it is seriously malfunctioning). Usually the main

Topological UML Modeling. DOI: http://dx.doi.org/10.1016/B978-0-12-805476-5.00005-8

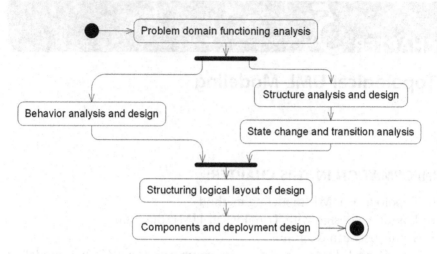

Figure 5.1 Topological UML modeling process and activities.

functionality is even an expanded hierarchy of cycles [40]. Therefore, a proper cycle analysis is necessary in the very beginning of software development lifecycle, because it enables careful analysis of system's operation and communication with the environment [91]. Operations of a class are addressed as responsibilities of this class. According to Larman's *"Applying UML and Patterns: An Introduction to Object-Oriented Analysis and Design and Iterative Development"* [58], responsibilities answer to two questions: *"What to do?"* and *"How to do?"*; and they are assigned to classes of objects during the object design. By using Topological UML the information of system functioning from TFM is transferred to design models and diagrams thus allowing marking and evaluating the most important objects and components within system and to assign proper responsibilities to the objects in a formal way.

Problem domain analysis and software system design with Topological UML modeling method consist of six activities as given in Fig. 5.1:

1. *Problem domain functioning analysis*—this is the first activity within Topological UML modeling and it states that the analysis of the problem domain should be performed. To do so, functioning description and functional requirements are used as input. Functioning description can be in any form; it needs to cover full description of problem domain functioning. Output of this activity is TFM (both the one representing functioning of problem domain, i.e., the situation as-is, and the one representing functionality of desired software system, i.e., the solution

to-be) which shows the system from computation independent viewpoint, mappings between functional features and functional requirements, and refined functional requirements. This activity ensures that proper attention is paid at the very beginning of the software development lifecycle by capturing various aspects of the desired system.

2. *Behavior analysis and design*—the next activity within Topological UML modeling process which is based on the results obtained in previous problem domain functioning analysis activity. By basing behavior analysis on TFM, we can clearly identify and design subsystems, use cases, actors, and relationships between them (topological use case diagram), messages and their sequence (sequence diagram), and workflows (activity and interaction overview diagram).

3. *Structure analysis and design*—the problem domain and solution domain representing TFM include enough information to identify system's structural artifacts and elements. By using this valuable information, we can design the domain model in the form of topological class diagram, communication diagram, and object diagram. As the object diagram shows a snapshot of the system at a given point in time, it is useful as an additional artifact when analyzing relationships between classes.

4. *State change and transition analysis*—the refined TFM and classes (either from topological class diagram or lifelines from communication diagram) are used to design state diagram for each class showing state changes and transitions. It is advised to analyze state changes of complex or most important objects in the system. The most important objects are those that are participating in the main functioning cycle of the system which is identified and specified during the construction of TFM during the very first activity within Topological UML modeling.

5. *Structuring logical layout of design*—logical layout of software design is structured in accordance with the defined subsystems in the system behavior analysis and design activity and the input of this activity is subsystems (use case diagram) and classes with their relationships (topological class diagram). The logical layout is depicted by using package diagram where each package initially represents one subsystem. The contents of packages are added from the topological class diagram accordingly to the use cases in each subsystem and the mappings between functional features and use cases. The output of this activity is package diagram structured according to subsystems and responsibilities of classes.

6. *Components and deployment design*—the input of this activity is packages from package diagram and nonfunctional requirements, and as the output a component design (component diagram) and deployment design (deployment diagram) are created.

The activities of Topological UML modeling within the software development project can be applied in any order and only part of the activities can be used. There is one restriction—inputs of each activity should be provided in order to produce intended outputs. Topological UML modeling method is guidelines of Topological UML profile application in software development; it does not restrict the use and application of Topological UML diagrams. Each modeling activity is described in detail in Part III, Topological UML Modeling Explained.

5.1.1 Top-Down Design With Topological UML Diagrams

Transitions between Topological UML diagrams according to Topological UML modeling method activity sequence are given in Fig. 5.2, where the diagrams are shown as nodes and the transitions between them as directed lines pointing from source diagram to destination diagram. Topological UML modeling does not include development of profile, timing, and composite structure diagrams as the TFM shows timing within functioning of a system; component diagram specifies structure of components. Profile diagram is not addressed while it is intended to specify a new profile of UML (not a software design). It is possible to automate transitions between Topological UML diagrams while the validation of the acquired diagrams is needed by the domain experts. The development of TFM can be partly automated as shown in *"Transforming Textual Use Cases to a Computation Independent Model"* [100], *"Knowledge Integration for Domain Modeling"* [115], and *"The Integrated Domain Modeling: A Case Study"* [117] where the business use cases are transformed into TFM.

The Topological UML diagrams that are used within Topological UML modeling are listed in Table 5.1, where a development order of the diagram is given as well as the diagrams to which it can be transformed or has information for development.

5.1.2 Seaming Causality Between Diagrams

As Topological UML profile introduces a new diagram type—the TFM—we need to show how the elements of TFM is used to spread the causality relationships and other information to different types of Topological

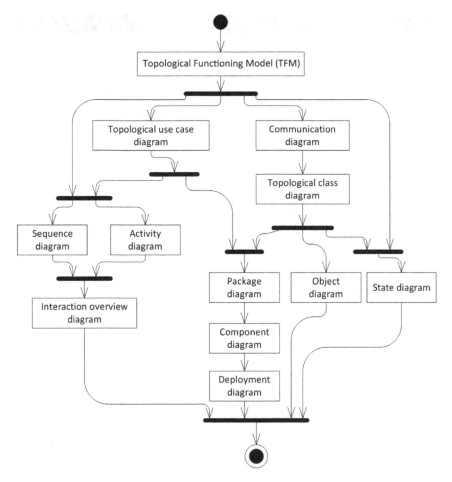

Figure 5.2 Transitions between Topological UML diagrams.

UML diagrams. At the same time, all mappings that exist between standard UML diagrams remain the same. The mappings between standard UML diagrams can be found in various books and researches, like [15,37,104,120,121]. Mappings between Topological UML diagrams are described in the form of table by giving element of one Topological UML diagram type and corresponding element in other kind of Topological UML diagram together with a brief description.

Mappings between elements of TFM and elements of communication and sequence diagrams are given in Table 5.2.

Mappings between elements of TFM and elements of activity diagram are given in Table 5.3.

Table 5.1 Diagrams Used Within Topological UML Modeling

No.	Diagram Type	Order	Information for	Notes
1.	Topological Functioning Model	1	Topological use case diagram, sequence diagram, activity diagram, communication diagram, state diagram	Initial TFM is developed by analyzing functional characteristics of the problem domain. The refinement of TFM includes adjusting TFM to the functional requirements of the desired software system since the requirements can introduce new functionality to the problem domain. By refining TFM the functional requirements are validated, i.e., the TFM shows missing, overlapping, conflicting, and incorrect requirements [8,91,95].
2.	Topological use case diagram	2	Sequence diagram, activity diagram, package diagram	The scope of use cases is set either by functional requirements or by system goals. The functionality represented by each use case is obtained from the TFM according to the mappings between functional features and functional requirements.
3.	Communication diagram	2	Topological class diagram	Communication diagram is used as an intermediate model between TFM and topological class diagram. It is developed by transforming TFM—the functional features representing the same object type are merged and the cause-and-effect relations become links between lifelines.
4.	Sequence diagram	3	Interaction overview diagram	Sequence diagram shows the messaging between actors and objects. Usually a set of sequence diagrams is created—one for each use case. Use case is used to set the scope of sequence diagram while TFM is used to set the messages and their order.
5.	Activity diagram	3	Interaction overview diagram	Activity diagram shows the workflow of a use case. Usually a set of activity diagrams is created—one for each use case. Use case is used to set the scope of activity diagram while TFM is used to set the action nodes and edges.
6.	Topological class diagram	3	Package diagram, state diagram, object diagram	Topological class diagram is used to represent a domain model and a system design model. The key idea behind domain model is a visual dictionary of abstractions. The topological relations between classes show the causal relations between entities in the problem and solution domains.
7.	Interaction overview diagram	4	–	Defines interactions through a variant of activity diagram in a way that promotes overview of the control flow. Interaction overview diagram focus on the overview of the flow of control.

(Continued)

No.	Diagram Type	Order	Information for	Notes
	Table 5.1 (Continued)			
8.	Object diagram	4	–	Object diagram can be developed during the refinement process of topological class diagram when the associations are analyzed. It is useful in situation when object of one type plays more than one role at a time. Object diagram can also be used to provide examples of system at a specific time.
9.	State diagram	5	–	State diagrams are used to show the state transitions of objects; one diagram is created for each object type.
10.	Package diagram	6	Component diagram	Package diagram is used to organize and group classes into logical structure—packages. Each package represents a subsystem and groups a set of cohesive responsibilities of classes.
11.	Component diagram	7	Deployment diagram	Component diagram represents modular, deployable, and replaceable parts of a system; one component is created for each package.
12.	Deployment diagram	8	–	Deployment diagram shows how instances of components are deployed on instances of nodes. The content of deployment diagram is denoted by components and nonfunctional requirements.

Table 5.2 Mapping TFM to Communication and Sequence Diagrams

No.	TFM Element	Communication and Sequence Diagram Element	Description
1.	Class specified by functional feature	Lifeline	Each functional feature specifies object which is performing action. During analysis of system object is specified by class.
2.	Operation specified by functional feature	Message	Each functional feature specifies an atomic business action which later is specified by topological operation.
3.	Sequence of functional features	Message sequence number (only in communication diagram) / Message order (only in sequence diagram)	Message sequence number is denoted by the sequence number of functional feature. The sequence of functional features is defined by problem domain expert.
4.	Logical relations	Message sending concurrency	Logical relations in TFM give additional information about execution concurrency of functional features, thus allowing to define concurrency within communication diagram.

Table 5.3 Mapping TFM to Activity Diagram

No.	TFM Element	Activity Diagram Element	Description
1.	Action of object specified by functional feature	Action	Each functional feature specifies an atomic business action which is represented by action of object and later is specified by topological operation. In activity diagram one action represents one functional feature from TFM.
2.	Cause-and-effect (i.e., topological) relationship	Edge	Functional features are connected by topological relationship which is represented by straight line with arrowhead at effect side (i.e., it points from cause to effect). In activity diagram one edge represents one topological relationship from TFM.
3.	Logical relationship with type *xor* (and partially *or*)	Decision and merge node	Logical relations in TFM give additional information about execution concurrency of functional features and decision-making within system. Exclusive or (*xor*) within activity diagram is represented with decision node and corresponding merge node. Disjunction (*or*) is represented in a mixture of decision and fork nodes.
4.	Preconditions of functional feature	Guards on edges outgoing from decision node	Preconditions of functional feature in TFM are represented as guards on edges incoming to corresponding action in activity diagram.
5.	Logical relationship with type *and* (and partially *or*)	Fork and join node	Logical relations in TFM give additional information about execution concurrency and decision-making within system. Conjunction (*and*) within activity diagram is represented with fork node and corresponding join node. Disjunction (*or*) is represented in a mixture of decision and fork nodes.
6.	Functional feature	Initial node	In basic scenario when input functional feature is transformed into an action, an initial node is added before this action. In more advanced scenario TFM can be split up in several parts and each part represented by its own activity diagram. In such case, the initial node is added before action which is obtained from the input functional feature of that TFM part.
7.	Functional feature	Final node	In basic scenario when output functional feature is transformed into an action, a final node is added after this action. In more advanced scenario TFM can be split up in several parts and each part represented by its own activity diagram. In such case, the final node is added after action which is obtained from the output functional feature of that TFM part.

No.	TFM Element	Topological Use Case Diagram Element	Description
: **Table 5.4 Mapping TFM to Topological Use Case Diagram**

No.	TFM Element	Topological Use Case Diagram Element	Description
1.	TFM or part of TFM	Subject	TFM itself defines subject of topological use case diagram. If TFM is divided into parts according to subsystems, then each part of TFM defines the subject.
2.	Entity of functional feature	Actor	Actor is an entity of input and output functional features.
3.	Functional features	Use case	Use case is defined by a set of functional features. All functional features within one set should be connected—there should be no separated functional features. The set of functional features included in one use case (i.e., the scope of use case) is denoted by expert, by functional requirement, or by goal.
4.	Topological relationship	Topological relationship	The topological relationship from input functional feature to the descendant functional feature denotes topological relationship pointing from actor to use case. The topological relationship from predecessor of output functional feature to the output functional feature denotes topological relationship pointing from use case to actor.
5.	Cause-and-effect (i.e., topological) relationship	Relationship between use cases	Relationship between use cases are denoted by the existence of topological relationship between functional features belonging to use cases.
6.	Logical relationship	Extend relationship	The type of relationship between use cases is denoted by the type of logical relationship in TFM. The disjunction (*or*) and exclusive or (*xor*) denote *extend* relationship between use cases.
7.	Cause-and-effect (i.e., topological) and logical relationship	Include relationship	The type of relationship between use cases is denoted by the type of logical relationship in TFM. The conjunction (*and*) denote *include* relationship between use cases. If there is no logical relationship between topological relationships in TFM, then it indicates that there exist include relationship between use cases.

Mappings between elements of TFM and elements of topological use case diagram are given in Table 5.4.

Mappings between elements of TFM and elements of topological class diagram are given in Table 5.5.

Mappings between elements of TFM and elements of state diagram are given in Table 5.6. Each functional feature specifies an object performing certain action. By transforming TFM into state diagrams a set of state diagrams is obtained. The count of obtained state diagrams is denoted by count of distinct objects specified by functional features.

No.	TFM Element	Topological Class Diagram Element	Description
	Table 5.5 Mapping TFM to Topological Class Diagram		
1.	Class specified by functional feature	Class	Each functional feature specifies object which is performing action thus during analysis of system the object is specified by class. A class in topological class diagram represents one class which is obtained by merging all functional features specifying the same class.
2.	Attributes of class specified by functional feature	Attribute of class	Each functional feature specifies an atomic business action which involves specification of affected data and data fields. Later this information can be specified as attributes of corresponding class.
3.	Operation specified by functional feature	Operation of class	Each functional feature specifies an atomic business action which later is specified by topological operation in TFM.
4.	Topological relationship	Topological relationship	Topological relationship within TFM is drawn between two functional features while in topological class diagram it is drawn between two topological operations. In fact, each topological operation is defined by one functional feature, so the topological relationship is transferred 1:1 from TFM into topological class diagram.
5.	Result of action and class specified by functional feature	Association	An association within topological class diagram can be added between class specified by functional feature and class specified by result of action of the same functional feature. By further analysis of the action context an aggregation or composition can be set of this association.

5.2 TOPOLOGICAL UML MODELING IN COMPARISON WITH OTHER MODELING METHODS

This section compares Topological UML modeling with UML modeling driven approaches discussed in Chapter 2, Software Designing With Unified Modeling Language Driven Approaches, object-oriented analysis and design (OOAD), Business Object-Oriented Modeling (B.O.O.M.), conceptual modeling, component-based development, and Topological Functioning Modeling for Model Driven Architecture (TFM4MDA). Each of the method is evaluated against a set of criterions divided into four groups:

- *Analysis and design models*—shows the summary of diagram types used and the transformation guidelines provided.
- *Problem domain analysis and design*—sets the emphasis on the evaluation of the existing and desired domain model designing and the identification of the boundaries of them.
- *Requirements management*—describes the requirements of management aspect of the compared methods (like requirements traceability).
- *Usage*—evaluates the practical application of each method in the software development.

Table 5.6 Mapping Topological Functioning Model TFM to State Diagram

No.	TFM Element	State Diagram Element	Description
1.	Object state specified by functional feature	State	Each functional feature specifies an object performing certain operation. If during execution of this action changes the state of object performing this action, functional feature specifies the new state of the object. Object state from functional feature is transformed into state in state diagram.
2.	Object state specified by functional feature	Initial state	When information from input functional feature is transformed into a state, an initial state is added before this state.
3.	Object state specified by functional feature	Final state	When information from output functional feature is transformed into a state, a final state is added after this state.
4.	Topological relationship	Transition	If during execution of action specified by functional feature is changed the state of object performing this action, then incoming topological relationship defines transition from previous state to the new state.
5.	Operation specified by functional feature	Event	Each functional feature specifies an atomic business action which later is specified by topological operation in TFM. If functional feature specifies the new state of object, the operation is transformed into the event triggering transition from one state to another.
6.	Operation specified by functional feature	Entry effect	If current functional feature specifies the new state of object, the operation is transformed into the entry effect of this new state.
7.	Operation specified by functional feature	Exit effect	If descendant functional feature specifies the new state of object, the operation of this descendant functional feature is transformed into the exit effect of current state.
8.	Preconditions of functional features	Guard condition	If current functional feature specifies the new state of object, the preconditions of this functional feature are transformed into the guard conditions.
9.	Logical relationship with type *and* (and partially *or*)	Fork and join	A logical relation in TFM gives additional information about execution concurrency of functional features, thus conjunction (and) within state diagram is represented with fork and corresponding join. Disjunction (*or*) indicates possible fork and join.

The criterions in each group are selected from a set of modeling methods and techniques reviews and guidelines [34,62,101,103] based on the purpose of Topological UML modeling.

The first evaluated group of criterions is analysis and design models and it consists of the following evaluation criterions:

1. *Count of diagrams used*—shows the number of diagrams used by each method.
2. *The first diagram created*—indicates the first diagram that is created by particular method (this criterion indicates the diagram that is

driving the further software development process, e.g., some methods are called use case driven).

3. *Transformations provided*—if method includes transformation guidelines for all diagrams addresses, then the value is *all*; if part of the diagrams are covered, then *partial*; and if no guidelines for transformations are given, then *none*.

4. *Transformation automation level*—if the transformation process can be done automatically (i.e., without presence of human), then the value is *automatic*; if some interaction is required by the human, then *semiautomatic*; or *manual* (no guidelines and mappings between diagrams and diagram elements are given).

The result of the evaluation against analysis and design models criterions is given in Table 5.7.

The second evaluated group of criterions is problem domain analysis and design and it consists of the following evaluation criterions:

1. *Representation of "as-is" domain model*—diagram types used to specify and analyze the existing functioning of the problem domain. This is an important criterion since it is needed to understand the functioning of the existing problem domain (e.g., business system) and only then introduce the new concepts and functions into it.

2. *Representation of "to-be" domain model*—diagram types used to specify and analyze the desired functioning of the solution.

3. *"As-is" boundary identification*—approach used for the existing (*as-is*) domain boundary identification (i.e., before the new software system is introduced to the problem domain).

4. *"To-be" boundary identification*—approach used for the desired (*to-be*) domain boundary identification (i.e., after the new software system is introduced to the problem domain) since the new software system can introduce a new functionality in the problem domain.

The result of the evaluation against problem domain analysis and design criterions is given in Table 5.8.

The next evaluated group of criterions is requirements management and it consists of following evaluation criterions:

1. *Functional requirements*—the way of the functional requirement specification.

No.	Criterion	Method	Evaluation
Table 5.7 Evaluation of Analysis and Design Models Criterions			
1.	Count of diagrams used	Topological UML modeling	12—all except profile diagram, timing diagram, and composite structure diagram
		OOAD with Unified Process	10—all except composite structure diagram, object diagram, profile diagram, and timing diagram
		B.O.O.M.	6—use case diagram, activity diagram, state diagram, class diagram, package diagram, and object diagram
		Conceptual modeling	5—class diagram, state diagram, use case diagram, sequence diagram, and profile diagram
		Component-based development	9—composite structure diagram, object diagram, profile diagram, interaction overview diagram, and timing diagram
		TFM4MDA	5—three UML diagrams: use case diagram, activity diagram, and class diagram; one diagram from TFM4MDA profile: TFM; and unspecified diagram type: problem domain objects graph
2.	The first diagram created	Topological UML modeling	TFM
		OOAD with Unified Process	Use case diagram
		B.O.O.M.	Use case diagram and class diagram (in parallel)
		Conceptual modeling	Class diagram
		Component-based development	Not specified, varies from case study to case study
		TFM4MDA	TFM
3.	Transformations provided	Topological UML modeling	All
		OOAD with Unified Process	Partial
		B.O.O.M.	Partial
		Conceptual modeling	Partial
		Component-based development	None
		TFM4MDA	All
4.	Transformation automation level	Topological UML modeling	Semiautomatic—some diagram types require additional actions from expert or designer
		OOAD with Unified Process	Semiautomatic—depending on the design patterns used
		B.O.O.M.	Manual
		Conceptual modeling	Semiautomatic
		Component-based development	Manual
		TFM4MDA	Semiautomatic

Table 5.8 Evaluation of Problem Domain Analysis and Design Criterions

No.	Criterion	Method	Evaluation
1.	Representation of *as-is* domain model	Topological UML modeling	TFM
		OOAD with Unified Process	Use case diagram
		B.O.O.M.	Business use cases and activity diagram
		Conceptual modeling	Partly by class diagram
		Component-based development	None
		TFM4MDA	TFM
2.	Representation of *to-be* domain model	Topological UML modeling	TFM, communication diagram, topological class diagram, and object diagram
		OOAD with Unified Process	Use case diagram, activity diagram, and class diagram
		B.O.O.M.	Use case diagram and class diagram
		Conceptual modeling	Class diagram
		Component-based development	Scenario and logical view of 4 + 1 architectural style
		TFM4MDA	TFM, class diagram with conceptual classes
3.	*As-is* boundary identification	Topological UML modeling	Initial TFM—the result of applying topological space closure operation
		OOAD with Unified Process	Intuitive—based on initial estimation of use cases
		B.O.O.M.	Business use cases—an initial estimation based on interviews
		Conceptual modeling	Intuitive
		Component-based development	None
		TFM4MDA	TFM as the result of topological space closure operation
4.	*To-be* boundary identification	Topological UML modeling	Refined TFM—the result of mapping TFM on functional requirements or goals
		OOAD with Unified Process	Intuitive—based on analysis of use cases
		B.O.O.M.	System use cases—identified and elaborated based on the business use cases
		Conceptual modeling	Intuitive
		Component-based development	Intuitive
		TFM4MDA	User goals finding in accordance with the TFM

2. *Nonfunctional requirements*—the way of the nonfunctional requirement specification.
3. *Requirements conformance*—evaluates the conformance of functional requirements to the existing domain functioning.
4. *Functional requirements traceability*—support of the functional requirements traceability between developed artifacts.
5. *Nonfunctional requirements traceability*—support of the nonfunctional requirements traceability between developed artifacts.

The result of the evaluation against requirements management criterions is given in Table 5.9.

The last evaluated group of criterions is usage and it consists of the following evaluation criterion:

1. *Type of validation*—evaluates how the method is validated. There can be three different ways of validating a method depending on the purpose of the validation and the conditions for empirical investigation [34]: *survey, case study,* and *experiment*. A survey is an investigation performed in retrospect when the method has been used for a certain period of time. A case study is an observational study in which data are collected for a specific purpose throughout the study. An experiment is a formal and controlled investigation (it also includes the theoretical examples).

The result of the evaluation against usage criterion is given in Table 5.10.

The results of comparison criterions show that the Topological UML modeling tends to holistically and formally cover all the system thus the count of applied diagrams to create the system's blueprint—its specification—is the largest. It uses all the diagrams available in Topological UML except profile diagram, timing diagram, and composite structure diagram. Since both Topological UML modeling and TFM4MDA are based on TFM, several characteristics of them are equal or similar, like the first diagram created which is TFM. As discussed in Chapter 4, Topological Unified Modeling Language, the TFM holistically covers the specification of the problem and solution domains thus allowing to formally seam together both domains and to eliminate the intuitive development of the specification. While using the TFM as a tool to carefully analyze the problem domain and design the solution domain, it is very important to not lose the information

Table 5.9 Evaluation of Requirements Management Criterions

No.	Criterion	Method	Evaluation
1.	Functional requirements	Topological UML modeling	Textual description, business use cases, etc.
		OOAD with Unified Process	Use case diagram
		B.O.O.M.	System use case diagram
		Conceptual modeling	Conceptual schema (all UML diagrams applied by this method)
		Component-based development	Use case diagram (the scenario view of 4 + 1 architecture style)
		TFM4MDA	Textual description, use case diagram
2.	Nonfunctional requirements	Topological UML modeling	Textual description
		OOAD with Unified Process	Textual specification within use cases
		B.O.O.M.	Textual specification within system use cases
		Conceptual modeling	None
		Component-based development	Components should conform to a characterization of a unit to be reusable
		TFM4MDA	Partially by textual specification within use cases
3.	Requirements conformance	Topological UML modeling	Mappings between requirements and the initial and refined TFM
		OOAD with Unified Process	Intuitive or based on knowledge of expert
		B.O.O.M.	Based on business use cases
		Conceptual modeling	Intuitive or based on knowledge of expert
		Component-based development	Intuitive or based on knowledge of expert
		TFM4MDA	Mappings between requirements and the TFM as-is
4.	Functional requirements traceability	Topological UML modeling	Trace links from requirements to functional features of TFM, use cases, topological class diagram, and other developed artifacts (Topological UML modeling enables traceability from the very beginning of software development lifecycle to the code and backward)
		OOAD with Unified Process	Requirements are traced to use cases and to other design and implementation artifacts.
		B.O.O.M.	Trace links from business use cases to system use cases and other developed artifacts
		Conceptual modeling	Intuitive; trace links between diagrams created in the conceptual schema
		Component-based development	Intuitive; trace links from Scenario view (use cases) to other views in the context of 4 + 1 architecture style
		TFM4MDA	Trace links between requirements, TFM, use cases, and other diagrams used

(Continued)

Table 5.9 (Continued)

No.	Criterion	Method	Evaluation
5.	Nonfunctional requirements traceability	Topological UML modeling	Trace links from nonfunctional requirements to component diagram and deployment diagram
		OOAD with Unified Process	Traced together with use cases
		B.O.O.M.	Traced together with system use cases
		Conceptual modeling	Not supported
		Component-based development	Intuitive; based on the experience of designer
		TFM4MDA	Not supported

Table 5.10 Evaluation of Usage Criterion

No.	Criterion	Method	Evaluation
1.	Type of validation	Topological UML modeling	Case study (as given in Part III, Topological UML Modeling Explained and [26])
		OOAD with Unified Process	Survey
		B.O.O.M.	Survey
		Conceptual modeling	Experiment (a conceptual modeling case study in [82] is shown in the context of already existing system so it cannot be considered as a real case study)
		Component-based development	Case study
		TFM4MDA	Experiment

gathered during construction of the TFM. The best way to do this is to transfer all the design decisions from TFM to other design diagrams and of course to the software code. In such case, we are going from more abstract models to more specialized models, thus adding more and more development-specific artifacts to design to get us to the executable software. TFM4MDA also uses a powerful tool to analyze functioning of the problem domain—the TFM, but the TFM4MDA lacks the ability to transfer responsibilities of objects from TFM to the classes. Other modeling methods like B.O.O.M., Unified Process, conceptual modeling, and component-based development rely on the abilities of the expert which is working on the development of specification. In most cases, there is no way to validate the result provided by the expert unless we are at the finish line of the software development process—getting an executable software. In the case of classical waterfall software development lifecycle there is a very high possibility that the software will not meet the goals stated by the owner of the product.

5.3 SUMMARY

Topological UML modeling is based on the formalism of TFM and the Topological UML profile. While TFM provides formal abstraction and understandability of the problem domain, other Topological UML diagrams allow to model system from different viewpoints. TFM is used in two forms—*as-is* and *to-be*, where the first one describes the existing functioning of the problem domain while the latter one—the required functioning of the solution (i.e., software system). Within Topological UML modeling TFM serves as the root model for behavior and structure specification and as a tool for validation of the functional requirements as well as of the software system. While using the TFM as a tool to carefully analyze the problem domain and design the solution domain, it is very important to not lose the information gathered during construction of the TFM. The best way to do this is to transfer all the design decisions from TFM to other design diagrams and of course to the software code. In such case, we are going from more abstract models to more specialized models, thus adding more and more development-specific artifacts to design to get us to the executable software.

The problem domain analysis and software design within Topological UML modeling consist of six activities, covering behavior, structure, layout, and deployment analysis and design. *By following the Topological UML modeling activities one by one, the system gets designed in top-down way and the developed design artifacts are in strong accordance with the functioning of problem domain, thus the Topological UML modeling ensures that causal trace links exist between artifacts of both problem and solution domains.*

By following the Topological UML modeling activities, designed software artifacts have the following characteristics:

- *High cohesion*—application of TFM for system functioning analysis and formal transformation of TFM to other diagram types ensures appropriate assignment of responsibilities to objects and classes (this actually is leading to the next statement).
- Every design artifact is an abstraction of a well-analyzed and understood problem domain artifact.
- *Low coupling with the rest of the system*—relations between elements initially are identified within TFM and defined as topological

relationships between functional features describing functioning of a problem and solution domains.

- *Well-defined interface*—the result of performing closuring operation of topological space is TFM reflecting functioning of system under consideration; the TFM obtained from topological space shows inputs and outputs (one of the functional characteristic of TFM). Topological UML modeling uses the inputs and outputs of TFM to define required and provided interfaces of system.

PART *III*

Topological UML Modeling Explained

CHAPTER 6

Problem Domain Functioning Analysis

INFORMATION IN THIS CHAPTER:

- Problem domain analysis
- Functional characteristics of system functioning
- Requirements checking and refinement
- Topological Functioning Model (TFM) development

6.1 INTRODUCTION

Problem domain functioning analysis is the first activity within Topological UML modeling during which a Topological Functioning Model (TFM) gets developed. During the analysis of the problem domain we model two aspects of the desired system—one representing functioning of problem domain, i.e., the situation *as-is*, and one representing functionality of desired software system, i.e., the solution *to-be*. This activity ensures that proper attention is paid at the very beginning of the software development lifecycle by capturing various aspects of the desired system. Such strategy allows to identify functional requirements which are not in accordance with the existing functioning of the problem domain. Thus, the stakeholders can make decision whether to change the existing business process or to adapt functional requirements to it.

Problem domain functioning analysis consists of three activities (see Fig. 6.1, where *Mappings* denotes the mappings between functional features and functional requirements):

1. *Topological space development*—topological space represents functioning of the system under consideration and its surrounding environment (i.e., finite set of TFM exists in topological space where each TFM shows functioning of a specific system), it is visualized by using oriented graph where functional features are vertices and

Topological UML Modeling. DOI: http://dx.doi.org/10.1016/B978-0-12-805476-5.00006-X

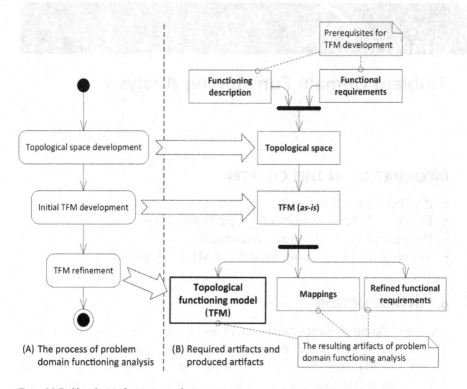

Figure 6.1 Problem domain functioning analysis activities.

cause-and-effect (causal) relationships—arcs between them directed from cause functional feature to the effect functional feature.

2. *Initial TFM development*—the TFM gets extracted from the topological space by analyzing functional features that belong to the desired system's functioning.

3. *TFM refinement*—functional requirements are mapped on functional features, thus checking the completeness of TFM and functional requirements. If required, we need to modify both the TFM and the functional features in order for the TFM to meet the desired system's functioning.

To perform the problem domain functioning analysis there are two prerequisites—functioning description of the business process or desired system and functional requirements which should be satisfied by the software system. The functioning description can be taken from different sources such as verbal descriptions like documents, interviews, user stories, diagrams, ontologies, schemas, business process descriptions, requirements specifications, as well as from mathematical expressions and expert knowledge about the system; it needs to cover full description of problem domain functioning.

The result of the problem domain functioning analysis is TFM (both the one representing functioning of problem domain and the one representing functionality of desired software system), mappings between functional features and functional requirements, and refined functional features. The TFM development activities are described in detail in the next sections (each section describes one activity).

6.2 ENTERPRISE DATA SYNCHRONIZATION SYSTEM CASE STUDY

Within the Part III, Topological UML Modeling Explained, we use a case study of enterprise data synchronization system development. The initial specification of enterprise data synchronization system consists of the following artifacts:

1. Informal description of data synchronization functioning, where nouns are denoted by *italic*, verbs are denoted by **bold**, and action preconditions and postconditions are underlined (see Section 6.2.1).
2. Functional and nonfunctional requirements defined for data synchronization software system (see Section 6.2.2).

6.2.1 Informal Enterprise Data Synchronization System Description

Scheduler every 5 min **reads** *configuration data* from *configuration file*. *Configuration data* **includes** following *parameters*: connection information of input data source, username and password for reading input data, flag to indicate if data should be taken from input data source, time at which to make import from input data source, connection information of target data source, username and password for editing data in target data source, path to import files folder, path to log folder.

After *configuration data* **is read**, *scheduler* **checks** if import from *source database* **should be performed**. *Import* from *source database* **is performed** at specified time which is given in *configuration data* as *parameter*. If import **should be performed** from *source database*, then *scheduler* **reads** all data from *source database* by using *query statement* given in *configuration file*. After all *data* **is read**, *scheduler* **checks** if read data structure is according to specification. Data from source databases has following structure: surname, forename, job title, address, e-mail address, telephone number, gender, start date, expiry date, department, and company code. If data structure is according to specification, then *scheduler* **puts** the read data into temporal *internal table*. After converting read data to temporal *internal table* every *row* from this table **is imported** into *target database*.

After *configuration data* is read and import from *source databases* **is performed** (if needed), *scheduler* **checks** *import folder*. If *CSV file* (the *import file*) **is found** in that folder, *scheduler* **reads** the *import file*. *Import file* has following structure: surname, forename, job title, address, e-mail address, telephone number, gender, start date, expiry date, department, and company code. *Scheduler* then **checks** that read *import file* **corresponds** to predefined *import file* structure. If *import file* structure is according to specification, then *scheduler* **converts** the read data into temporal *internal table*. After converting read data into temporal *internal table* every *row* from this table **is imported** into *target database*. If *import file* structure is not prepared according to specification, the *import file* **is skipped, moved** to *processed files folder* and a *log file* **is created** in *log files folder* stating that particular *import file* was not imported into *target database*.

For every *row scheduler* **checks** if *data* from a particular *row* already **exists** in *target database*. If *data* from the particular *row* **exists** then **update** of *existing data* **is performed** in *target database*. If *data* from the particular *row* **does not exist** then **insert** of *new data* **is performed** in *target database*. By updating or inserting data in *target database scheduler* **prepares** *log file* in *log files folder* for every import file and for every time data is imported from *source database*. In *log file* **is logged** every data *row* from *temporal internal table* in order to unify *log files* from different data sources. For every *row* from *source data* an *import status* **is logged**. There are two *import statuses:* *successful* and *error*. *Successful* status **is logged** when *import* **is successful** for particular row. *Error* status **is logged** when *import* **is not successful** for particular row. If *error* **is logged** then *error description* also **is logged** in order to allow *data import manager* to watch for *un-imported data*. After data import is completed the *log file* **is archived**. After importing data from *import file*, the *import file* **is moved** to *processed files folder*.

6.2.2 Functional and Nonfunctional Requirements

The enterprise data synchronization system has the following functional requirements:

- *FR1*—Employee data synchronization should be done between input data sources and target data source. This requirement includes requirements FR1.1–FR1.7.
- *FR1.1*—By starting synchronization process a configuration information should be taken from configuration file.
- *FR1.2*—If needed, data from source database should be taken.
- *FR1.3*—Data should be taken from import files in CSV format.
- *FR1.4*—If import CSV file is with wrong data structure, the processing of particular file should be skipped and faulty import file should be logged.
- *FR1.5*—All data obtained from either source database or import files should be placed in target database.
- *FR1.6*—When importing data in target database all rows from source data should be logged together with import status for each particular data row.

The enterprise data synchronization system has the following nonfunctional requirements:

- *NFR1*—Employee data synchronization mechanism should be implemented in a way that it runs every 5 min after previous data synchronization has been completed.
- *NFR2*—Employee data synchronization mechanism should be deployed separately from any other systems and components.
- *NFR3*—Executable files responsible for logging should be deployed separately of other components.
- *NFR4*—Employees responsible for source data preparation should not have access to employee data synchronization mechanism.

6.3 TOPOLOGICAL SPACE DEVELOPMENT

The first activity to develop a TFM of system under consideration is the development of topological space which consists of two actions (see Fig. 6.2):

1. *Definition of physical or business functional characteristics*—functional characteristics are defined in the form of functional features that graphically are drawn as vertices of a directed graph.

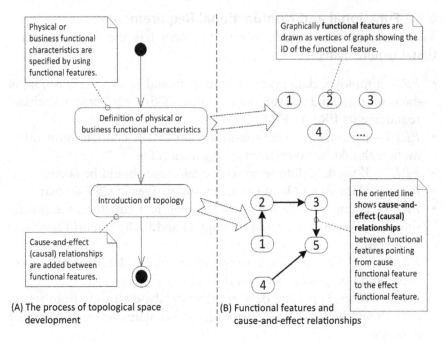

Figure 6.2 Development of topological space.

2. *Introduction of topology* Θ—cause-and-effect (causal) relationships are added between functional features. Graphically causal relationships are drawn as oriented arcs between vertices pointing from cause functional feature to the effect functional feature. Causal relationship is binary relationship linking together only two functional features.

To develop the topological space of problem domain, the functioning description of the system is used. The functioning description can be taken from different sources such as verbal descriptions like documents [86], interviews, user stories, business use cases (discussed in [104]), diagrams, ontologies, schemas, business process descriptions, requirements specifications, as well as from mathematical expressions and expert knowledge about the system; it needs to cover full description of problem domain functioning.

Definition of physical or business functional characteristics, i.e., the development of functional features, consists of the following activities [9]:

1. Definition of objects and their properties from the problem domain description.
2. Identification of external systems and partially dependent systems.
3. Definition of functional features using verb analysis in the problem domain description, i.e., by finding meaningful verbs.

In the case of having functioning description of the system as a textual description, all the required information can be visualized within text. For example, the informal description of enterprise data synchronization functioning given in Section 6.2.1 is analyzed by taking into account nouns (denoted by *italic*), verbs (denoted by **bold**), and action preconditions and postconditions (denoted by underline).

As a result, a set of functional features X_{id} are defined. At the lowest abstraction level one functional feature should describe only one atomic business action (it cannot be further divided into a set of business actions) [91]. By using the topological characteristic *continuous mapping* of TFM, the abstraction level of functional features can be changed at any time when needed (e.g., the initial TFM can be detailed out by lowering the abstraction level of functional features thus showing more or less detailed description of problem domain functioning). Each functional feature is a unique tuple as shown by equation X_{id} = <Id, A, Op, R, O, Cl, St, PreCond, PostCond, E, Es, S> Eq. (4.4) in Chapter 4, Topological Unified Modeling Language, where:

- *Id*—identifier of functional feature,
- *A*—action of object O,
- *Op*—operation which will provide functionality defined by action A (can be acquired when the class diagram is synthesized),
- *R*—result of action A,
- *O*—object that receives the result or that is used in action A (e.g., a role, a time period, a catalogue),
- *Cl*—class which will represent object O in static viewpoint of system (can be acquired when the class diagram is synthesized),
- *St*—new state of object O after performing action A,
- *PreCond*—a set of preconditions C_{id},
- *PostCond*—a set of postconditions C_{id},
- *E*—entity responsible for performing action A,
- *Es*–indicates if execution of action A could be automated (i.e., performed without human interaction), and
- *S*—subordination of functional feature (can be internal or external).

Each precondition or postcondition is a condition C_{id} described by unique tuple $C_{id} = <Id,\ Cond,\ oCond>$ Eq. (4.5) in Chapter 4, Topological Unified Modeling Language, where:

- *Id*—identifier of condition,
- *Cond*—condition or an atomic business rule, and
- *oCond*—identifier of opposite condition, i.e., $C_i = -C_j$.

Condition is considered as an atomic business rule.

Within enterprise data synchronization software system development project has been defined 33 functional features (see Table 6.1).

Id	Object Action A	Precondition PreCond	Entity E	Object O	Subordination S
	Table 6.1 Functional Features of Enterprise Data Synchronization System				
1	Defining data synchronization parameters		Data import manager	Configuration	External
2	Creating data synchronization parameters		Data import manager	Configuration	External
3	Acquiring synchronization parameters		Configuration	Configuration	Inner
4	Checking if import from source database should be performed		Configuration	Configuration	Inner
5	Defining source data		Source data manager	SourceDataSource	External
6	Creating data in source database		Source database	SourceDataSource	External
7	Reading all data from source database	If import should be performed from source database	Scheduler	SourceDataSource	Inner
8	Checking if read data structure is according to specification		Scheduler	Scheduler	Inner
9	Putting the read data into temporal internal table	If data structure is according to specification	Scheduler	Scheduler	Inner
10	Importing every row from internal table into target database		Scheduler	Scheduler	Inner

(*Continued*)

Id	Object Action A	Precondition PreCond	Entity E	Object O	Subordination S
					Table 6.1 (Continued)
11	Checking import folder		Scheduler	ImportFolder	Inner
12	Creating data for CSV import file		Source data manager	ImportFile	External
13	Creating CSV import file		Import file	ImportFile	External
14	Reading the import file	If CSV file (the import file) is found in import folder	Scheduler	ImportFile	Inner
15	Checking if import file data structure is according to specification		Scheduler	Scheduler	Inner
16	Converting the read data from import file into temporal internal table	If import file structure is according to specification	Scheduler	Scheduler	Inner
17	Skipping importing of import file	If import file structure is not prepared according to specification	Scheduler	Scheduler	Inner
18	Moving import file to processed files folder		Scheduler	ImportFile	Inner
19	Creating log file in log files folder		Scheduler	Logger	Inner
20	Writing into log file that particular import file was not imported into target database		Data import manager	Logger	External
21	Receiving log file for unimported CSV file		Data import manager	Logger	External
22	Checking if data from a particular row already exists in target database		Scheduler	TargetDataSource	Inner
23	Updating existing data in target database	If data from the particular row exists	Target database	TargetDataSource	External
24	Receiving updated information		Target database	TargetDataSource	External
25	Insert new data in target database	If data from the particular row does not exist	Target database	TargetDataSource	External
26	Receiving new information		Target database	TargetDataSource	External

(Continued)

Table 6.1 (Continued)

Id	Object Action A	Precondition PreCond	Entity E	Object O	Subordination S
27	Creating log file in log files folder for import file processing	If data is read from import file	Scheduler	Logger	Inner
28	Logging data row from temporal internal table		Data import manager	Logger	Inner
29	Logging successful status	If import is successful for particular row	Data import manager	Logger	Inner
30	Logging error status	If import is not successful for particular row	Data import manager	Logger	Inner
31	Logging error description	If error is logged	Data import manager	Logger	Inner
32	Archiving log file	If data import is completed	Data import manager	Logger	External
33	Receiving archived import log file		Data import manager	Logger	External

Introduction of topology Θ (in other words, creation of topological space) means establishing cause-and-effect (causal) relationships T_{id} between identified functional features. Cause-and-effect (causal) relationship T_{id} is a binary relationship relating two functional features X_{id} represented as arcs of a directed graph oriented from a cause vertex to an effect vertex. The synonym for cause-and-effect relationship is topological relationship. Each cause-and-effect relationship is a unique tuple $T_{id} = <\text{Id}, X_c, X_e, L_{out}, L_{in}>$ Eq. (4.6) in Chapter 4, Topological Unified Modeling Language, where:

- *Id*—unique identifier of cause-and-effect relationship,
- X_c—cause functional feature,
- X_e—effect functional feature,
- L_{out}—set of logical relationships between cause-and-effect relationships on outgoing arcs of cause functional feature X_c (optional), and
- L_{in}—set of logical relationships between cause-and-effect relationships on incoming arcs of effect functional feature X_e (optional).

Topological space Z is a system represented by equation $Z = N \cup M$ Eq. (4.2) in Chapter 4, Topological Unified Modeling Language, where N is a set of inner system functional features and M is a set of external functional features (i.e., the external functional features show links and communication with the external environment). Topological space represents the system under consideration together with the environment in which this system exists. Together, functional features and cause-and-effect relationship make topological space of the system under consideration.

The identified cause-and-effect relationships between the defined functional features for enterprise data synchronization system case study are illustrated by the means of the topological space (see Fig. 6.3), where functional features are added as vertices of directed graph and cause-and-effect relationships as arcs between vertices pointing from cause functional feature to the effect functional feature. Functional features are given in Table 6.1.

It is acknowledged that every business and technical system is a subsystem of the environment. TFM enables careful analysis of system's operation and communication with the environment through analysis of functional cycles—a common thing for all system (technical, business, or biological) functioning should be the main functional feedback, visualization of which is an oriented cycle. Thus, it is stated that at least one directed closed loop (i.e., cycle) must be present in every topological model of system functioning. This cycle shows the main functionality that has a vital importance in the system's life. Usually it is even an expanded hierarchy of cycles. By interrupting this

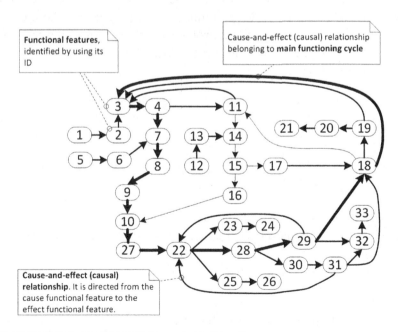

Figure 6.3 Topological space of enterprise data synchronization system.

main cycle the system can no longer function or it functions faulty [86]. Therefore, a proper cycle analysis is necessary in the TFM construction, because it enables careful analysis of system's operation and communication with the environment. To better illustrate main cycle in graph representation of TFM, the arcs belonging to this cycle are drawn with bolder lines. In Fig. 6.3 is clearly visible that cause-and-effect relations form functioning cycles. In enterprise data synchronization system case study the main functioning cycle represents getting data from source database and import files and editing those data in target database, and is as follows:

$$3 \to 4 \to 7 \to 8 \to 9 \to 10 \to 27 \to 22 \to 28 \to 29 \to 18 \to 3.$$

6.4 INITIAL TOPOLOGICAL FUNCTIONING MODEL DEVELOPMENT

The next activity within problem domain functioning analysis after topological space development is the development of TFM. To do so we need to complete the following two actions (see Fig. 6.4):

1. *Separation of TFM from topological space*—done by applying the closuring operation over a set of system's inner functional features.
2. *Identification of logical relations*—the presence of logical relations within TFM denotes forking, joining, decision-making, and merging during the functioning of the problem and solution domains. They are identified by analyzing preconditions and postconditions of functional features.

Logical relation L_{id} shows the logical relationship conjunction (*and*), disjunction (*or*), or exclusive or (*xor*) between two or more cause-and-effect relationships T_{id}. The type of logical relation denotes system execution behavior (e.g., decision-making, parallel actions). Each logical relation is a unique tuple $L_{id} = \ <Id, T, Rt>$ Eq. (4.7) in Chapter 4, Topological Unified Modeling Language, where:

- *Id*—identifier of logical relationship,
- *T*—set of cause-and-effect relationships belonging to this logical relationship, and
- *Rt*—logical relationship type (*and, or*, or *xor*).

Separation of TFM from topological space is done by applying the closure operation as shown by the equation $X = [N]$ Eq. (4.3) in Chapter 4, Topological Unified Modeling Language, over a set of

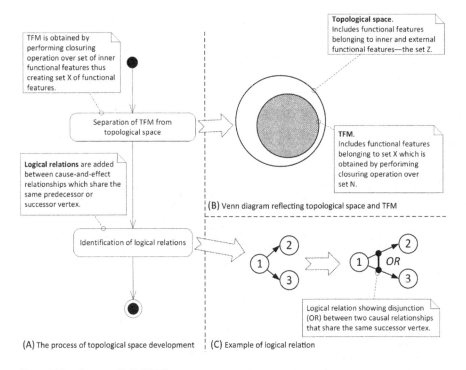

Figure 6.4 Development of initial TFM.

system's inner functional features (the set N), where $X\eta$ is an adherence point of the set N and capacity of X is the number n of adherence points of N. Initial TFM can be called *TFM as-is* where *as-is* means that the TFM represents the functioning of the problem domain without the impact of planned software system. Construction of initial TFM can be iterative. Iterations are needed if the information collected for TFM development is incomplete or inconsistent or there have been introduced changes in system functioning or in software requirements.

According to the equation $Z = N \cup M$ Eq. (4.2) given in Chapter 4, Topological Unified Modeling Language, all the identified functional features given in Table 6.1 are split into two sets, where N is a set of internal system functional features and M is a set of functional features of other systems that interact with the system or of the system itself, which affect the external ones:

- $N = \{3, 4, 7, 8, 9, 10, 11, 14, 15, 16, 17, 18, 19, 22, 27, 28, 29, 30, 31\}$
- $M = \{1, 2, 5, 6, 12, 13, 20, 21, 23, 24, 25, 26, 32, 33\}$

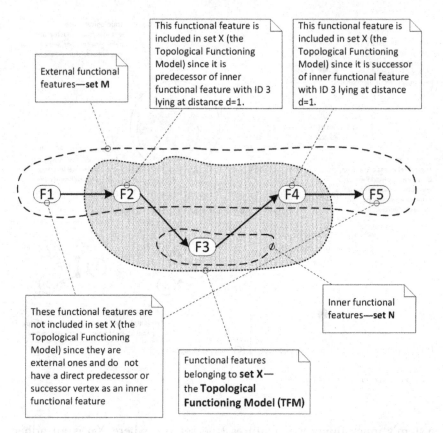

Figure 6.5 Functional features belonging to set N, M, and X.

In order to get all of the system's functionality—the set X—the closuring operation (see equation X = [N] Eq. (4.3) in Chapter 4, Topological Unified Modeling Language) is applied over the set N. During the closuring operation, all the vertices in set N are analyzed by taking into account successor and predecessor vertices of all vertices in set N. As a result, the obtained set X includes all the vertices from set N and all the vertices from set M which are adjacent to the vertices in set N. It is assumed here that all vertices adjacent to vertex from set N lie at the distance d = 1 from it. A visualization example of closuring operation by analyzing abstract functional features F1, F2, F3, F4, and F5 is given in Fig. 6.5.

In the context of enterprise data synchronization system development case study the closuring operation revealing how functional features are added to set X is given in Table 6.2 where with

Table 6.2 Closuring Operation Over the Set N	
Functional Feature From Set N	**Adjacent Functional Features**
3	2, 4, 11, 18, 19
4	3, 7, 11
7	4, 6, 8
8	7, 9
9	8, 10
10	9, 16, 27
11	3, 4, 14, 18
14	11, 13, 15
15	14, 16, 17
16	10, 15
17	15, 18
18	3, 11, 17, 19, 29, 31
19	3, 18, 20
22	23, 25, 27, 28, 29, 31
27	10, 22
28	22, 29, 30
29	18, 22, 28, 32
30	28, 31
31	18, 22, 30, 32

underline is denoted external functional features that are belonging to set M.

The obtained set X (*the TFM*) after applying closuring operation is as follows:

X = {2, 3, 4, 6, 7, 8, 9, 10, 11, 13, 14, 15, 16, 17, 18, 19, 20, 22, 23, 25, 27, 28, 29, 30, 31, 32}.

The resulting TFM is given in Fig. 6.6.

Identification of logical relations between cause-and-effect relationships consists of two steps since there are two kinds of logical relationships L_{id}—one kind is between arcs that are outgoing from functional features X_{id} and the other kind is between arcs that are incoming to functional features X_{id}. The logical relationships between outgoing arcs are denoted with L_{out} and the logical relationships between incoming arcs with L_{in}, thus the identification of

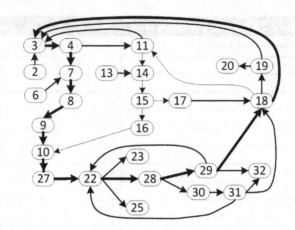

Figure 6.6 TFM representing enterprise data synchronization system functioning.

logical relations between cause-and-effect (i.e., topological) relationships consists of two actions:

1. Identification of logical relations L_{out} between cause-and-effect relationships T_{id} that are outgoing from functional feature X_{id} (see Section 6.4.1).
2. Identification of logical relations L_{in} between cause-and-effect relationships T_{id} that are incoming to functional feature X_{id} (see Section 6.4.2).

Within TFM can be defined three types of logical relations L_{id}: conjunction (*and*), disjunction (*or*), and exclusive disjunction (*xor*). Within each logical relation L_{id} participate two or more cause-and-effect relationships T_{id}. The following two subsections cover the identification of logical relations L_{out} and L_{in}.

6.4.1 Identification of Logical Relations Between Outgoing Cause-and-Effect Relationships

Logical relations L_{out} between cause-and-effect relationships that are outgoing from functional feature indicate necessity of decision-making or branching. In the case of making decision only part of effect functional features is executed, but in the case of branching all of the effect functional features are executed (i.e., system performs parallel processing) [23].

The analysis of logical relations L_{out} is critical when transforming TFM into other diagram types, while these relations contain information about decision-making, parallel execution, and branching. Thus, by using TFM and logical relations L_{id} it is possible to build advanced diagrams of other type (e.g., activity and topological use case diagrams). This is in opposition to the opinion in [6] that TFM contains information sufficient to create only basic activity diagrams (i.e., without forking, joining, and decisions).

Depending on the relationship type Rt of logical relation L_{out}, system execution behavior is defined as follows:

- *Conjunction* (*and*)—system is running in parallel by executing all effect functional features of cause-and-effect relationships participating in this logical relation,
- *Disjunction* (*or*)—system can be running in parallel by executing one, part of, or all effect functional features of cause-and-effect relationships participating in this logical relation, and
- *Exclusive disjunction* (*xor*)—only one effect functional feature of cause-and-effect relationships participating in this logical relation is executed.

The algorithm of identifying logical relations L_{out} between outgoing arcs of functional features is given in Fig. 6.7 while the rules for identification of logical relation L_{out} type are given in Table 6.3, where X_e denotes effect functional features and C_{id} denotes preconditions of X_e.

To better understand identification of logical relations a small fragment of TFM representing enterprise data synchronization system functioning from Fig. 6.6 is used consisting of four functional features: 22, 23, 25, and 28 in Fig. 6.8. The functional feature 23 has a precondition C_1 (*If data from the particular row exists*) and functional feature 25 has a precondition C_2 (*If data from the particular row does not exist*) while functional feature 28 has no preconditions as given in Table 6.1. The relation between preconditions C_1 and C_2 is as follows: $C_1 = C_2$; thus, indicating that between the arcs that are outgoing from functional feature 22 to functional features 23 and 25 ($22 \rightarrow 23$ and $22 \rightarrow 25$) the logical relation with type exclusive disjunction (xor) exist. Since functional feature 28 has no preconditions logical relations with type conjunction (and) are added

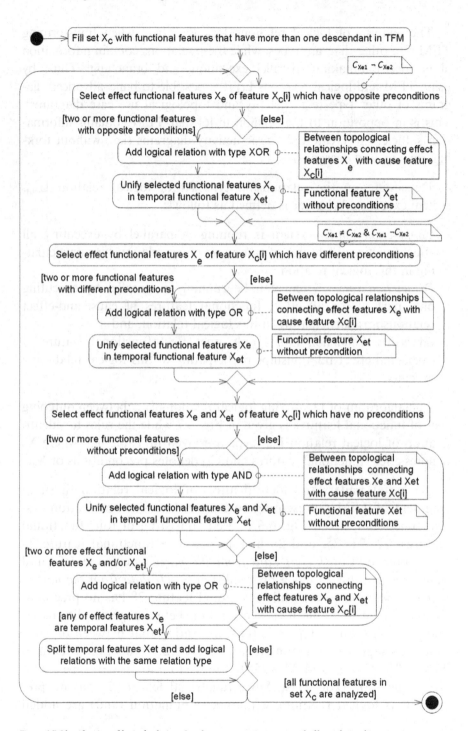

Figure 6.7 Identification of logical relations L_{out} between outgoing cause-and-effect relationships.

Relation Type	X_e		C_{id}	Example of L_{out}
Table 6.3 Rules for Identification of Logical Relations L_{out}				
and	X_{e1}	Ø		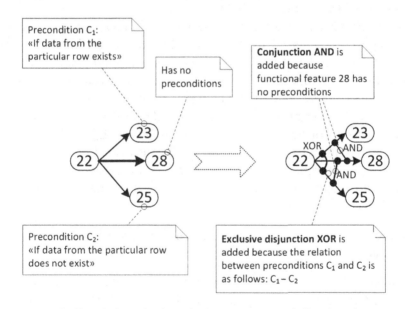
	X_{e2}	Ø		
or	X_{e1}	C_1	$C_1 \neq C_2$ & $C_1 \neq C_2$	
	X_{e2}	C_2		
xor	X_{e1}	C_1	$C_2 = C_1$	
	X_{e2}	C_2		

Precondition C_1:
«If data from the particular row exists»

Has no preconditions

Conjunction AND is added because functional feature 28 has no preconditions

Precondition C_2:
«If data from the particular row does not exist»

Exclusive disjunction XOR is added because the relation between preconditions C_1 and C_2 is as follows: $C_1 - C_2$

Figure 6.8 Example of logical relation identification between outgoing cause-and-effect relationships.

between cause-and-effect relationship $22 \rightarrow 23$ and $22 \rightarrow 28$, and $22 \rightarrow 25$ and $22 \rightarrow 28$.

The resulting TFM with logical relations on outgoing cause-and-effect relationships of enterprise data synchronization system is given in Fig. 6.9.

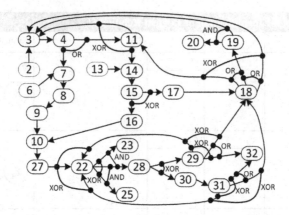

Figure 6.9 TFM representing enterprise data synchronization system functioning and logical relations between out-going cause-and-effect relationships.

6.4.2 Identification of Logical Relations Between Incoming Cause-and-Effect Relationships

Logical relations L_{in} between cause-and-effect relationships that are incoming to functional feature indicate that there is decision or branching made before the effect functional feature. If there was branching before the effect functional feature, then before executing this functional feature there should be joining and system can continue its execution only after all arcs are joined [23]. This reflects the mathematical foundations of Petri nets [21]. Logical relations L_{in} contain important information when transforming TFM into other diagram types, e.g., activity diagram. Depending on the type of logical relation L_{in} in the activity diagram join (Rt = and) and decision-making should be created (Rt = or or xor).

Depending on the relation type of logical relation L_{in}, system execution behavior is defined as follows:

- *Conjunction (and)*—system is executing in parallel thus effect functional feature X_e can be executed only when all direct predecessor functional features (i.e., all cause functional features X_c in the distance d = 1) of cause-and-effect relationships T_{id} participating in logical relation L_{id} are executed,
- *Disjunction (or)*—system can be executing in parallel by executing one, part of, or all cause functional features X_c of effect functional feature X_e at the distance d = 1 of cause-and-effect relationships T_{id} participating in this logical relation, and

Table 6.4 Rules for Identification of Logical Relations L_{in}

Relation Type	Source Relation L_{out}	Corresponding Relation L_{in}
and		
or		
xor		

- *Exclusive disjunction* (*xor*)—only one cause functional feature X_c of effect functional feature X_e at the distance $d = 1$ of cause-and-effect relationships T_{id} participating in this logical relation L_{id} is executed.

Relation type of logical relations L_{in} is denoted by corresponding logical relation L_{out} (for relationships which are branched within TFM) and by the preconditions and postconditions (for the relationships that come from the inputs of TFM). The rules for identification of logical relations L_{in} between incoming arcs of functional features are given in Table 6.4, where L_{out} denotes logical relations between outgoing arcs, and L_{in} denotes logical relations between incoming arcs.

The algorithm for identification of logical relations L_{in} between incoming arcs of functional features is given in Fig. 6.10. To find required functional features within TFM, graph traversing algorithms are used (e.g., backtracking algorithm [64]). The identification process of logical relations L_{in} is different from the identification process of logical relations L_{out}. The main difference is in the fact that logical relations L_{in} are added according to the existing logical relations L_{out} and preconditions and postconditions of functional features, while logical relations L_{out} are added by taking into account only preconditions of functional features.

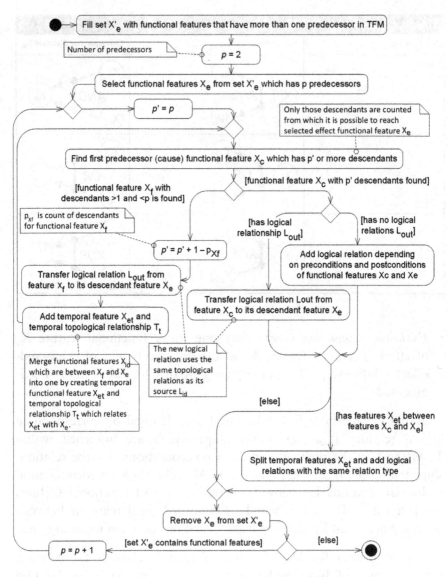

Figure 6.10 Identification of logical relations between incoming cause-and-effect relationships.

To better understand identification of logical relations a small fragment of TFM representing enterprise data synchronization system functioning from Fig. 6.6 is used consisting of following functional features: 3, 4, 7, 8, 9, 10, 11, 14, 15, 16, and 27 in Fig. 6.11 where it is clearly visible that only one vertex has more than one predecessor—functional feature 10. So, we should define the correct logical relation

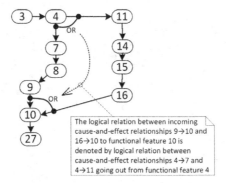

Figure 6.11 Example of logical relation identification between incoming cause-and-effect relationships.

L_{in} between the following two cause-and-effect relationships: $9 \to 10$ and $16 \to 10$. By traversing the TFM graph, the first found predecessor (cause) functional feature which has two or more descendants is functional feature 4. According to the algorithm given in Fig. 6.10 we should transfer logical relation L_{out} from outgoing arcs from cause functional feature 4 to its descendant functional feature's 10 incoming arcs. Thus, the logical relation between cause-and-effect relationships $9 \to 10$ and $16 \to 10$ is *or*—the same as between the cause-and-effect relationships $4 \to 7$ and $4 \to 11$.

The TFM as given in Fig. 6.12 shows logical relations between cause-and-effect relationships. The logical relations are divided into two sets:

- L_{out}—logical relations between cause-and-effect relationships which are outgoing from functional feature and
- L_{in}—logical relations between cause-and-effect relationships which are incoming into functional feature.

6.5 REFINING TOPOLOGICAL FUNCTIONING MODEL

The last activity to develop a TFM of system under consideration is the refinement of initial TFM. By mapping functional requirements to functional features, the latter are validated in conformance with the constructed TFM. Functional features specify functionality that exists in the problem domain, but requirements specify functionality that should exist in the solution domain. Therefore, it is possible to make mappings between requirements and functional features of the TFM. As a result of requirements validation, both TFM and requirements are checked.

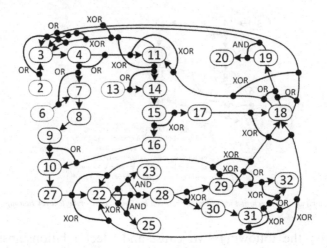

Figure 6.12 TFM representing enterprise data synchronization system functioning and logical relations between cause-and-effect relationships.

TFM is refined by completing the following actions (see Fig. 6.13):

1. *Mapping functional requirements to functional features*—there are five types of mappings between functional features on functional requirements: *one to one, many to one, one to many, one to zero,* and *zero to one.*
2. *Checking for missing and incomplete functional requirements*—if mapping with type *one to many* or *zero to one* is added, it indicates that requirements do not cover the full functionality of the problem domain; missing functional requirements should be added or existing ones extended and mappings should be updated.
3. *Checking for missing functional features*—if at least one mapping with type *one to zero* is added, it indicates that the functional requirements introduce new functionality to the problem domain; missing functional features and cause-and-effect relationships should be defined and mappings should be updated.
4. *Searching for overlapping functional requirements*—if mapping with type *many to one* is added, it indicates that functional requirements overlap the specification of what will be implemented in accordance with one functional feature.

In [88] it is suggested to represent requirement mappings between functional requirements and functional features by using

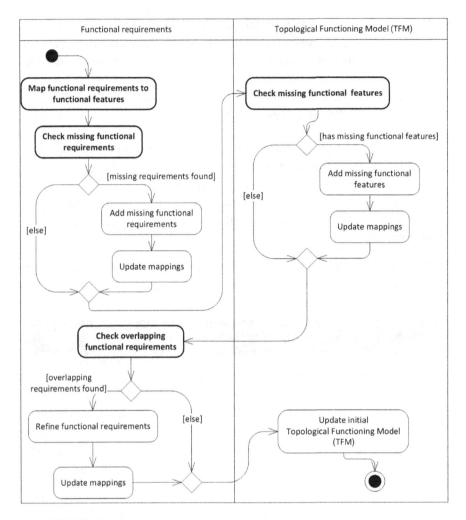

Figure 6.13 TFM refinement process.

arrow predicates. An arrow predicate is a construct in universal categorical logic.

There are five types of mappings and corresponding arrow predicates defined for mapping requirements onto TFM [9]:

1. *One to one*—one requirement completely specifies what will be implemented in accordance with one functional feature.
2. *Many to one*—set of requirements overlap the specification of what will be implemented in accordance with one functional feature.

3. *One to many*—one requirement incompletely specifies some functional feature, or one requirement completely specifies several functional features. It can be so because of one of the following reasons:

   a. the requirement joins several requirements and can be split up or
   b. functional features are more detailed than the functional requirements.

4. *One to Zero*—one requirement specifies some new or undefined functionality. In this particular case, it is necessary to define possible changes in the problem domain functioning.

5. *Zero to one*—specification does not contain any requirement corresponding to the defined functional feature. This means that it could be a missing requirement.

Graphical representations of arrow predicates are given in Table 6.5.

Table 6.5 Arrow Predicates Used to Map Functional Requirements to Functional Features			
No.	Type	Description	Graphical Representation
1.	One to one	Inclusion predicate is used if the functional requirement A completely specifies what will be implemented in accordance with the functional feature B	A ⟹ B
2.	Many to one	Covering predicate is used if functional requirements $A_1, A_2, \ldots, A_n$ overlap the specification of what will be implemented in accordance with the functional feature B	A_1 ... A_n → B [cov]
		Disjoint (component) predicate is used if functional requirements $A_1, A_2, \ldots, A_n$ together completely specify the functional feature B and do not overlap each other	A_1 ... A_n → B [disj]
3.	One to Many	Projection is used if some part of the functional requirement A incompletely specifies some functional feature B	A → B
		Separating family of functions is used if one functional requirement A completely specifies several functional features $B_1, \ldots, B_n$	A → B_1 ... B_n [1-1]

The mappings between functional requirements and functional features allow to:

- *Check for missing requirements*—presence of *one to many* (with *projection* predicate) or *zero to one* mapping type indicates that requirements do not cover the full functionality of the problem domain. Missing functional requirements should be added or existing ones extended and mappings should be updated in order to cover main functional cycle of the problem domain.
- *Check for missing functional features*—if at least one mapping with type *one to zero* exists, it indicates that the functional requirements introduce new functionality to the problem domain. Missing functional features and cause-and-effect relationships should be defined and mappings should be updated.
- *Identify overlapping functional requirements*—presence of *many to one* (with *covering* predicate) mapping type or if there is existence of more than one functional requirement with more than one mapping type associated with some functional feature which indicates that a number of functional requirements define functionality that will be implemented by the same functional feature.

As a result of this activity we get refined TFM representing the functionality of the desired software system (refined TFM can be addressed as *TFM to-be*), mappings between functional features and functional requirements, and refined functional requirements.

The established mappings from functional requirements to functional features within enterprise data synchronization system are given in Table 6.6. As you can see in Table 6.6 all the mappings between functional requirements and functional features in our case study are with type one to many. This means that each functional requirement completely specifies several functional features and we have no missing functional requirements or functional features, and functional requirements do not overlap. Thus, the refined TFM is equal to the initial TFM. Since in this case study use cases are used to model requirements, the set of mappings of functional requirements include both functional features and functional requirements.

Table 6.6 Mappings for Functional Requirements to Functional Features

Functional Requirements	Functional Features	Mapping Type	Graphical Representation
FR1.1	2, 3, 4	One to many	FR1.1 [1-1] → 2, 3, 4
FR1.2	6, 7, 8, 9	One to many	FR1.2 [1-1] → 6, 7, 8, 9
FR1.3	11, 13, 14, 15, 16, 17	One to many	FR1.3 [1-1] → 11, 13, 14, 15, 16, 17
FR1.4	18, 19, 20	One to many	FR1.4 [1-1] → 18, 19, 20
FR1.5	10, 27, 22, 23, 25	One to many	FR1.5 [1-1] → 10, 27, 22, 23, 25
FR1.6	28, 29, 30, 31, 32	One to many	FR1.6 [1-1] → 28, 29, 30, 31, 32

6.6 SUMMARY

Problem domain functioning analysis is the first activity within Topological UML modeling during which a TFM gets developed. A case study of enterprise data synchronization system is used to explain each step of the problem domain functioning analysis. During the analysis of the problem domain we model two aspects of the desired system—one representing functioning of problem domain, i.e., the situation *as-is*, and one representing functionality of desired software system, i.e., the solution *to-be*. This activity ensures that proper attention is paid at the very beginning of the software development lifecycle by capturing various aspects of the desired system. Such strategy allows to identify functional requirements which are not in accordance with the existing functioning of the problem domain. Thus, the stakeholders can make decision whether to change the existing business process or to adapt functional requirements to it.

Problem domain functioning analysis consists of three activities:

1. *Topological space development*—topological space represents functioning of the system under consideration and its surrounding environment.
2. *Initial TFM development*—the TFM gets extracted from the topological space by analyzing functional features that belong to the desired system's functioning.
3. *TFM refinement*—functional requirements are mapped on functional features, thus checking the completeness of TFM and functional requirements.

CHAPTER 7

Behavior Analysis and Design

INFORMATION IN THIS CHAPTER:

- Consuming Topological Functioning Model (TFM) for formal behavior analysis and design
- Formal development of use cases
- Determination of subsystems, communication between systems and users
- Workflow modeling in accordance with solution domain functioning

7.1 INTRODUCTION

Behavior analysis and design is the next activity within Topological UML modeling. It is based on the results obtained within previous Topological UML modeling activity—problem domain functioning analysis. By basing behavior analysis on Topological Functioning Model (TFM), we are identifying and designing subsystems, use cases, actors, and relationships between them (topological use case diagram), messages and their sequence (sequence diagram), and workflows (activity and interaction overview diagram). Behavior analysis and design consists of following four activities:

1. *Use case analysis*—it is based on refined functional requirements, refined TFM, and mappings between functional features and functional requirements. The very first step is identification of use cases. The next step is to map functional features onto use cases according to mappings between functional requirements and functional features thus creating the scenario of each use case. When functional features have been mapped onto use cases, the identification of actors is performed. Since actors in use case diagram show interaction between system and external systems or entities [78], they are obtained from topological space. The cause-and-effect relationships

Topological UML Modeling. DOI: http://dx.doi.org/10.1016/B978-0-12-805476-5.00007-1

between functional features define two kinds of relationships within topological use case diagram—the topological relationship (i.e., the communication) between use case and actor, and dependencies between use cases, while logical relations between topological relationships within TFM defined the type of dependencies between use cases. As a result of this activity we get topological use case diagram showing use cases, actors, relationships between them, and subsystems.

2. *Messages and their sequence analysis*—to analyze messages and how they are sent, a sequence diagram is used. The sequence diagram is developed by taking all the required information from topological use case diagram and TFM. Scope of each sequence diagram is set by the scope of corresponding use case. Actors are added to sequence diagrams directly from the corresponding use case. At the same time the TFM allows establishing objects with lifelines (objects from functional features), messages they send each other (cause-and-effect relationships). As a result of messages and their sequence analysis we get sequence diagram for each use case showing the objects and message sending between them.

3. *Workflows analysis*—to analyze workflows activity diagrams are used. Each activity diagram gets developed in accordance with use cases, TFM, and mappings between functional features and functional requirements. Scope of each activity diagram is set by the scope of corresponding use case. The activity diagram contains the description of the same functionality that is included into corresponding use case. The TFM and mappings between functional features and functional requirements allow establishing actions and the control flow between actions—functional features are transformed into action nodes and topological relationships into activity edges. The logic of control flow (i.e., decision, merge, fork, and join) is defined in accordance with the logical relations. As a result of this activity we get activity diagram for each use case representing its workflow.

4. *Workflows and messaging analysis*—this activity is used to formally develop interaction overview diagrams which basically merges together activity and sequence diagrams (interaction overview diagrams are specialization of activity diagrams that represent interactions). While the first one gives the information about control flow, the latter shows objects and messaging between them. The obtained diagram can be helpful in order to better understand the overall process of system and the control flow relations between sequence diagrams.

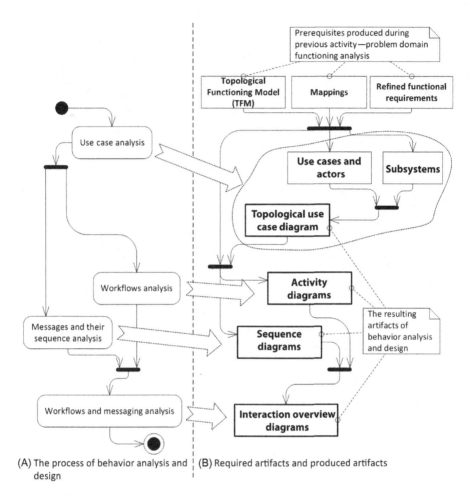

Figure 7.1 Process of system behavior analysis and design.

The process of behavior analysis and design is given in Fig. 7.1 while each of the four activities are described in the further sections of this chapter (each section describes one activity).

7.2 USE CASE ANALYSIS

Use case analysis and design consists of the following four actions (see Fig. 7.2):

1. *Identification of use cases*—the use cases are created according to the functional requirements of the required system or the system goals.

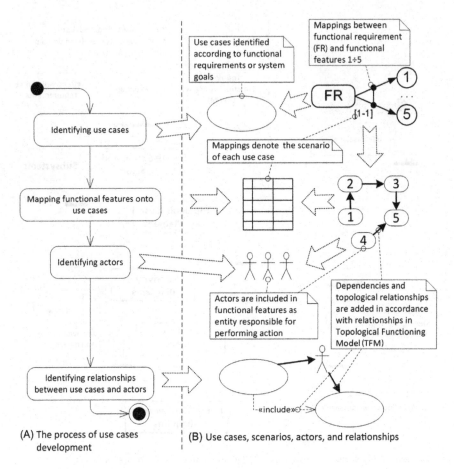

Figure 7.2 Use case analysis process.

2. *Mapping functional features onto use cases*—functional features onto use cases are mapped according to mappings between functional features and functional requirements thus creating the scenario of each use case.
3. *Identification of actors*—since actors in use case diagram show interaction between system and external systems or entities [78], they are obtained from topological space.
4. *Establishing relationships between use cases and actors*—the cause-and-effect relationships from TFM between functional features define two kinds of relationships within topological use case diagrams—the topological relationship (i.e., the communication) between use case and actor and the dependencies between use cases,

while the logical relations between cause-and-effect relationships define the stereotype of the dependency between use cases (i.e., *«include»* and *«exclude»*).

To develop topological use case diagram, the TFM, refined functional requirements, and mappings between functional features and functional requirements are used. These artifacts have been developed during the previous Topological UML modeling activity—problem domain functioning analysis (see Chapter 6, Problem Domain Functioning Analysis).

Identification of use cases is performed by creating one use case for each requirement. The alternative is to use system goals which are identified by the problem domain experts. If system goals need to be identified during problem domain analysis a TFM4MDA approach can be used [88]. TFM4MDA uses goals [60] in order to identify use cases and concepts from the description of the system (in the form of informal description, expert interviewing, etc.).

To illustrate analysis of use cases, we use enterprise data synchronization system development case study introduced in Chapter 6, Problem Domain Functioning Analysis. Within the case study every functional requirement is modeled with a corresponding use case, thus we have identified the following seven use cases (see Fig. 7.3):

- *FR1*—employee data synchronization,
- *FR1.1*—obtaining configuration information,
- *FR1.2*—obtaining data from source database,
- *FR1.3*—obtaining data from import files,

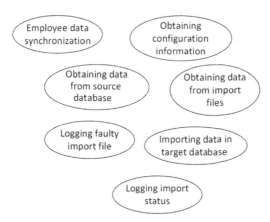

Figure 7.3 Use cases identified in enterprise data synchronization system case study.

- *FR1.4*—logging faulty import file,
- *FR1.5*—importing data in target database, and
- *FR1.6*—logging import status.

The next step is to *map functional features onto use cases* according to mappings between functional features and functional requirements by expert. The expert finds an input and an output functional feature for each use case—all functional features that correspond to particular use case should be in one chain.

In the context of case study, the following mappings exist between use cases and functional features:

- Employee data synchronization—this use case includes requirements FR1.1–FR1.7,
- Obtaining configuration information—includes functional features {2, 3, 4},
- Obtaining data from source database—{6, 7, 8, 9},
- Obtaining data from import files—{11, 13, 14, 15, 16, 17},
- Logging faulty import file—{18, 19, 20},
- Importing data in target database—{10, 27, 22, 23, 25}, and
- Logging import status—{28, 29, 30, 31, 32}.

When functional features have been mapped onto use cases, the *identification of actors* is performed. Since actors in use case diagram show interaction between system and external systems or entities [78], they are obtained from topological space. The actors are entities from functional features and the set of actors are identified by Eq. (7.1), where E is a set of functional features defining external entities, X is a set of functional features belonging to TFM, and N is a set of inner functional features:

$$E = X \backslash N \qquad (7.1)$$

In the context of enterprise data synchronization system development case study, within Chapter 6, Problem Domain Functioning Analysis, we have developed TFM which consists of the following 26 functional features:

X = {2, 3, 4, 6, 7, 8, 9, 10, 11, 13, 14, 15, 16, 17, 18, 19, 20, 22, 23, 25, 27, 28, 29, 30, 31, 32}.

All the inner functional features belonging to this TFM is as follows:

N = {3, 4, 7, 8, 9, 10, 11, 14, 15, 16, 17, 18, 19, 22, 27, 28, 29, 30, 31}.

By applying Eq. (7.1) we get the following set of functional features defining entities as actors for collaboration between the system and other parties (Table 7.1 shows entities for each functional feature belonging to set E):

$$E = \{2, 6, 13, 20, 23, 25, 32\}.$$

In total within case study we have identified the following four actors (see Fig. 7.4):

- Data import manager,
- Source database,
- Import file, and
- Target database.

Table 7.1 Entities for Functional Features Included in Set E

Functional Feature Id	Entity E	Subordination S
2	Data import manager	External
6	Source database	External
13	Import file	External
20	Data import manager	External
23	Target database	External
25	Target database	External
32	Data import manager	External

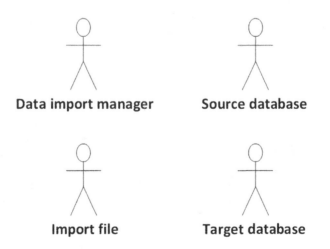

Data import manager   **Source database**

Import file   **Target database**

Figure 7.4 Actors identified from TFM.

The cause-and-effect relationship between one functional feature belonging to set E and the other to set N defines topological relationship between use case and actor. For a better understanding take a look at Fig. 7.5, where topological relationship is added between use case *logging import status* and actor *data import manager*.

The final action is to *establish relationships between use cases* according to mappings between functional features and them. According to these mappings *«include»* and *«extend»* relationships are automatically established between use cases by analyzing logical relations L_{out} between topological relationships. Logical relations should be analyzed for the first predecessor functional feature (which has two or more descendants, but within the scope of predecessor use case) of the use case's input functional features:

- The *«include»* relationship is added in two cases:
  1. No branching for the predecessor functional features and
  2. Logical relation L_{out} with type *and*.

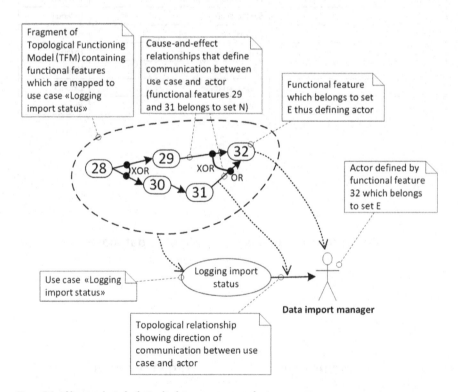

Figure 7.5 Adding topological relationship between use case and actor.

- The *«extend»* relationship is denoted by presence of logical relation L_{out} with type *or* and *xor* on the topological relationships outgoing from functional feature.

The designed topological use case diagram is supplemented with the information of subsystems. The scope of subsystems is determined by analyzing functional cycles within TFM—subsystems are extracted from TFM by applying closuring operation on the set of functional features belonging to a particular functioning cycle.

According to the mappings between functional features and requirements and logical relations in TFM the *«include»* and *«extend»* relationships are automatically established between use cases. Since actors in use case diagram show interaction between system and external systems or entities, they are obtained from topological space—actors are *entities* (E) from functional features and the set of actors are identified by Eq. (7.1). Topological relation between one functional feature belonging to set E and the other to set X defines relation between use case and actor since all use cases are mapped to functional features. The developed topological use case diagram is given in Fig. 7.6.

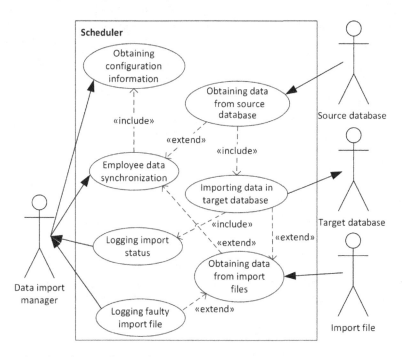

Figure 7.6 Topological use case diagram of enterprise data synchronization system.

As a result of use case analysis activity, we have developed topological use case diagram showing use cases, actors, relationships between them, and subsystems.

7.3 MESSAGES AND THEIR SEQUENCE ANALYSIS

Messaging and their sequence analysis consist of three actions (see Fig. 7.7) in which one sequence diagram is developed for each use case:

1. *Setting scope of sequence diagram*—one sequence diagram is created for each use case, thus through the mappings between use cases and TFM, the sequence diagram formally gets all the necessary information.
2. *Adding lifelines*—through the mappings between use case and TFM, the lifelines are added as entities from functional features.
3. *Establishing messages between objects and their sequence*—cause-and-effect relationships between functional features within TFM set the messaging between objects, while logical relations set the required interaction operator.

Use cases, TFM, and mappings between functional features and functional requirements are used to develop sequence diagrams. The *scope of each sequence diagram is set* by the scope of corresponding use

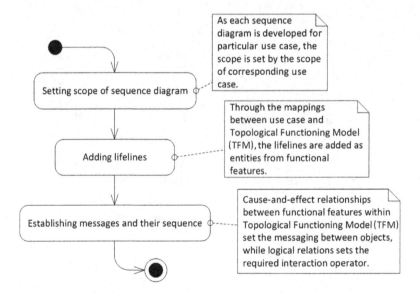

Figure 7.7 Messages and their sequence analysis process.

case (i.e., the sequence diagram contains the description of the same functionality that is included in the corresponding use case). Actors are added to sequence diagrams directly from the corresponding use case. The TFM and mappings allow establishing objects with lifelines (merged functional features), messages they send each other (cause-and-effect relationships). If one use case has included another use case (e.g., A includes B), then the sequence diagram for use case A should include interaction use (*ref*) for the sequence diagram of use case B.

Messages between objects and their sequence are established by transforming part of TFM according to the scope of the corresponding use case. During TFM transformation all vertices with the same type of objects should be merged. While merging these vertices all topological relations between them are kept. The cause-and-effect relations from TFM serve as message sending between objects. The interaction operators are added by taking into consideration logical relations L_{out}:

- *alt*—added for logical relations L_{out} with type *or* and *xor*,
- *opt*—added for logical relations L_{out} with type *or*, and
- *par*—added for logical relations L_{out} with type *and*.

In the case of adding interaction operators *alt* and *opt* their guards are set as the preconditions of the corresponding effect functional feature. To better understand the TFM transformation into sequence diagram, take a look at Fig. 7.8, where on the left side is given

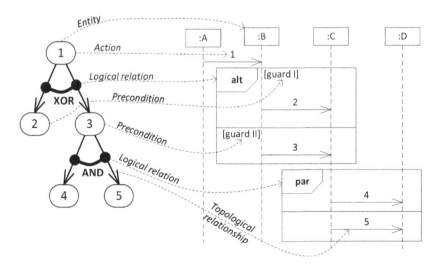

Figure 7.8 Mappings between elements of TFM and sequence diagram.

fragment of TFM and on the right side fragment of sequence diagram (the dashed arrows from TFM to sequence diagram show corresponding elements of TFM in the sequence diagram).

Since in enterprise data synchronization system development case study use cases are used to model requirements, the use cases define the number and the scope of sequence diagrams. The scope of sequence diagrams defines a set of functional features that are included in each use case. A total set of seven sequence diagrams is created. Sequence diagram for use case *importing data in target database* (which reflects functional requirement FR1.5) is given in Fig. 7.9.

As FR1.5 mappings also include functional requirement FR1.6, the corresponding sequence diagram contains *ref* interaction use to sequence diagram *logging import status*. The mappings between

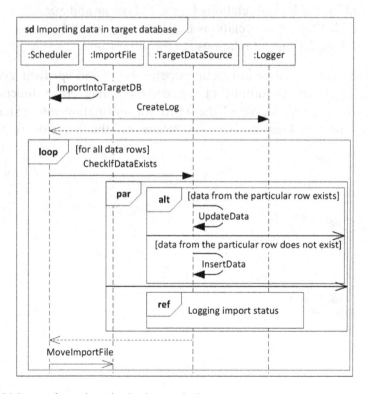

Figure 7.9 Sequence diagram importing data in target database.

Id	Object Action (A)	Precondition (PreCond)
Table 7.2 Part of Functional Features Defined for Enterprise Data Synchronization System		
10	Importing every row from internal table into target database	
22	Checking if data from a particular row already exists in target database	
23	Updating existing data in target database	If data from the particular row exist
25	Insert new data in target database	If data from the particular row do not exist
27	Creating log file in log files folder for import file processing	If data are read from import file
28	Logging data row from temporal internal table	
29	Logging successful status	If import is successful for particular row
30	Logging error status	If import is not successful for particular row
31	Logging error description	If error is logged
32	Archiving log file	If data import is completed

functional requirements FR1.5, FR1.6, and functional features are as follows:

- *FR1.5*—importing data in target data base—{10, 27, 22, 23, 25, FR1.6} and
- *FR1.6*—logging import status—{28, 29, 30, 31, 32}.

Description of the functional features mapped for functional requirements FR1.5 and FR1.6 is given in Table 7.2.

As a result of messages and their sequence analysis activity we have developed sequence diagram for each use case showing the lifelines and message sending between them.

7.4 WORKFLOWS ANALYSIS

Analysis and design of workflows consist of three actions (see Fig. 7.10) in which one activity diagram is developed for each use case:

1. *Setting scope of activity diagram*—one activity diagram is created for each use case, thus through the mappings between use cases and TFM, the activity diagram formally gets all the necessary information.

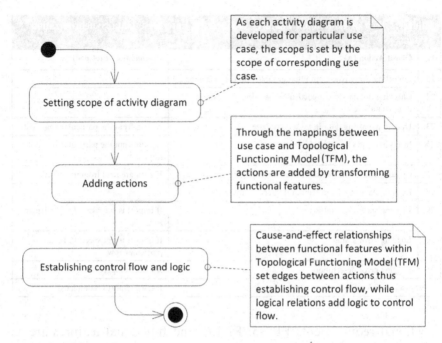

As each activity diagram is developed for particular use case, the scope is set by the scope of corresponding use case.

Setting scope of activity diagram

Through the mappings between use case and Topological Functioning Model (TFM), the actions are added by transforming functional features.

Adding actions

Cause-and-effect relationships between functional features within Topological Functioning Model (TFM) set edges between actions thus establishing control flow, while logical relations add logic to control flow.

Establishing control flow and logic

Figure 7.10 Workflows analysis process.

2. *Adding actions*—actions are added by transforming functional features from corresponding part of TFM into actions.
3. *Establishing control flow and logic*—cause-and-effect relationships between functional features within TFM are added as edges between actions thus establishing the control flow while logical relations between cause-and-effect relationships define the logic of control flow (i.e., decision, merge, fork, and join).

Workflows within system are analyzed and designed by using the activity diagram. Use cases, TFM, and mappings between functional features and functional requirements are used to develop activity diagrams. *Scope of each activity diagram is set* by the scope of corresponding use case (i.e., the activity diagram contains the description of the same functionality that is included into corresponding use case). The TFM and mappings allow *establishing actions and the control flow* between actions—functional features are transformed into action nodes and topological relationships into activity edges. *The logic of control flow* (i.e., decision, merge, fork, and join) is defined in accordance with the logical relations L_{out} within TFM as shown in the activity diagram pattern in Table 7.3.

Table 7.3 Rules for Identification of Logical Relations L$_{out}$ and Patterns for Transforming TFM Into Activity Diagram

Rt	X$_e$	C$_{id}$		Example of L$_{out}$	Pattern of Activity Diagram
and	X$_{e1}$	Ø			
	X$_{e2}$	Ø			
or	X$_{e1}$	C$_1$	C$_1$≠C$_2$ & C$_1$≠C$_2$		
	X$_{e2}$	C$_2$			
xor	X$_{e1}$	C$_1$	C$_2$ = C$_1$		
	X$_{e2}$	C$_2$			

An example showing TFM to activity diagram transformation is given in Fig. 7.11, where on the upper side is given fragment of TFM and on the lower side corresponding fragment of activity diagram (the dashed arrows from TFM to activity diagram shows corresponding elements of TFM in the activity diagram).

Since in enterprise data synchronization system development case study use cases are used to model requirements, the use cases define the number and the scope of activity diagrams. The scope of activity diagrams defines a set of functional features that are included in each use case. A total set of seven activity diagrams is created. Activity diagram for use case *importing data in target database* (which reflects functional requirement FR1.5) is given in Fig. 7.12. As FR1.5 mappings also include functional requirement FR1.6, the corresponding activity diagram contains *ref* interaction use to activity diagram *logging import status*. Mappings between functional requirements and functional features together with description of those functional features are given in Section 7.3.

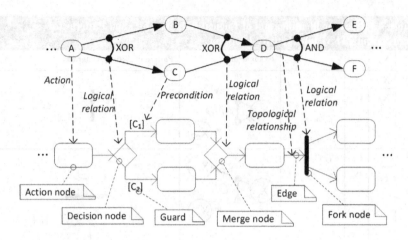

Figure 7.11 Example of TFM to activity diagram transformation.

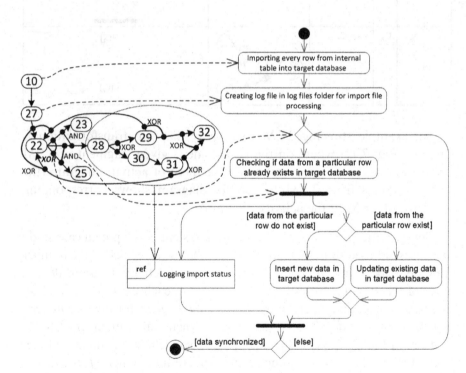

Figure 7.12 Activity diagram representing workflow of use case importing data in target database *and corresponding part of TFM.*

As a result of workflows analysis activity, we have developed activity diagram for each use case showing the actions, edges between action, control flow, and the logic of control flow.

7.5 WORKFLOWS AND MESSAGING ANALYSIS

To tie together workflows and messaging, interaction overview diagrams are used. To develop interaction overview diagram, the activity diagrams

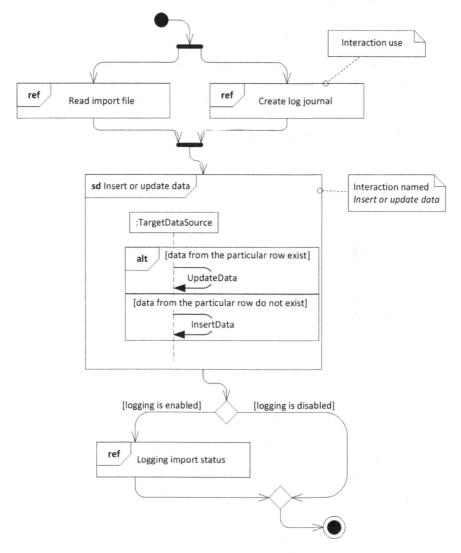

Figure 7.13 Example of interaction overview diagram.

(representing the workflow of use case) and sequence diagrams (showing the objects and messages they send each other) are merged together.

The workflow and messaging design together is represented with interaction overview diagram which define interactions through a variant of activity diagram in a way that promotes overview of the control flow. Interaction overview diagram focuses on the overview of the flow of control where the nodes are of type interaction or interaction use. The lifelines and the messages do not appear at this overview level [78].

The interaction overview diagrams are developed by merging created activity diagrams and sequence diagrams. While the first one gives the information about control flow, the latter shows objects and messaging between them. The obtained diagram can be helpful in order to better understand the overall process of system and the control flow relations between sequence diagrams. An example of interaction overview diagram is given in Fig. 7.13.

As a result of workflows and messaging analysis activity we have developed interaction overview diagrams.

7.6 SUMMARY

Behavior analysis and design is the next activity within Topological UML modeling following the first activity—problem domain functioning analysis. During behavior analysis and design a set of behavioral diagrams is developed for the system under consideration based on the previously developed artifacts—TFM and mappings between functional requirements to functional features. The behavioral diagrams are developed by transforming previously created artifacts thus assuring that the analysis and design is going in accordance with the required functioning. By basing behavior analysis on TFM, we are identifying and designing subsystems, use cases, actors, and relationships between them (topological use case diagram), messages and their sequence (sequence diagram), and workflows (activity and interaction overview diagram). Behavior analysis and design consists of the following four activities:

1. *Use case analysis*—it is based on refined functional requirements, refined TFM, and mappings between functional features and

functional requirements. As a result of this activity we get topological use case diagram showing use cases, actors, relationships between them, and subsystems.

2. *Messages and their sequence analysis*—the sequence diagram is developed by taking all the required information from topological use case diagram and TFM. As a result of messages and their sequence analysis we get sequence diagram for each use case showing the objects and message sending between them.

3. *Workflows analysis*—each activity diagram gets developed in accordance with use cases, TFM, and mappings between functional requirements and functional features. As a result of this activity we get activity diagram for each use case representing its workflow.

4. *Workflows and messaging analysis*—this activity is used to formally develop interaction overview diagrams which basically merge together activity and sequence diagrams.

CHAPTER 8

Structure Analysis and Design

INFORMATION IN THIS CHAPTER:

- Consuming Topological Functioning Model (TFM) for formal structure analysis and design
- TFM transformation into structure diagrams
- Formal development of classes and their relationships

8.1 INTRODUCTION

Structure analysis and design is an activity within Topological UML modeling process. This activity is based on the results obtained within the very first Topological UML modeling activity—problem domain functioning analysis in which Topological Functioning Model (TFM) is developed for the system under consideration. The TFM holistically represents the functioning of the problem and solution domains. As a holistic model, TFM includes necessary information to develop diagrams reflecting structure of the solution domain. Structure analysis and design consists of the following activities:

1. *Analysis of objects structure and communication*—it is based on the TFM transformation into communication diagram. When transforming TFM into communication diagram the following TFM elements are used: functional features (source for lifeline identification and message sending from object to object), cause-and-effect relationships (from which lifeline to which lifeline the message is sent and the message sending sequence), and logical relations (message sending concurrency).
2. *Domain model development*—domain model is represented by using topological class diagram which is developed by transforming communication diagram. It is used for adding classes and operations to the topological class diagram, where lifelines are transformed into classes while messages into operations. After the classes and

Topological UML Modeling. DOI: http://dx.doi.org/10.1016/B978-0-12-805476-5.00008-3

topological relationships between them have been established, the attributes are added to the classes taking the necessary information from corresponding functional feature.

3. *Modeling snapshots of the system*—object diagram serves to take a look at a complete or partial view of the structure of a modeled system at a specific time moment. It can be used instead of a topological class diagram in situations that involve more than one object of the same class acting in different roles or to provide examples of a system at a specific time.

The process of structure analysis and design is given in Fig. 8.1, while each of the activities is described in the further sections of this chapter (each section describes one activity). Additional section is designated for initial topological class diagram refinement.

The main goal of structure analysis and design is to develop a topological class diagram which contains classes together with their attributes and responsibilities. To identify classes and assign the right responsibility

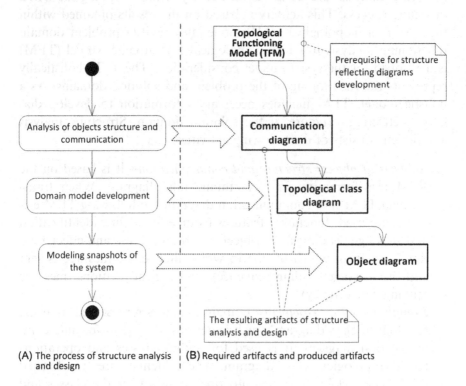

(A) The process of structure analysis and design

(B) Required artifacts and produced artifacts

Figure 8.1 Structure analysis and design process.

to each one of them a TFM is used. This chapter shows the transformation of TFM into communication diagram and communication diagram into topological class diagram (together with refinement of it).

8.2 ANALYSIS OF OBJECTS AND THEIR COMMUNICATION

Analysis of objects and their communication is based on the TFM transformation into communication diagram. When transforming TFM into communication diagram the following TFM elements are used:

* *Functional features*—source for lifeline identification and message sending from object to object;
* *Cause-and-effect relationships*—from which lifeline to which lifeline the message is sent and the message sending sequence; and
* *Logical relations*—message sending concurrency.

The development process of communication diagram is given in Fig. 8.2.

To develop communication diagram, a TFM of the system is used. The TFM is constructed during the very first Topological UML modeling activity—problem domain functioning analysis (see Chapter 6, Problem Domain Functioning Analysis). In order to obtain a communication diagram, it is necessary to check if each functional feature of the TFM reflects only one type of object. If some functional feature reflects more than one type of object, then it is needed to decompose it to the level where one functional feature uses only one type of objects. If TFM has been successfully checked it can be transformed into communication diagram.

The first step in transformation is to merge functional features with objects of the same type in one lifeline (the lifeline represents the *class* (Cl) attribute of the functional feature). While merging functional features into lifelines the relationships with other lifelines should be retained (if there is more than one topological relationship, then only one link is added between lifelines). The count of topological relationships between merged functional features denotes the count of messages sent between lifelines represented by those functional features. Messages can be obtained from functional features because one functional feature represents one atomic business action. The message that is sent to a lifeline is an *operation* (Op) attribute of the functional feature (e.g., if functional

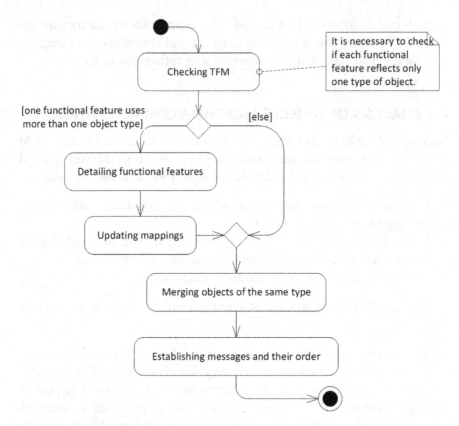

Figure 8.2 Development of communication diagram.

feature B is descendant of functional feature A, then in communication diagram the lifeline representing A sends a message to lifeline representing B and this message is the value of *operation* (Op) attribute of B). Actors to communication diagram are added from the input functional features—value of the *entity* (E) attribute is used.

For a better understanding of TFM to communication diagram transformation, a small fragment of TFM consisting of two functional features A and B is used, where A is an input functional feature of TFM. An example showing TFM to communication diagram transformation is given in Fig. 8.3, where:

• On the upper side is given fragment of TFM consisting of two functional features A and B linked together with cause-and-effect relationship pointing from functional feature A to functional feature B and

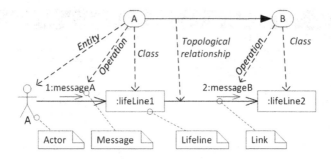

Figure 8.3 Example of TFM to communication diagram transformation.

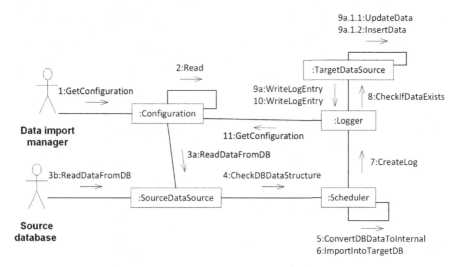

Figure 8.4 Communication diagram representing data synchronization with source database.

- On the lower side is given fragment of communication diagram (the dashed arrows from TFM to communication diagram show corresponding elements of TFM in the communication diagram).

The developed communication diagram representing data synchronization with source data base in the context of enterprise data synchronization system development case study is given in Fig. 8.4, while Table 8.1 contains all the functional features of developed TFM where column *Id* contains identifier of functional feature, *Lifeline* shows values of functional features' *class* (Cl) element, and *Message* shows *operation* (Op) element. Elements defining functional feature's tuple are given in Eq. (4.4).

Table 8.1 Functional Features' Specification for Communication Diagram		
Id	Lifeline	Message
2	Configuration	CreateConfiguration
3	Configuration	Read
4	Configuration	IsImportFromDBNeeded
6	SourceDataSource	CreateData
7	SourceDataSource	ReadDataFromDB
8	Scheduler	CheckDBDataStructure
9	Scheduler	ConvertDBDataToInternal
10	Scheduler	ImportIntoTargetDB
11	ImportFolder	CheckImportFolder
13	ImportFile	CreateImportFile
14	ImportFile	ReadImportFile
15	Scheduler	CheckImportFileStructure
16	Scheduler	ConvertImportFileDataToInternal
17	Scheduler	SkipImportFile
18	ImportFile	MoveImportFile
19	Logger	CreateLog
20	Logger	WriteLogEntry
22	TargetDataSource	CheckIfDataExists
23	TargetDataSource	UpdateData
25	TargetDataSource	InsertData
27	Logger	CreateLog
28	Logger	WriteLogEntry
29	Logger	WriteLogEntry
30	Logger	WriteLogEntry
31	Logger	WriteLogEntry
32	Logger	ArchiveLog

As a result of this activity the partial domain model in the form of communication diagram is created.

8.3 DOMAIN MODEL DEVELOPMENT

Domain model development is based on topological class diagram development. The topological class diagram is developed by transforming communication diagram and adding additional information from corresponding TFM thus ensuring that the classes, their responsibilities, and relationships are added in strong conformance with the required functionality and domain functioning. Domain model development by means of topological class diagram consists of four activities (see Fig. 8.5):

1. *Adding classes and operations*—lifelines from communication diagram are transformed into classes and messages into operations.
2. *Adding topological relationships between classes*—links from communication diagram are transformed into topological relationships while the direction of message sending defines the direction of topological relationship.
3. *Identifying attributes*—it is achieved by taking into consideration attributes of the object represented by functional feature in TFM.
4. *Refining initial topological class diagram*—it is aimed to lower abstraction level of topological class diagram by adding additional information, including relationships between classes. By lowering abstraction level, the diagram gets additional information which is needed during the software development and later also during its maintenance (this activity is covered in next section).

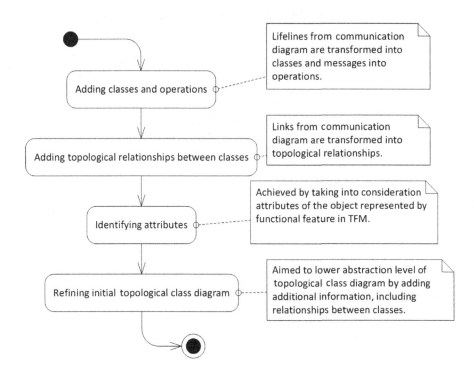

Figure 8.5 Development of topological class diagram.

At first the communication diagram is used for *adding classes and operations* to the topological class diagram—lifelines are transformed into classes and messages into operations. The next step is *adding topological relationships* between classes. Since the notation of topological class diagram allows variations of topological relationship graphical representation, it is advised to draw only one directed arrow in the same direction between classes (the arrow will show the cause and the effect operations). The example of communication diagram to topological class diagram transformation is given in Fig. 8.6, where on the left side is given fragment of communication diagram and on the right side fragment of topological class diagram.

After the classes and topological relationships between them have been established the next step is *identification of attributes*. This can be achieved by taking into consideration attributes of the object represented by functional feature. If the functional feature is well specified, the *class* attribute of it is determined. If the *class* attribute is not determined, it can be specified in several ways (e.g., by analyzing functioning description of the system and searching nouns that represent attributes of the object [26], performing expert interviews [104], or by using ontology [125]).

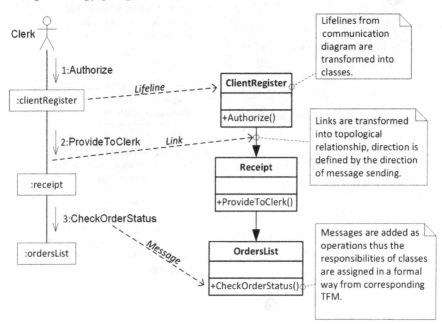

Figure 8.6 Example of communication to topological class diagram transformation.

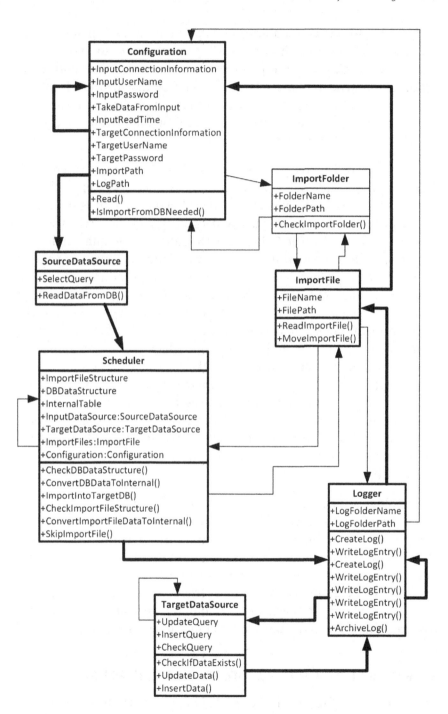

Figure 8.7 Initial topological class diagram of enterprise data synchronization system.

By transforming communication diagram an initial topological class diagram is obtained (with attributes, operations, and topological relations between classes). A topological relation shows the control flow within the system. If static relations should be included (such as associations, generalization, etc.), then initial topological class diagram should be refined. The refinement process of initial topological class diagram is described in the next section.

The developed topological class diagram in the context of enterprise data synchronization system development case study is given in Fig. 8.7. With bolder lines in developed topological class diagram is maintained the main functional cycle which is defined within the previously constructed TFM in Chapter 6, Problem Domain Functioning Analysis. In enterprise data synchronization system case study the main functioning cycle represents getting data from source data base and import files and editing those data in target database. By interrupting this main cycle the system can no longer function or it functions faulty [86]. Thus, the visualization with bolder lines for topological relationships and classes clearly shows the classes and relationships which have the main responsibility assigned to them. This reflects the idea that the holistic domain representation by the means of TFM enables identification of all necessary domain concepts and, even, enables to define their necessity for a successful implementation of the system. The responsibilities of classes are assigned as operations; thus, by using TFM in software development the classes are identified and responsibilities are assigned directly from the problem domain.

Topological class diagram given in Fig. 8.7 can be considered as initial because it contains classes and topological relations between them and it is at high abstraction level. By reviewing and refining initial class diagram associations, generalizations, dependencies, and other relationships defined in UML are added. In this way the abstraction level of diagram is lowered and structural relations between classes are added. The refinement of initial topological class diagram is covered within the case study explored in the next section.

8.4 REFINEMENT OF TOPOLOGICAL CLASS DIAGRAM

The refinement of topological class diagrams is aimed to lower abstraction level of it. By lowering abstraction level, the diagram gets additional information which is needed during the software development and later also during its maintenance. The refinement process consists of six actions [28] (see Fig. 8.8):

1. *Identifying generalizations*—to find a generalization you need to look for the same responsibilities, topological relationships, attributes, and operations that are common to two or more classes. The set of common responsibilities, topological relationships, attributes, and operations can be elevated to a more general class.
2. *Identifying structural relationships between classes*—the identification of physical relationships between entities involved in the system consists of three steps—at first aggregations are added, then followed by compositions, and finally associations are added.
3. *Defining interfaces*—interfaces are identified by the operations and the signals that cross the boundary of the system under consideration.

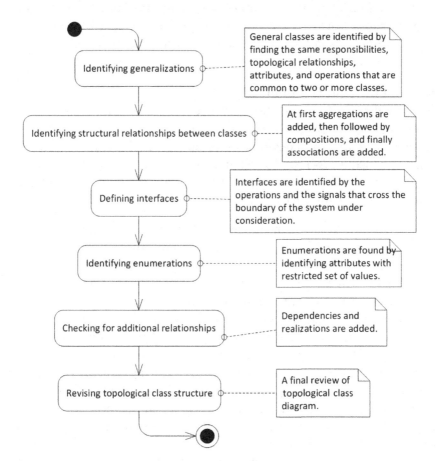

Figure 8.8 Refinement process of topological class diagram.

These operations and signals can be found by analyzing both the TFM and the topological space of the system (the TFM shows the functioning of the system, while topological space shows the system within the surrounding environment). This analysis shows the inputs (*provided interfaces*) and outputs (*required interfaces*) of the system.

4. *Identifying enumerations*—by reviewing initial topological classes of the system under consideration enumeration candidates can be found, e.g., attributes which can contain only a restricted set of values can be transformed into enumeration containing set of these restricted values.
5. *Checking for additional relationships*—it includes identification of dependencies and realizations.
6. *Revising topological class structure.*

The actions of refinement process are described in detail in the subsequent subsections. As a result of applying refinement process, a rich topological class diagram with lower abstraction level is obtained.

8.4.1 Identifying Generalizations

A generalization is a relationship between a general kind of thing (called the generalized class or parent) and a more specific kind of thing (called the specialization class or child). Generalization sometimes is called an *is-a-kind-of* relationship. If child class has one parent class, then it is single inheritance. If child class has two or more parent classes, then it is multiple inheritance.

The generalizations can be identified in two ways. The first way is to review initial topological classes which are obtained from the communication diagram and TFM. To find a generalization you need to look for the same responsibilities, topological relationships, attributes, and operations that are common to two or more classes. The set of common responsibilities, topological relationships, attributes, and operations can be elevated to a more general class. If this general class does not exist it should be created. Since topological relationships define control flow within system, by introducing general classes and generalization relationships it is possible that the more general class is placed at the end of topological relationship and the more specific class is placed at the beginning of topological relationship (see Fig. 8.9). In order to help identifying generalizations, during the review process of initial topological classes, an additional attention can be paid on

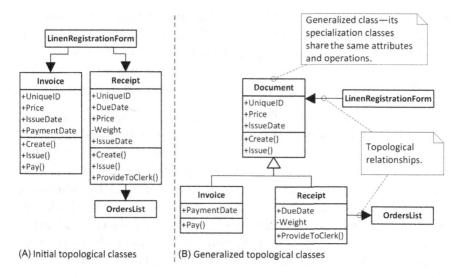

Figure 8.9 Initial topological classes and generalized topological classes.

anywhere where the initial topological classes indicate that there is more than one *kind of* thing (e.g., two kinds of documents—invoice and receipt (see Fig. 8.9b)). This indicates a possible generalization.

The second way is by doing additional interviews with stakeholders. During interviews the interviewees are asked if any of the classes are variations on others [104]. By applying both ways in generalization identification a more formal (by reviewing initial topological classes) and less formal (by making interviews) approaches are used. The reviewing process is more formal because it is based on sets of already existing information. Reviewing and introduction of generalization relationships (together with parent classes) can be automated. By using together reviewing and interviewing an additional model checking gets performed.

8.4.2 Identifying Structural Relationships Between Classes
The identification of physical relationships between entities involved in the system consists of three steps. At first it is needed to *check and find the whole and part relationships*—aggregations and compositions.

Aggregation is a *has a* relationship meaning that an object of the whole has objects of the part [37]. If objects are related with an aggregation, then by destroying the object of the whole, the objects of the part is not destroyed. Aggregation is a special kind of association. According to guidelines given in [104], aggregation can be placed between objects if a part object can belong to more than one whole object and the part continues to exist when the whole is destroyed. Words that suggest aggregation include *collection, list*, and *group*.

Composition is a form of aggregation, with strong ownership and coincident lifetime as part of the whole. Parts with nonfixed multiplicity may be created after the composite itself, but once created they live and die with it. This means that, in a composite aggregation, an object may be a part of only one composite at a time and by destroying whole, the parts are destroyed with it [37]. According to guidelines given in [104], composition can be placed between objects if a part is totally *owned* by the whole and the part ceases to exist when the whole is destroyed. Words that suggest composition include *composed of* and *component*.

After identification of aggregations and compositions, the next step is *identification of associations between classes*. An *association* is a structural relationship that specifies that objects of one thing are connected to objects of another. Given an association connecting two classes, it is possible to relate objects of one class to objects of the other class [77]. According to guidelines given in [15], associations can be placed between objects if it is needed to navigate from objects of one type to objects of another. This is a data-driven view of associations.

8.4.3 Defining Interfaces

An interface is a collection of operations that are used to specify a service of a class or a component. Graphically, an interface may be rendered as a stereotyped class in order to expose its operations and other properties. Interfaces may also be used to specify a contract for a use case or subsystem [77].

A line around the topological class diagram which is obtained by applying transformations on the TFM can be drawn, thus showing the boundary of the system under consideration. The next step is to identify the operations and the signals that cross this boundary. These operations and signals can be found by analyzing both the TFM and the topological space of the system (the TFM shows the functioning of the system, but topological space shows the system within the surrounding environment). This analysis shows the inputs and outputs

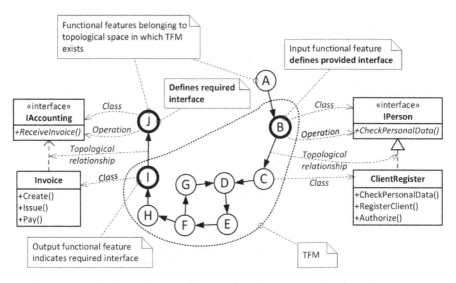

Figure 8.10 Fragment of topological space and examples of provided and required interfaces.

of the system. The input functional features within TFM indicate the *provided interfaces*, but the output functional features indicate the *required interfaces*. Required (imported) interfaces are modeled by using dependency relationships, and provided (exported) interfaces are modeled by using realization relationships. An example of showing analysis of TFM and topological space and the resulting interfaces is given in Fig. 8.10, where in the middle is given fragment of TFM and on the sides fragment of topological class diagram (the dashed arrows from TFM to topological class diagram show corresponding elements of TFM in the topological class diagram).

By using the guidelines given in *"The Unified Modeling Language User Guide"* [15] it is possible to model interfaces within the system as seams between different parts of the system.

8.4.4 Identifying Enumerations

An enumeration is a data type whose values are enumerated in the model as enumeration literals. Enumeration is a kind of data type, whose instances may be any of a number of user-defined enumeration literals. An enumeration may be shown using the classifier notation (a rectangle) with the keyword *«enumeration»*.

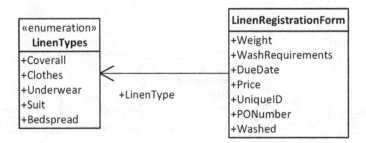

Figure 8.11 Example of identified enumeration for linen registration form.

The enumeration within a system can be found in two ways. The first way is to review initial topological classes which are obtained from the TFM of the system under consideration. To find enumerations at first you need to look for attributes which can contain only a restricted set of values. In the context of the laundry system, an example of the restricted set of values is the requested washing type. The second thing is to search for objects which can change its state value during its lifetime. In the context of the laundry system, an example of such object is washing request. The washing request can have different states, e.g., *new, registered, in washing, completed, paid.* The second way is by doing additional interviews with stakeholders. During the interviews the interviewees are asked if any of the attributes has only limited list of allowed values or if there exist states of things involved into system. If such lists of values or states exist, then enumerations should be defined for each such list. An example of identified enumerations is given in Fig. 8.11.

8.4.5 Checking for Additional Relationships
The checking of additional relationships includes identification of dependencies and realizations.

A *dependency* is a relationship that states that one thing uses the information and services of another thing, but not necessarily the reverse. Dependency relationship should be used to show that one thing is using another. Most often dependencies between classes are used to show that one class uses operations from another class or it uses variables or arguments typed by the other class. Dependencies also most often show required interfaces of a class. Dependencies do not model structural relationships.

Realization is a semantic relationship between classifiers in which one classifier specifies a contract that another classifier guarantees to carry out.

8.4.6 Revising Topological Class Structure

The final step in topological class diagram refinement is the revising of topological class structure. The revising of topological class structure should be done using following guidelines (revising guidelines for generalizations are based on guidelines given in *"UML for the IT Business Analyst"* [104]):

1. Any classes that have the same topological relationships or associations to other classes should be identified. If such classes exist, a decision of adding additional generalized class should be made. If generalized class is added, then common topological relationships and associations should be moved to it.
2. Any classes that have the same attributes or operations as other classes should be identified. If such classes exist, a decision of adding additional generalized class that will contain common attributes and operations should be made.
3. Every generalized class in the topological class diagram should be justified. The point of introducing a generalized class is to provide a convenient, single place to put rules that affect a number of specialized classes. There should be at least one attribute, operation, or relationship that can be ascribed to the generalized class.
4. As a final revising step of generalized classes is that each generalized class should have at least two specializations, with two exceptions:
   a. The generalized class is concrete and
   b. It is anticipated that more specializations will be added in the future.
5. Since the system is connected with the environment (through inputs and outputs), at least one provided and one required interface should be identified. Revising of interfaces should follow these rules:
   a. The count of operations defined within provided interfaces should be the same as count of input functional features within TFM.
   b. The count of operations defined within required interfaces should be the same as count of output functional features within TFM.

After the revising process has been finished, the initial topological class diagram is refined and the abstraction level of it has been lowered. Mainly the abstraction level should be lowered in order to introduce generalized classes, structural relationships, and interfaces.

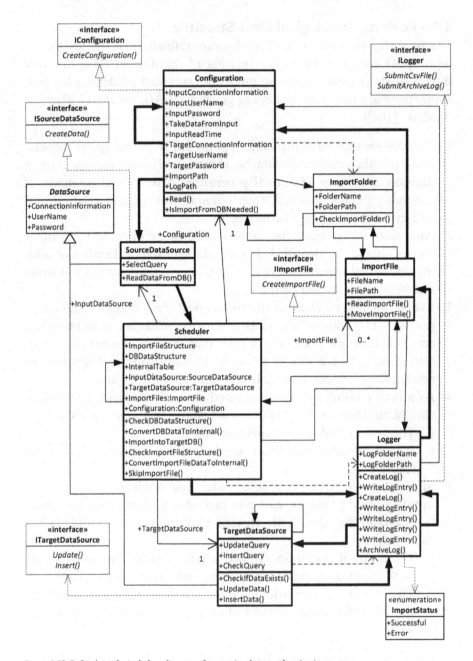

Figure 8.12 Refined topological class diagram of enterprise data synchronization system.

The refined topological class diagram of enterprise data synchronization system is given in Fig. 8.12, where with bolder topological relationships is denoted main functioning cycle and during refinement process have been added the following artifacts:

- Generalizations—an abstract generalized class *DataStructure* speciali-zations of which are classes *SourceDataSource* and *TargetDataSource*;
- Structural relationships—associations between multiple classes, e.g., *Scheduler* and *SourceDataSource*;
- Interfaces—both provided (*IConfiguration, ISourceDataSource*, and *IImportFile*) and required (*ILogger* and *ITargetDataSource*);
- Enumerations—an enumerator *ImportStatus* which lists all the statuses of import result;
- Dependencies and realizations—in addition to dependency and realization relationships used to relate classes with interfaces and enumerations an additional dependency was identified between classes *Configuration* and *ImportFolder*.

8.5 MODELING SYSTEM SNAPSHOTS

To model a snapshot of a system, its structure representing view is required—it can be either communication diagram or topological class diagram. Since object diagram shows a complete or partial view of the structure of a modeled system at a specific time moment [78] it can be used instead of a topological class diagram in situations that involve more than one object of the same class acting in different roles [104] or to provide examples of a system at a specific time. An object diagram focuses on particular set of object instances and attributes, and the links between the instances. A set of object diagrams provides insight into how a view of system is expected to evolve over time. Only those aspects of a model that are of current interest need to be shown on an object diagram. When topological class diagram is transformed into a set of object diagrams, the classes become instance specifications, and associations—links. As a result of modeling system snapshots activity, a set of object diagrams is created describing the objects details of the domain model.

8.6 SUMMARY

Structure analysis and design is an activity within Topological UML modeling process. This activity is based on the results obtained within the very first Topological UML modeling activity—problem domain functioning analysis in which TFM is developed for the system under consideration. The TFM holistically represents the functioning of the problem and solution domains. As a holistic model, TFM includes necessary information to develop diagrams reflecting structure of the solution domain. Topological UML modeling models structure by means of the topological class diagram. To design a structure reflecting diagrams, the following activities are performed:

- *Analysis of objects structure and communication*—initially TFM is transformed into communication diagram showing objects and messages they send each other.
- *Domain model development*—afterward the communication diagram is further transformed into topological class diagram. The operations are obtained during TFM transformation to communication diagram and the attributes are added from TFM while transforming communication diagram into topological class diagram. The responsibilities of classes are assigned as operations; thus, by using TFM in software development the classes are identified and responsibilities are assigned directly from the problem domain.
- *Modeling snapshots of the system*—object diagram serves to take a look at a complete or partial view of the structure of a modeled system at a specific time moment. It can be used instead of a topological class diagram in situations that involve more than one object of the same class acting in different roles or to provide examples of a system at a specific time.

CHAPTER *9*

Object State Change and Transition Analysis

INFORMATION IN THIS CHAPTER:

- Consuming Topological Functioning Model (TFM) for formal object state change and transition analysis
- TFM transformation into state diagrams

9.1 INTRODUCTION

Object state change and transition analysis is an activity within Topological UML modeling process following structure analysis and design activity. It is based on the state diagram development. Object state change and transition analysis consists of one activity—analyzing object state changes and transitions (see Fig. 9.1). Initially we need to scale down Topological Functioning Model (TFM). States for each class are obtained from the functional features of TFM (functional feature has an attribute that defines the new state of the object). State transitions are obtained by transforming cause-and-effect relationship between functional features. The special states (initial state and final state) are added to the obtained state diagram as inputs and outputs of TFM.

To perform object state change and transition analysis, the refined TFM and classes (either from topological class diagram or lifelines from communication diagram) are used as a source information for state diagram. Development of TFM is described in Chapter 6, Problem Domain Functioning Analysis, while structure analysis in which classes are developed—in Chapter 8, Structure Analysis and Design. As a result of object state change and transition analysis is one state diagram for each class. It is advised to analyze state changes of complex or most important objects in the system. The most important objects are those that are participating in the main functioning cycle of the system.

Topological UML Modeling. DOI: http://dx.doi.org/10.1016/B978-0-12-805476-5.00009-5

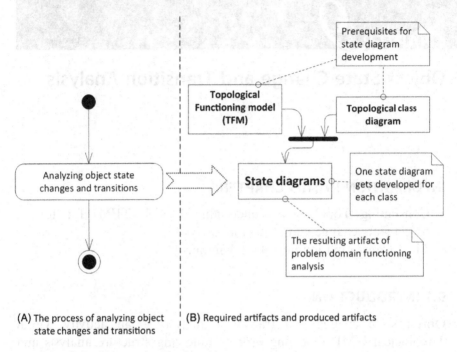

(A) The process of analyzing object   (B) Required artifacts and produced artifacts
state changes and transitions

Figure 9.1 Analyzing object state changes and transitions.

9.2 OBJECT STATE CHANGE AND TRANSITION ANALYSIS

Object state change and transition analysis is based on the TFM transformation into a set of state diagrams. The input of this activity is refined TFM and classes (either from topological class diagram or lifelines from communication diagram) and the output of this activity is one state diagram for each class. Each functional feature specifies an object performing certain action. The count of obtained state diagrams is denoted by count of distinct objects specified by functional features. It is advised to analyze state changes of complex or most important objects in the system as outlined by Podeswa in *"UML for the IT Business Analyst"* [104]. The most important objects are denoted by TFM—the functional features that are included into main functional cycle denote them, thus the identification of most important objects is done in a formal way.

The first action is to scale down TFM which is performed by removing functional features which does not represent the object under consideration but in the same time retaining cause-and-effect relations. For example, assume that TFM consists of three functional features A, B, and C and are in the following causal chain: $A \rightarrow B \rightarrow C$. The A and C represent the same object while B represents another object. The resulting (scaled down) TFM is as follows: $A \rightarrow C$.

States for each class are obtained from the functional features of refined TFM (functional feature has an attribute named *newState* as shown in Section 4.3.1). If the execution of functional feature involves the change of the corresponding object's state, then the attribute *newState* has value, otherwise the value is not set. State transitions are obtained by transforming cause-and-effect relationship between functional features [27].

The special states (initial state and final state) are added to the obtained state diagram as follows:

• The *initial state* is added before the states that are obtained from the functional features which are the inputs of the downscaled TFM,

No.	TFM Element	State Diagram Element	Description
Table 9.1 Mappings Between Elements of TFM and State Diagram			
1.	Object state from functional feature	State	If execution of functional feature's action changes the state of object performing this action, it specifies the new state of the object.
2.	Object state from functional feature	Initial state	When information from input feature is transformed into a state, an initial state is added before this state.
3.	Object state from functional feature	Final state	When information from output feature is transformed into a state, a final state is added after this state.
4.	Cause-and-effect relationship	Transition	If execution of functional feature's action changes the state of object performing this action, then corresponding cause-and-effect relationship defines transition from previous state to the new state.
5.	Operation from functional feature	Event	Each functional feature specifies an atomic business action which later is specified by topological operation in TFM. If functional feature specifies the new state of object, the operation is transformed into the event triggering transition from one state to another.
6.	Operation from functional feature	Entry effect	If current functional feature specifies the new state of object, the operation is transformed into the entry effect of this new state.
7.	Operation from functional feature	Exit effect	If descendant functional feature specifies the new state of object, the operation of this descendant functional feature is transformed into the exit effect of current state.
8.	Preconditions from functional feature	Guard condition	If current functional feature specifies the new state of object, the preconditions of this functional feature are transformed into the guard conditions.
9.	Logical relationship with type *and* (and partially *or*)	Fork and join	A logical relation in TFM gives additional information about execution concurrency of functional features, thus conjunction (*and*) within state diagram is represented with fork and corresponding join. Disjunction (*or*) indicates possible fork and join.

i.e., the ones which has no predecessors, or at the smallest distance to the input functional features of full TFM.

- The *final state* is added after the states that are obtained from the functional features which are the outputs of the downscaled TFM, i.e., the ones which has no descendants, or at the smallest distance to the output functional features of full TFM.

Mappings between elements of TFM and state diagram are described in Table 9.1 giving corresponding elements of TFM and state diagram together with a description of each mapping.

The example of transforming generic example of TFM into state diagram is given in Fig. 9.2, where the left part shows fragment of TFM and right part corresponding state diagram.

In the context of enterprise data synchronization system, this chapter discusses state diagram created for one of the main object—*Logger*. Table 9.2 contains specification of functional features that are used to define state diagram for object *Logger*.

The first action is to scale down TFM which is performed by removing functional features that do not represent the object under consideration but in the same time retaining cause-and-effect relations.

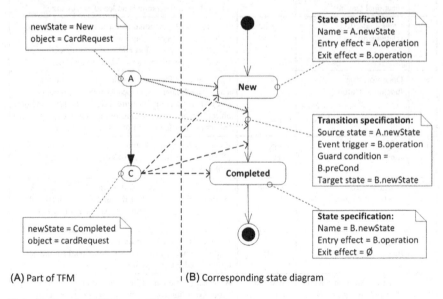

(A) Part of TFM   (B) Corresponding state diagram

Figure 9.2 Example of TFM to state diagram transformation.

Id	Object Action	Precondition	New State
Table 9.2 Functional Features Specifying Functioning of Object *Logger*			
19	Creating log file in log files folder		Completing logging
20	Writing into log file that particular import file was not imported into target database		Completing logging
27	Creating log file in log files folder for import file processing	If data is read from import file	Creating log file
28	Logging data row from temporal internal table		Logging data row
29	Logging successful status	If import is successful for particular row	Logging status
30	Logging error status	If import is not successful for particular row	Logging status
31	Logging error description	If error is logged	Logging status
32	Archiving log file	If data import is completed	Archiving

In the context of enterprise data synchronization system development case study from all the functional features belonging to TFM (X = {2, 3, 4, 6, 7, 8, 9, 10, 11, 13, 14, 15, 16, 17, 18, 19, 20, 22, 23, 25, 27, 28, 29, 30, 31, 32}) we should leave only the following eight functional features: {19, 20, 27, 28, 29, 30, 31, 32}. These functional features represent the object *Logger*. Fig. 9.3 shows both the full TFM of enterprise data synchronization system (left side) and the scaled down containing only functional features representing object *Logger* (right side). Within scaled down TFM with the interrupted relationships between functional features are denoted relationships that have been retained while removing functional features defining other objects.

The specification of functional features {19, 20, 27, 28, 29, 30, 31, 32} given in Table 9.2 shows that the object *Logger* in total has five different states:

1. *Archiving*,
2. *Completing logging*,
3. *Creating log file*,
4. *Logging data row*, and
5. *Logging status*.

The resulting state diagram is given in Fig. 9.4.

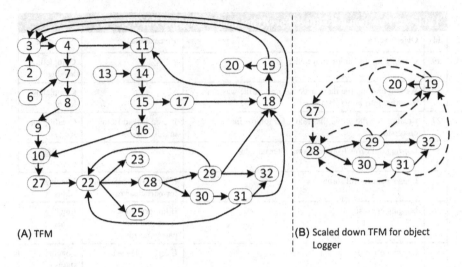

Figure 9.3 Full TFM and scaled down for object Logger.

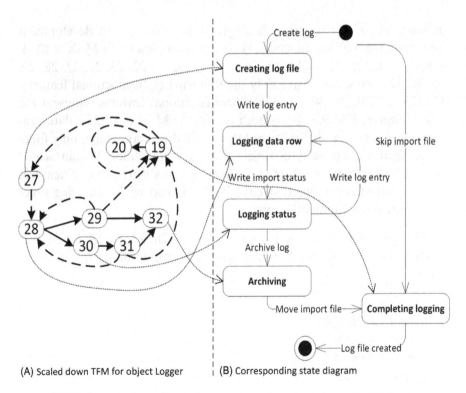

Figure 9.4 TFM of enterprise data synchronization system functioning and state diagram for object Logger.

9.3 SUMMARY

Object state change and transition analysis is an activity within Topological UML modeling process following structure analysis and design activity. It is based on the state diagram development. The state changes and transitions within a system are formally analyzed by using TFM—it is transformed into a set of state diagrams (one state diagram for each class). It is advised to analyze state changes of complex or most important objects in the system. The most important objects are those that are participating in the main functioning cycle of the system. Classes involved in system are identified and specified while developing communication diagram and topological class diagram within Topological UML modeling activity structure analysis and design. States for each class are obtained from the functional features of TFM (functional feature has an attribute that defines the new state of the object), while state transitions are obtained by transforming cause-and-effect relationship between functional features. The special states (initial state and final state) are added to the obtained state diagram as inputs and outputs of TFM. Thus, the state diagrams are developed in a formal way by transforming domain model.

CHAPTER 10

Structuring Logical Layout of Software Design

INFORMATION IN THIS CHAPTER:

- Structuring logical layout of software design
- Transforming subsystems and classes with relationships into packages with relationships
- Formal package diagram development

10.1 INTRODUCTION

Logical layout of software design is structured in accordance with the defined subsystems in the behavior analysis and design activity and classes with their relationships as developed within structure analysis and design activity. The logical layout is depicted by using package diagram where each package initially represents one subsystem. The package is a general-purpose mechanism for organizing modeling elements into groups, i.e., classes in groups or in namespaces and the relationships between them. Packages are used to arrange modeling elements (e.g., classes, interfaces, components, nodes, diagrams, collaborations, use cases, other packages) into larger chunks that it is possible to manipulate them as a group. Packages can also be used to present different views of system's architecture and they can be incorporated into components to build up their internal structure. Well-designed packages group elements that are semantically close and that tend to change together. The process of structuring the logical layout of software design is given in Fig. 10.1.

10.2 DESIGNING PACKAGES

Initially packages are added to package diagram as subsystems from topological use case diagram which gets developed within Topological UML modeling behavior analysis and design activity. The contents of packages are added from the topological class diagram accordingly to

Topological UML Modeling. DOI: http://dx.doi.org/10.1016/B978-0-12-805476-5.00010-1

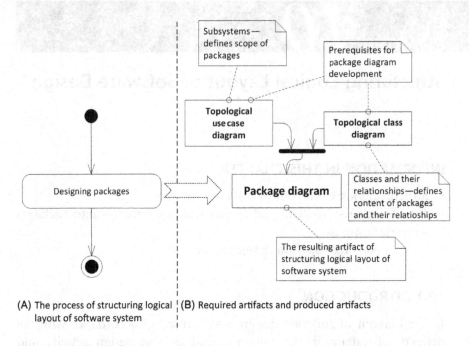

(A) The process of structuring logical layout of software system

(B) Required artifacts and produced artifacts

Figure 10.1 Structuring the logical layout of software design.

the use cases in each system and the mappings between functional features and use cases. Thus, each package gets a set of classes that are responsible for particular subsystem. If needed the initial packages can be split up by grouping classes by their responsibilities. The output of this activity is package diagram structured according to subsystems and responsibilities of classes.

The developed package diagram in the context of enterprise data synchronization system development case study is given in Fig. 10.2, where one package added as topological use case diagram of enterprise data synchronization system (see Fig. 7.3) contains only one subsystem *Scheduler*. The graphical representation used in Fig. 10.2 shows package *Scheduler* without revealing its internal details.

Another way of representing package is by revealing its details. According to UML, a package can contain any element, i.e., classes, interfaces, components, nodes, use cases, diagrams, and other packages grouped into it. Every element that is included in the package is defined within it. If we destroy the package, all the elements within it are destroyed as well. Fig. 10.3 shows package *Scheduler* revealing its internal details—classes and interfaces. The classes and interfaces

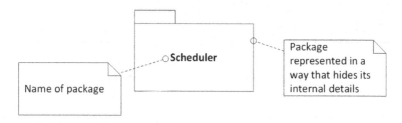

Figure 10.2 Initial package diagram of enterprise data synchronization system.

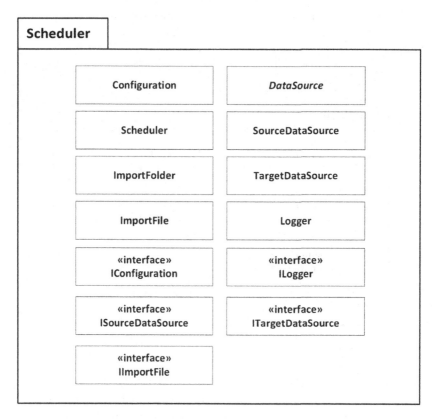

Figure 10.3 Package diagram showing internal details.

are added by following mappings between topological use case diagram and topological class diagram. In the context of enterprise data synchronization system development case study all the classes and interfaces are added from topological class diagram developed during structure analysis and design activity (see Fig. 8.12) to the package *Scheduler*.

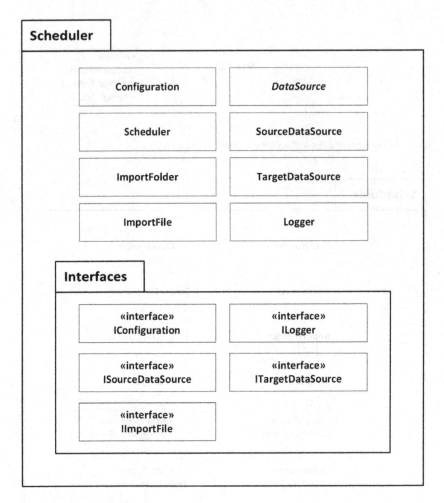

Figure 10.4 Package diagram with additional package for interfaces.

As package *Scheduler* contains classes and interfaces, we can make groupings of similar elements by adding additional packages, e.g., by grouping all interfaces in a special package with name *Interfaces* (see Fig. 10.4).

10.3 SUMMARY

Logical layout of software design is structured in accordance with the defined subsystems in the behavior analysis and design activity and classes with their relationships as developed within structure analysis and design activity. The logical layout is depicted by using package diagram where each package initially represents one subsystem. Packages are used to arrange modeling elements (e.g., classes, interfaces, components, nodes, diagrams, collaborations, use cases, other packages) into larger chunks that it is possible to manipulate them as a group. Initially packages are added to package diagram as subsystems from topological use case diagram which gets developed within Topological UML modeling behavior analysis and design activity. The contents of packages are added from the topological class diagram accordingly to the use cases in each system and the mappings between functional features and use cases. Thus, each package gets a set of classes that are responsible for particular subsystem. If needed the initial packages can be split up by grouping classes by their responsibilities. The output of this activity is package diagram structured according to subsystems and responsibilities of classes.

CHAPTER 11

Components and Deployment Design

INFORMATION IN THIS CHAPTER:

- Designing components
- Planning deployment

11.1 INTRODUCTION

Components are designed in accordance with packages and nonfunctional requirements while deployment is planned for the designed components in accordance with nonfunctional requirements. The components and deployment design consist of two consequent activities (see Fig. 11.1):

- *Designing components*—the components design is depicted by using component diagram showing the internal parts, connectors, and ports that implement a component. Component represents a modular part of a system that encapsulates its contents. It defines its behavior in terms of provided and required interfaces.
- *Planning deployment*—the planned deployment is reflected by using deployment diagram which commonly is used to specify how the components of a system are distributed across the infrastructure and how they are related together. To model such a view deployment diagrams use just two kinds of elements—nodes (i.e., components of a system or the infrastructure artifacts) and relationships that link nodes together.

11.2 DESIGNING COMPONENTS

Components designing within Topological UML modeling are performed according to the packages and nonfunctional requirements. The input of this activity is package diagram and nonfunctional

Topological UML Modeling. DOI: http://dx.doi.org/10.1016/B978-0-12-805476-5.00011-3

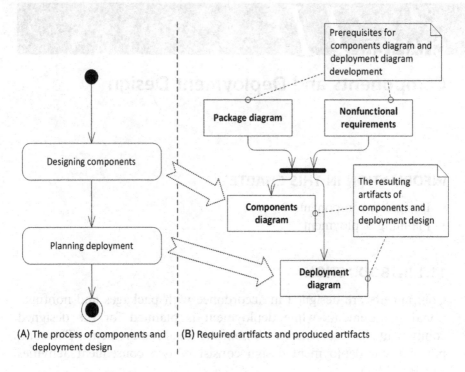

(A) The process of components and   (B) Required artifacts and produced artifacts
    deployment design

Figure 11.1 Overview of designing components and planning deployment.

requirements. The components designing process consists of two
subsequent actions (see Fig. 11.2):

- *Defining components*—the initial components are designed, one component for each package.
- *Refining components*—initial components are refined according to nonfunctional requirements. For example, the nonfunctional requirements
  may include security requirements by stating that executable files
  responsible from logging into system should be deployed separately
  from other components.

As the output a component diagram is developed showing the
internal parts, connectors, and ports that implement a component.
When the component is instantiated, copies of its internal parts are
also instantiated.

The developed component diagram in the context of enterprise data
synchronization system development case study is given in Fig. 11.3,

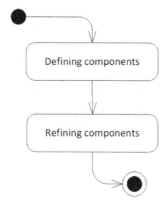

Figure 11.2 Components designing process.

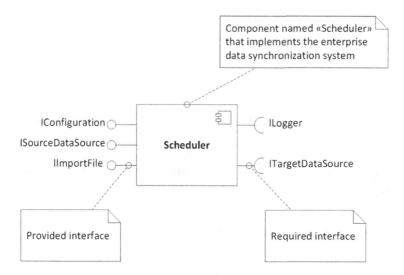

Figure 11.3 Component diagram of enterprise data synchronization system.

where one component is added as package diagram of enterprise data synchronization system (see Fig. 10.2) contains only one package *Scheduler*. The graphical representation used in Fig. 11.3 shows interfaces of component *Scheduler*—lollipop is used for provided interfaces while socket for required interfaces.

Another way of graphically showing required interfaces and provided interfaces is by using realization and dependency relationships. In both cases the relationship is oriented from component to the

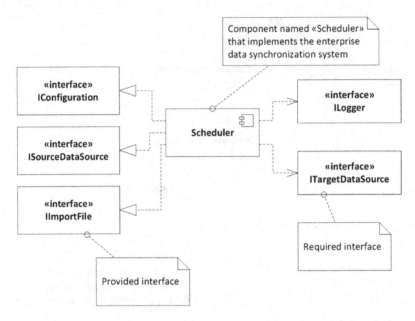

Figure 11.4 Component diagram of enterprise data synchronization system.

corresponding interface. Component diagram given in Fig. 11.4 uses realization and dependency relationships to show required and provided interfaces while in the meantime it is the same component diagram as given in Fig. 11.3, just using a slightly different graphical representation.

11.3 DEPLOYMENT PLANNING

Deployment planning within Topological UML modeling is made according to the components and nonfunctional requirements. During the deployment planning the components are assigned to the nodes as specified by nonfunctional requirements. As the output a deployment diagram is created which represents the assignment of software artifacts to nodes. A deployment diagram is commonly used to specify how the components of a system are distributed across the infrastructure and how they are related together. To model such a view deployment diagrams use just two kinds of elements—nodes (a computational resource upon which artifacts may be deployed for execution) and relationships that link nodes together. Deployment diagram shows the static deployment view of architecture. Deployment diagram is typically related to a component diagram in a way that nodes typically enclose one or more components and it shows the configuration of runtime processing nodes and the artifacts that live on them.

The developed deployment diagram in the context of enterprise data synchronization system development case study is given in Fig. 11.5, where one component named *Scheduler* is added to a single node named *Application server.*

To get a more detailed insight of the enterprise data synchronization system and how it is related to other nodes in infrastructure, we can add more nodes to the deployment diagram thus revealing all the communication links between different types of nodes, e.g., other servers or workstations. In such scenario in the context of enterprise data synchronization system development case study all the required and provided interfaces show relationships between nodes that contain components realizing interfaces which are required and provided by the *Scheduler* component (see Fig. 11.6), where:

- Provided interfaces are available on *Data manager workstation* node (interface *IConfiguration*), *Source database server* node (interface *ISourceDataSource*), and *File server* node (interface *IImportFile*).

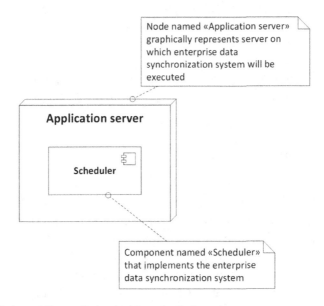

Figure 11.5 Deployment diagram of enterprise data synchronization system.

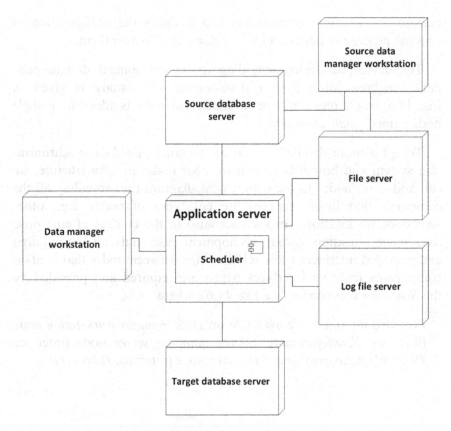

Figure 11.6 Deployment diagram showing relationships with other nodes.

- Required interfaces are available on *Log file server* node (interface *ILogger*) and *Target database server* node (interface *ITargetDataSource*).

11.4 SUMMARY

Components and deployment design is an activity within Topological UML modeling. It follows the structuring logical layout of software design activity and concludes the Topological UML modeling process. Components are designed in accordance with packages and nonfunctional requirements while deployment is planned for the designed components in accordance with nonfunctional requirements. The components design is depicted by using component diagram showing the internal parts, connectors, and ports that implement a component while the planned deployment is reflected by using deployment diagram which is commonly used to specify how the components of a system are distributed across the infrastructure and how they are related together. Deployment diagram shows the static deployment view of architecture and it is related to a component diagram in a way that nodes typically enclose one or more components and it shows the configuration of runtime processing nodes and the artifacts that live on them.

BIBLIOGRAPHY

[1] Alksnis G., Osis J. Category Theory and Computer Science. Computer Science, Applied Computer Systems (Computer Science, Vol. 5), Vol. 8, Scientific Proceedings of Riga Technical University, Riga, 2001, pp. 59−67.

[2] Ambler S. Agile Modeling: Effective Practices for EXtreme Programming and the Unified Process, John Wiley & Sons, New York, 2002, 400.

[3] Ambler S. Elements of UML 2.0 Style, Cambridge University Press, New York, 2005, 200.

[4] Arlow J., Neustadt I. UML 2 and the Unified Process: Practical Object-Oriented Analysis and Design, second ed., Addison-Wesley, Upper Saddle River, NJ, 2005, 624.

[5] Asnina E. The Formal Approach to Problem Domain Modelling Within Model Driven Architecture. Proceedings of the 9th International Conference "Information Systems Implementation and Modelling" (ISIM'06), Jan Štefan MARQ, Přerov, Czech Republic, 2006, pp. 97−104.

[6] Asnina E. A Formal Holistic Outline for Domain Modeling// Advances in Databases and Information Systems. 13th East-European Conference, ADBIS 2009: Associated Workshops and Doctoral Consortium, Local Proceedings, JUMI Publishing House Ltd, Riga, Latvia, 2009, pp. 400−407.

[7] Asnina E., Gulbis B., Osis J., Alksnis G., Donins U., Slihte A. Backward Requirements Traceability within the Topology-Based Model Driven Software Development. Proceedings of the 3rd International Workshop on Model-Driven Architecture and Modeling-Driven Software Development, SciTePress, Beijing, China, 2011, pp. 36−45.

[8] Asnina E., Osis J. Computation independent models: bridging problem and solution domains, in: Osis J., Nikiforova O. (Eds.), Model-Driven Architecture and Modeling Theory-Driven Development: ENASE 2010, 2nd MDA&MTDD Whs, SciTePress, Portugal, 2010, pp. 23−32.

[9] Asnina E., Osis J. Topological Functioning Model as a CIM-Business Model, Model-Driven Domain Analysis and Software Development: Architectures and Functions, IGI Global, Hershey, NY, 2011, pp. 40−64.

[10] Asnina E., Osis J., Jansone A. Formal specifications of topological relations, in: Caplinskas A., Dzemyda G., Lupeikiene A., Vasilecas O. (Eds.), Databases and Information Systems VII: Selected Papers from the Tenth International Baltic Conference, DB&IS 2012 (Frontiers in Artificial Intelligence and Applications), Vol. 249, IOS Press, Amsterdam, 2013, pp. 175−188.

[11] Batra D., Satzinger J. Contemporary approaches and techniques for the systems analyst, Journal of Information Systems Education 17 (3) (2006) 257−265.

[12] Baumeister H., Koch N., Mandel L. Towards a UML Extension for Hypermedia Design. «UML»'99: The Unified Modeling Language, Beyond the Standard (Lecture Notes in Computer Science), Vol. 1723, Springer, Berlin, Germany, 1999, pp. 614−629.

[13] Booch G. Object Oriented Analysis and Design with Applications, second ed., Addison-Wesley, Upper Saddle River, NJ, 1993, 608.

[14] Booch G., Maksimchuk R., Engel M., Young B., Conallen J., Houston K. Object-Oriented Analysis and Design with Applications, third ed., Addison-Wesley, Upper Saddle River, NJ, 2007, 720.

[15] Booch G., Rumbaugh J., Jacobson I. The Unified Modeling Language User Guide, second ed., Addison-Wesley, Upper Saddle River, NJ, 2005, 475.

[16] Breu R., Hinkel U., Hofmann C., Klein C., Paech B., Rumpe B., et al. Towards a Formalization of the Unified Modeling Language. ECOOP'97 – Object-Oriented Programming. 11th European Conference (Lecture Notes in Computer Science), Vol. 1241, Springer, Berlin, Germany, 1997, pp. 344–366.

[17] Burton-Jones A., Meso P. Conceptualizing systems for understanding: An empirical test of decomposition principles in object-oriented analysis, Information Systems Research 17 (1) (2006) 38–60.

[18] Buschmann F., Meunier R., Rohnert H., Sommerlad P., Stal M. Pattern-Oriented Software Architecture: A System of Patterns, John Wiley & Sons Ltd, West Sussex, 1996, 476.

[19] Darwin I. Java Cookbook, second ed., O'Reilly, Sebastopol, 2004, 864.

[20] DeLoach S., Hartrum T. A theory-based representation for object-oriented domain models, IEEE Transactions on Software Engineering 26 (6) (2000) 500–517.

[21] Desel J., Juhás G. "What is a Petri Net?" Informal Answers for the Informed Readers. Unifying Petri Nets, Advances in Petri Nets (Lecture Notes in Computer Science), Vol. 2128, Springer, Berlin, Germany, 2001, pp. 1–25.

[22] Dobing B., Parsons J. Dimensions of UML Diagram Use: Practitioner Survey and Research Agenda. Principle Advancements in Database Management Technologies: New Applications and Frameworks, Information Science Reference, Hershey, NY, 2010, pp. 271–290.

[23] Donins U. Semantics of Logical Relations in Topological Functioning Model. Proceedings of the 7th International Conference on Evaluation of Novel Approaches to Software Engineering (ENASE 2012), 2012.

[24] Donins U. Software Development with the Emphasis on Topology. Advances in Databases and Information Systems (Lecture Notes in Computer Science), Vol. 5968, Springer-Verlag, Berlin, Germany, 2010, pp. 220–228.

[25] Donins U. Topological Business Systems Modeling and Software Systems Design, RTU Publishing House, Riga, Latvia, 2011, 65 (in Latvian).

[26] Donins U., Osis J. Topological Modeling for Enterprise Data Synchronization System: A Case Study of Topological Model-Driven Software Development. Proceedings of the 13th International Conference on Enterprise Information Systems, Vol. 3, SciTePress, Beijing, China, 2011, pp. 87–96.

[27] Donins U., Osis, J., Asnina, E., Jansone, A. Formal Analysis of Objects State Changes and Transitions. Proceedings of the 7th International Conference on Evaluation of Novel Approaches to Software Engineering (ENASE 2012), 2012.

[28] Donins U., Osis J., Slihte A., Asnina E., Gulbis B. Towards the Refinement of Topological Class Diagram as a Platform Independent Model. Proceedings of the 3rd International Workshop on Model-Driven Architecture and Modeling-Driven Software Development, SciTePress, Beijing, China, 2011, pp. 79–88.

[29] D'Souza D., Wills A. Objects, Components, and Frameworks with UML: The Catalysis Approach, Addison-Wesley, Upper Saddle River, NJ, 1998, 816.

[30] Erickson J., Siau K. Theoretical and practical complexity of modeling methods, Communications of the ACM 50 (8) (2007) 46–51.

[31] Evans A., Kent S. Core Meta-Modelling Semantics of UML: The pUML Approach. «UML»'99: The Unified Modeling Language, *Beyond the Standard* (Lecture Notes in Computer Science), Vol. 1723, Springer, Berlin, Germany, 1999, pp. 140–155.

[32] Evermann J., Wand Y. Ontological modeling rules For UML: An empirical assessment, Journal of Computer Information Systems 46 (5) (2006) 14–29.

[33] Evermann J., Wand Y. Towards Ontologically-Based Semantics for UML Constructs. Conceptual Modeling – ER 2001. 20th International Conference on Conceptual Modeling (Lecture Notes in Computer Science), Vol. 2224, Springer, Berlin, Germany, 2001, pp. 341–354.

[34] Fenton N., Pfleeger S. Software Metrics: A Rigorous and Practical Approach, second ed., Coriolis Group, Scottsdale, AZ, 1996, 649.

[35] Fowler M. Why use the UML? Software Development 6 (3) (1998).

[36] Fowler M. Patterns of Enterprise Application Architecture, Addison-Wesley, Upper Saddle River, NJ, 2002, 560.

[37] Fowler M. UML Distilled: A Brief Guide to the Standard Object Modeling Language, third ed., Addison-Wesley, Upper Saddle River, NJ, 2003, 208.

[38] France R., Rumpe B. «UML»'99: The Unified Modeling Language, Beyond the Standard (Lecture Notes in Computer Science), Vol. 1723, Springer, Berlin, Germany, 1999, 724.

[39] Gamma E., Helm R., Johnson R., Vlissides J. Design Patterns: Elements of Reusable Object-Oriented Software, Addison-Wesley, Upper Saddle River, NJ, 1994, 416.

[40] Grundspenkis J. Fault Localisation Based on Topological Feature Analysis of Complex System Model. Diagnostics and Identification, Zinatne, Riga, 1974, pp. 38–48, in Russian.

[41] Harel D. Statecharts: A visual formalism for complex systems, Science of Computer Programming 8 (3) (1987) 231–247.

[42] He X. Formalizing U.M.L. Semantics. 25th Annual International Computer Software and Applications Conference (COMPSAC'01), IEEE Computer Society, Chicago, IL, 2001, p. 277.

[43] International Electronical Commission. http://www.iec.ch/.

[44] International Organization for Standardization (ISO). http://www.iso.org/.

[45] International Organization for Standardization (ISO). ISO/IEC/IEEE 42010:2011 "Systems and software engineering – Architecture description," 2011, p. 37.

[46] ISO/IEC 19501:2005. Information technology – Open Distributed Processing – Unified Modeling Language (UML) Version 1.4.2. http://www.iso.org/iso/home/store/catalogue_tc/catalogue_detail.htm?csnumber = 32620.

[47] ISO/IEC 19505-1:2012. Information technology – Object Management Group Unified Modeling Language (OMG UML) – Part 1: Infrastructure. http://www.iso.org/iso/home/store/catalogue_tc/catalogue_detail.htm?csnumber = 32624.

[48] ISO/IEC 19505-2:2012. Information technology – Object Management Group Unified Modeling Language (OMG UML) – Part 2: Superstructure. http://www.iso.org/iso/home/store/catalogue_tc/catalogue_detail.htm?csnumber = 52854.

[49] Jacobson I., Christerson M., Jonsson P., Overgaard G. Object-Oriented Software Engineering: A Use Case Driven Approach, Addison-Wesley, Upper Saddle River, NJ, 1992, 552.

[50] Jones C. Positive and negative innovations in software engineering, International Journal of Software Science and Computational Intelligence 1 (2) (2009) 20–30.

[51] Kent S. The Unified Modeling Language. Formal Methods for Distributed Processing: A Survey of Object-Oriented Approaches, Cambridge University Press, Cambridge, 2001, pp. 126–151.

[52] Kim S., Carrington D. Formalizing the UML Class Diagram Using Object-Z. «UML»'99: The Unified Modeling Language, *Beyond the Standard* (Lecture Notes in Computer Science), Vol. 1723, Springer, Berlin, Germany, 1999, pp. 83–98.

[53] Kleppe A., Warmer J., Bust W. MDA Explained. The Model Driven Architecture: Practice and Promise, Addison-Wesley, Upper Saddle River, NJ, 2003, 192.

[54] Kobryn C. UML 2001: A Standardization Odyssey, Communications of the ACM 42 (10) (1999) 29–37.

[55] Kruchten P. The 4 + 1 view model of architecture, IEEE Software 12 (16) (1995) 42–50.

[56] Kruchten P. The Rational Unified Process: An Introduction, Addison-Wesley, Upper Saddle River, NJ, 2003, 336.

[57] Lano K., Kolahdouz-Rahimi S. Model-Driven Development of Model Transformations. Theory and Practice of Model Transformations (Lecture Notes in Computer Science), Vol. 6707, Springer-Verlag, Berlin, Germany, 2011, pp. 47–61.

[58] Larman C. Applying UML and Patterns: An Introduction to Object-Oriented Analysis and Design and Iterative Development, third ed., Prentice Hall, Upper Saddle River, NJ, 2005, 736.

[59] Lazar I., Motogna S., Parv B., Lazar C. Realizing Use Cases for Full Code Generation in the Context of fUML. Proceedings of the 2nd International Workshop on Model-Driven Architecture and Modeling Theory-Driven Development, SciTePress, Portugal, 2010, pp. 80–89.

[60] Leffingwell D., Widrig D. Managing Software Requirements: A Use Case Approach, second ed., Addison-Wesley, Upper Saddle River, NJ, 2003, 544.

[61] Li D., Li X., Stolz V. QVT-based model transformation using XSLT, ACM SIGSOFT Software Engineering Notes 36 (1) (2011) 1–8.

[62] Loniewski G., Insfran E., Abrahao S. A systematic Review of the Use of Requirements Engineering Techniques in Model-Driven Development. Model Driven Engineering Languages and Systems (Lecture Notes in Computer Science), Vol. 6395, Springer-Verlag, Berlin, Germany, 2010, pp. 213–227.

[63] Loudon K. C + + Pocket Reference, O'Reilly, Sebastopol, 2003, 138.

[64] Luger G. Artificial Intelligence: Structures and Strategies for Complex Problem Solving, fifth ed., Addison-Wesley, Upper Saddle River, NJ, 2005, 928.

[65] Mellor S., Balcer M. Executable UML: A Foundation for Model-Driven Architecture, Addison-Wesley, Upper Saddle River, NJ, 2002, 416.

[66] Mens T., Van Gorp P. A taxonomy of model transformation, Electronic Notes in Theoretical Computer Science 152 (2006) 125–142.

[67] Miller, J., Mukerji, J. (Eds.). MDA Guide Version 1.0.1. http://www.omg.org/cgi-bin/doc?omg/03-06-01.pdf.

[68] Nagel C., Evjen B., Glynn J., Watson K., Skinner M. Professional C# 4.0 and NET 4, John Wiley & Sons, New York, 2010, 1536.

[69] Nielsen M., Havelund K., Wagner K., George C. The RAISE language, method and tools, Formal Aspects of Computing 1 (1) (1989) 85–114.

[70] OMG. Common Warehouse Metamodel Specification Version 1.1. http://www.omg.org/spec/CWM/1.1/PDF/.

[71] OMG. Unified Modeling Language Specification Version 1.1. http://www.omg.org/cgi-bin/doc?ad/97-08-11.

[72] OMG. Unified Modeling Language Specification Version 1.3. http://www.omg.org/spec/UML/1.3/PDF.

[73] OMG. Unified Modeling Language Specification Version 1.5. http://www.omg.org/spec/UML/1.5/PDF/.

[74] OMG. Meta Object Facility (MOF) Core Specification Version 2.0. http://www.omg.org/spec/MOF/2.0/PDF/.

[75] OMG. UML Testing Profile Version 1.0. http://www.omg.org/spec/UTP/1.0/PDF/.

[76] OMG. Service Oriented Architecture Modeling Language (SoaML). http://www.omg.org/spec/SoaML/1.0/Beta2/PDF.

[77] OMG. Unified Modeling Language Infrastructure Version 2.4.1. http://www.omg.org/spec/UML/2.4.1/Infrastructure/PDF/.

[78] OMG. Unified Modeling Language Superstructure Version 2.4.1. http://www.omg.org/spec/UML/2.4.1/Superstructure/PDF/.

[79] OMG. OMG Unified Modeling Language TM (OMG UML) Version 2.5. http://www.omg.org/spec/UML/2.5/PDF/.

[80] OMG. OMG Systems Modeling Language (OMG SysML). http://www.omg.org/spec/SysML/1.2/PDF.

[81] OMG. OMG Formally Released Versions of UML. http://www.omg.org/spec/UML/.

[82] Olive A. Conceptual Modeling of Information Systems, Springer, Berlin, Germany, 2007, 455.

[83] Osis J. Extension of Software Development Process for Mechatronic and Embedded Systems. Proceedings of the 32nd International Conference on Computer and Industrial Engineering, University of Limerick, Limerick, Ireland, 2003, pp. 305–310.

[84] Osis J. Formal computation independent model within the MDA life cycle, International Transactions on Systems Science and Applications 1 (2) (2006) 159–166.

[85] Osis J. Software Development with Topological Model in the Framework of MDA. Proceedings of the 9th CAiSE/IFIP8.1/EUNO International Workshop on Evaluation of Modeling Methods in Systems Analysis and Design (EMMSAD'2004) in connection with the CAiSE'2004, Vol. 1, RTU, Riga, 2004, pp. 211–220.

[86] Osis J. The Topological Model of System Functioning, Vol. 6, Automatics and Computer Science, Riga, Latvia, 1969, pp. 44–50, in Russian.

[87] Osis J., Asnina E. A Business Model to Make Software Development Less Intuitive. Proceedings of the 2008 International Conference on Innovation in Software Engineering, IEEE Computer Society CPS, Los Alamitos, USA, Vienna, Austria, 2008, pp. 1240–1246.

[88] Osis J., Asnina E. Enterprise Modeling for Information System Development within MDA. Proceedings of the 41st Annual Hawaii International Conference on System Sciences (HICSS 2008), IEEE Computer Society, Chicago, IL, 2008, p. 491.

[89] Osis J., Asnina E. Derivation of Use Cases from the Topological Computation Independent Business Model, Model-Driven Domain Analysis and Software Development: Architectures and Functions, IGI Global, Hershey, NY, 2011, pp. 65–89.

[90] Osis J., Asnina E. Is modeling a treatment for the weakness of software engineering? in: Garcia Diaz V., Cueva Lovelle J., García-Bustelo B. (Eds.), Handbook of Research on Innovations in Systems and Software Engineering, IGI Global, Hershey, NY, 2015, pp. 411–427.

[91] Osis J., Asnina E. Topological Modeling for Model-Driven Domain Analysis and Software Development: Functions and Architectures, Model-Driven Domain Analysis and Software Development: Architectures and Functions, IGI Global, Hershey, NY, 2011, pp. 15–39.

[92] Osis J., Asnina E., Grave A. Computation Independent Modeling within the MDA. Proceedings of the IEEE International Conference on Software Science, Technology and Engineering, IEEE Computer Society Nr. E3021, Herzlia, Israel, 30–31 October 2007, pp. 22–34.

[93] Osis J., Asnina E., Grave A. Computation independent representation of the problem domain in MDA, e-Informatica Software Engineering Journal 2 (1) (2008) 29–46.

[94] Osis J., Asnina E., Grave A. Formal Problem Domain Modeling within MDA, Communications in Computer and Information Science (CCIS), Vol. 22, Software and Data Technologies, Berlin, Germany: Springer-Verlag, 2008, pp. 387–398.

[95] Osis J., Asnina, E., Grave, A. MDA Oriented Computation Independent Modeling of the Problem Domain. Proceedings of the 2nd International Conference on Evaluation of Novel Approaches to Software Engineering (ENASE 2007), Barcelona, Spain, 2007, pp. 66–71.

[96] Osis J., Donins U. An Innovative Model Driven Formalization of the Class Diagrams. Proceedings of the 4th International Conference on Evaluation of Novel Approaches to Software Engineering (ENASE 2009), INSTICC Press, Portugal, 2009, pp. 134–145.

[97] Osis J., Donins U. Formalization of the UML Class Diagrams. Evaluation of Novel Approaches to Software Engineering (Communications in Computer and Information Science (CCIS)), Vol. 69, Springer-Verlag, Berlin, Germany, 2010, pp. 180–192.

[98] Osis J., Donins U. Modeling Formalization of MDA Software Development at the Very Beginning of Life Cycle. Advances in Databases and Information Systems, 13th East-European Conference, ADBIS 2009: Associated Workshops and Doctoral Consortium, Local Proceedings, JUMI Publishing House Ltd, Riga, Latvia, 2009, pp. 48–61.

[99] Osis J., Donins U. Platform Independent Model Development by Means of Topological Class Diagrams. Proceedings of the 2nd International Workshop on Model-Driven Architecture and Modeling Theory-Driven Development, SciTePress, Portugal, 2010, pp. 13–22.

[100] Osis J., Slihte A. Transforming Textual Use Cases to a Computation Independent Model. Proceedings of the 2nd International Workshop on Model-Driven Architecture and Modeling Theory-Driven Development, SciTePress, Portugal, 2010, pp. 33–42.

[101] Osis J., Solomencevs A. Comparison of Topological Functioning Model for Software Engineering with BPMN Approach in the Context of Model Driven Architecture. Proceedings of the 11th International Conference on Evaluation of Novel Approaches to Software Engineering (ENASE 2016), [S.l.]: SciTePress, Italy, Rome, 27–28 April, 2016, 2016, pp. 337–348.

[102] Owre S., Rushby J., Shankar N. PVS: A Prototype Verification System. 11th International Conference on Automated Deduction (Lecture Notes in Artificial Intelligence), Vol. 607, Springer, Berlin, Germany, 1992, pp. 748–752.

[103] Pardillo J. A Systematic Review on the Definition of UML Profiles. Model Driven Engineering Languages and Systems (Lecture Notes in Computer Science), Vol. 6394, Springer-Verlag, Berlin, Germany, 2010, pp. 407–422.

[104] Podeswa H. UML for the IT business analyst, second ed., Course Technology PTR, Boston, MA, 2009, 372.

[105] Rumbaugh J., Blaha M., Premerlani W., Eddy F., Lorensen W. Object-Oriented Modeling and Design, Prentice Hall, Englewood Cliffs, NJ, 1991, 528.

[106] Rumbaugh J., Jacobson I., Booch G. The Unified Modeling Language Reference Manual, second ed., Addison-Wesley, Upper Saddle River, NJ, 2004, 721.

[107] Scott K. The Unified Process Explained, Addison-Wesley, Upper Saddle River, NJ, 2001, 208.

[108] Sejans J., Nikiforova N. Practical Experiments with Code Generation from the UML Class Diagram. Proceedings of the 3rd International Workshop on Model-Driven Architecture and Modeling-Driven Software Development, SciTePress, Beijing, China, 2011, pp. 57–67.

[109] Shalloway A., Trott J. Design Patterns Explained: A New Perspective on Object-Oriented Design, second ed., Addison-Wesley, Upper Saddle River, NJ, 2004, 480.

[110] Shekhovstov V. On the Evolution of Quality Conceptualization Techniques. The Evolution of Conceptual Modeling (Lecture Notes in Computer Science), Vol. 6520, Springer-Verlag, Berlin, Germany, 2011, pp. 117–136.

[111] Siau K., Cao Q. Unified modeling language (UML): A complexity analysis, Journal of Database Management 12 (1) (2001) 26–34.

[112] Siau K., Cao Q. How complex is the unified modeling language? Advanced Topics in Database Research 1 (2002) 294–306.

[113] Siau K., Loo P. Identifying difficulties in learning UML, Information Systems Management 23 (3) (2006) 43–51.

[114] Simons, A., Graham, I. 37 Things That Don't Work in Object-Oriented Modeling with UML. Proceedings of ECOOP 98 Workshop on Precise Behavioral Semantics. Universitat Muchen, 1998, pp. 209–232.

[115] Slihte A., Osis J., Donins U. Knowledge Integration for Domain Modeling. Proceedings of the 3rd International Workshop on Model-Driven Architecture and Modeling-Driven Software Development, SciTePress, Beijing, China, 2011, pp. 46–56.

[116] Slihte A., Osis J., Donins U., Asnina E., Gulbis B. Advancements of the Topological Functioning Model for Model Driven Architecture Approach. Proceedings of the 3rd International Workshop on Model-Driven Architecture and Modeling-Driven Software Development, SciTePress, Beijing, China, 2011, pp. 91–100.

[117] Slihte A., Osis J. The Integrated Domain Modeling: A Case Study, Databases and Information Systems. Proceedings of the 11th International Baltic Conference, Baltic DB&IS 2014, TUT Press, 2014, pp. 465–470.

[118] Solomencevs A., Osis J. The Algorithm for Getting a UML Class Diagram from Topological Functioning Model, Proceedings of 10th International Conference on Evaluation of Novel Approaches to Software Engineering, SciTePress, Portugal, 2015, pp. 341–351.

[119] Spivey J. The Z Notation: A Reference Manual, second ed., Prentice Hall, NJ, 1992, 150.

[120] Stevens P., Pooley R. Using U.M.L.: Software Engineering with Objects and Components, second ed., Addison-Wesley, Harlow, 2006, 250.

[121] Van Der Straeten R., Mens T., Simmonds J., Jonckers V. Using Description Logic to Maintain Consistency between UML Models. «UML» 2003 – The Unified Modeling Language, Modeling Languages and Applications (Lecture Notes in Computer Science), Vol. 2863, Springer-Verlag, Berlin, Germany, 2003, pp. 326–340.

[122] Szlenk M. UML Static Models in Formal Approach. Balancing Agility and Formalism in Software Engineering (Lecture Notes in Computer Science), Vol. 5082, Springer-Verlag, Berlin, Germany, 2008, pp. 129–142.

[123] Unified Process iterative development: https://commons.wikimedia.org/wiki/File:Development-iterative.png.

[124] Warmer J., Kleppe A. The Object Constraint Language: Getting Your Models Ready for MDA, second ed., Addison-Wesley, Upper Saddle River, NJ, 2003, 240.

[125] Xueming L., Parsons J. Ontological Semantics for the Use of UML in Conceptual Modeling, ER (Tutorials, Posters, Panels & Industrial Contributions), 2007, pp. 179–184.

[126] Zhao Y., Zong-Yuan Y., Xie J. Pi-Calculus Based Assembly Mechanism of UML State Diagram and Validation of Model Refinement. Proceedings of International Conference on Electronic Computer Technology 2009 (ICECT 2009). Macau, China, 2009, pp. 604–609.

Printed in the United States
By Bookmasters